RECLAIMING CATHOLICISM

Treasures Old and New

RECLAIMING CATHOLICISM
Treasures Old and New

Edited by
THOMAS H. GROOME
and
MICHAEL J. DALEY

ORBIS BOOKS

Maryknoll, New York 10545

Second Printing, May 2010

Founded in 1970, Orbis Books endeavors to publish works that enlighten the mind, nourish the spirit, and challenge the conscience. The publishing arm of the Maryknoll Fathers and Brothers, Orbis seeks to explore the global dimensions of the Christian faith and mission, to invite dialogue with diverse cultures and religious traditions, and to serve the cause of reconciliation and peace. The books published reflect the views of their authors and do not represent the official position of the Maryknoll Society. To learn more about Maryknoll and Orbis Books, please visit our website at www.maryknollsociety.org.

Library of Congress Cataloging-in-Publication Data

Reclaiming Catholicism : treasures old and new / edited by Thomas H. Groome and Michael J. Daley.
    p. cm.
 Includes bibliographical references and index.
 ISBN 978-1-57075-863-8 (pbk.)
 1. Catholic Church—United States. 2. United States—Church history. I. Groome, Thomas H. II. Daley, Michael J., 1968–
  BX1406.3.R43 2010
  282'.73—dc22

                  2009034705

Contents

PART II: PERSONALITIES

PART III: PRACTICES

Preface

THOMAS H. GROOME

This book mines the treasury of pre–Vatican II American Catholicism for the spiritual riches to be gleaned from its perspectives, personalities, and popular practices. The American Catholic community prior to the Second Vatican Council (1962–1965) can be numbered among the most vital expressions of Catholicism in the history of the church. It was a vast network of vibrant parishes, with myriad associations, organizations, and impressive plants as well as overflowing Sunday Mass attendance; it boasted as many as eight million students enrolled in Catholic schools, the largest independent educational system in the history of the world; it sponsored a huge coalition of hospitals and social services, fraternities and sororities; it had priests, sisters, and brothers galore, enough to export thousands as missionaries, while its seminaries and novitiates were bulging at the seams. "They" must have been doing something very right back then. Of course, that *was* then, and this is now; yet, it is surely true that *reclaimed* spiritual wisdom from that era can enrich the faith lives of Catholics today.

Reclaiming—Not Regressing

I grew up on an Irish farm that had a bog across the way. For hundreds of years, that bog provided good turf to heat the homes of the local people; the sweet smell of a turf fire on a winter's night was as pleasing as any apple pie in the oven. But gradually the bog got cut away, and then went into disuse, left lying fallow, soggy and overgrown. During my childhood, however, the government launched what it called a "*reclamation* project" of the bog. Gradually it was cleared of underbrush and drained. When *reclaimed*, it proved to be amazingly fertile soil for vegetables and fruits; it flourishes to this day. That was my first encounter with the word *reclaiming*; we use it in the title of this collection with echoes of what it meant for that Irish bog.

To reclaim is neither naïve nor nostalgic toward the past; it certainly does not mean to regress or to simply repeat what was. Instead, the task is to claim again as our own the potential that the past still holds for our present and future, to reappropriate and then build upon its wisdom for our time. We're convinced that by bringing appreciation, reservation, and imagination to its defining perspectives, personalities, and practices, we can reclaim great spiritual wisdom from those glory days of American Catholicism to enrich the faith-life of people today.

Treasures Old and New

In what scripture scholars identify as a summary statement in the Gospel of Matthew, Jesus says: "Every scribe who has been instructed in the kingdom of heaven is like the head of a household who brings forth from the storeroom [some translations have "the treasure"] both the new and the old" (Mt 13:52). In other words, those who are wise for the reign of God should ever return to the traditions of the community to reclaim old truths that can become as new for another time. That Christian faith should have such enduring vitality is also echoed in Jesus' conversation with the Samaritan woman at the well. There he promised to her and to Christians ever after that his Gospel would be like fresh waters, "welling up to eternal life" (Jn 4:14). Nothing is more deadly than stagnant waters; nothing is more life-giving than fresh waters. The intent of our project here is to tap into the fresh waters that spring from the Catholicism of our immediate fore-parents in faith.

Most Catholics who grew up prior to Vatican II experienced that great council as what good Pope John XXIII promised it would be, a monumental project of *aggiornamento*—updating and renewing—of the Church, or as John quipped informally, "an opening of the window to let in fresh air." Later, Pope John Paul II rightly hailed Vatican II as "a providential event," one "of utmost importance in the two-thousand-year history of the church," and "the beginning of a new era." At the time and since then, Vatican II has proved to be an unstoppable outpouring of the Holy Spirit to renew and reform the

Church. Its whole project might be summarized as reclaiming a radical theology of baptism from the early Christian communities, radical in that baptism is the root (Latin, *radix*) of who Christians are and should be as disciples of Jesus.

In sum, Vatican II took seriously our baptismal bonding with Jesus Christ as "priest, prophet, and ruler." Thus, it renewed our calling to "full, conscious, and active participation" in the Church's worship[1] —to be a priestly people; to side with those "who are poor or in any way afflicted"[2]—to be a prophetic people; and "made one body with Christ by baptism . . . [as] sharers in the mission of the whole Christian people"[3]—to be a co-responsible community.

On the ground, this was experienced as a transformed and participatory liturgy, emphasizing both word and sacrament and celebrated in the local language; as heightened emphasis on the church's social teachings, making clear the mandate of our faith to work for God's reign of love and holiness, to do God's will of justice and peace "*on earth* as it is done in heaven"; as deepened awareness of the communal nature of the Church, to be a "body of Christ" that works together to continue Jesus' ministries and saving mission to the world. Add in ecumenical outreach to other Christians and interfaith dialogue with other religions, the renewal of religious life, the emergence of parish and diocesan councils (a first seed of democracy), retrieving the call of every Christian (not just vowed religious) to holiness of life, and so on and on. For the younger generations who didn't live through it, all this and more is now taken for granted; but for those of us of prior vintage, Vatican II was an earthquake with now forty years of aftershocks.

Most of the council's reforms were, in fact, a *ressourcement* or we might say a reclamation of convictions and practices from the early Christian communities. Yet the typical Catholic of the time did not recognize its deep continuity with the treasury of Christian tradition. Instead many experienced it as a great discontinuity with that to which they'd grown accustomed; it was as if the rug had been pulled out from under them.

A New Moment of Opportunity for Reclamation

Of course, it would be hard to imagine any real reform and renewal without some feelings of discontinuity. But just imagine, almost overnight, we went from the priest beginning Mass with his back to the people, behind an altar railing, turned toward—typically—an imposing granite altar, and whispering in Latin with a gaggle of altar boys at his feet, to his facing outward across a table with a cheery, "Good morning everyone" and a warm invitation to worship together as a community of priestly people. Or imagine again, the Catholic Church went into the council still referring to Protestants as "heretics" and came out of it calling them "our brothers and sisters in Christ." Such changes (some prefer the euphemistic "developments") were bound to feel traumatic. Many Catholics, once rock-solid confident that they knew their faith and its practices, suddenly lost their sure footing.

With hindsight, too, many of the changes were poorly catechized and were often overstated to the point that people heard only a call to abandon old ways. For example, when the Church decided to suspend the *law* of Friday abstinence—other than during Lent—people should have been encouraged to continue this practice as a good ascetical discipline (actually, the 1966 papal document announcing the change urged as much). Yet, it was most often presented as "It's no longer a sin to eat meat on Fridays," and the long tradition of Friday abstinence—dating back to the early centuries—was simply abandoned. We could have reclaimed such a practice and, while not placing it under "pain of sin," continued to do it voluntarily; what a good opportunity to feel solidarity with the poor who rarely have meat, to contribute what we save to a good cause, to remember the Lord's crucifixion on Good Friday. With regard to this, and to other such good practices, our book suggests that it may not be too late to *reclaim* them.

There is also a widespread phenomenon now of adolescent and young adult Catholics returning to the perspectives and practices of pre–Vatican II Catholicism. Some even feel that they were cheated out of something very valuable by their baby-boomer parents who set aside too many of the old Catholic ways. The danger here, however, is of regression rather than reclamation, of going back to repeat rather than building upon the enduring wisdom of that era. For example, in the aftermath of Vatican II, the Catholic Church rightly re-centered our focus on Jesus, on sacred scripture, and on the liturgy. Among other things, these reforms reduced the sometimes excessive attention to Mary in Catholic piety. Now, however, with the reforms well in place, we have a new moment of opportunity to reclaim an authentic Marian devotion for our time that rather than undoing the good work of the council will advance it (e.g., with all Mariology rooted in Christology, scripture, and fostering discipleship to Jesus). So, there is much riding on how we proceed with *reclamation*.

In this volume we have asked our distinguished authors to engage in a threefold hermeneutic (interpretation and presentation) of their topics, one that is *appreciative*, *critical*, and *constructive* regarding some perspective, practice, or personality of pre–Vatican II Catholicism. These essays are *appreciative* in that they raise up the underlying values and wisdom of Catholicism from immediately prior to Vatican II; they are *critical* as needed in that they recognize the shortcomings—now clearer from hindsight. The defining intent, however, is to move beyond both appreciation and critique to *creative* appropriation of the spiritual wisdom from those days to ours. The combination of all three—appreciation, reservation, and imagination—is what makes for *Reclaiming Catholicism*.

Take, for example, the Rosary, so long a cherished prayer of Catholics but recently fallen off in popular practice. It is surely worth reclaiming; its mantra-like rhythm and contemplative spirit could still be a gentling prayer practice in our busy world. And even if the "nightly family Rosary" would be a challenge for most, it could be recited in other contexts, such as on a car ride—alone or as a family; it might temper road rage or distract a while from "Are we there yet?" By way of reservation, however, note that the traditional three sets of five decades focused exclusively on the Christ of faith; the mysteries went from "The finding of the child Jesus in the temple" (fifth Joyful mystery) to "The agony in the garden" (first Sorrowful one), skipping entirely the public life of Jesus. Here Pope John Paul II has led the way in creative retrieval. He affirmed the Rosary as "a treasure to be rediscovered," recognized its limitations, and then added the "mysteries of light"—five great moments from the public ministry of Jesus. This is the kind of appreciative, critical, and creative reclaiming that you will find in this book.

Our contributors include some of the finest theologians and pastoral leaders of our time; our authors read like a "who's who" list of Catholic scholars. And we've invited them to write from personal memory as well—all satisfy the required age. So here you will find the best of "narrative theology" set to the purpose of reclaiming the spiritual wisdom from the defining perspectives, personalities, and practices of pre–Vatican II American Catholicism. Read on and personally experience why Jesus urged us to constantly return to the "storeroom" of our faith to find *treasures old and new*.

Boston College
March 17, 2009
Feast of St. Patrick

Notes

1. Constitution on the Liturgy #14, in *Documents of Vatican II*, ed. Walter Abbott (New York: America Press, 1966), 144.

2. Constitution on Church in Modern World #1, in Abbott, *Documents*, 199–200.

3. Ibid., # 31, in Abbott, *Documents*, 57.

Introduction

A Generation X Catholic: "Back in the Day" Is Not My Day

MICHAEL J. DALEY

As one proof for the substance of their faith tradition, Catholics have long gloried in their famous converts—those persons who have left another religious tradition, or none at all, to become Catholic. Names like the English churchman John Henry Newman, the English writer G. K. Chesterton, the German intellectual and eventual Auschwitz martyr Edith Stein, and the Catholic Worker movement cofounder Dorothy Day all come to mind. An impressive, though recent list, indeed. Surely, if these persons have found a home in the Catholic Church, there must be something of value here.

To this list I'd like to add perhaps the most famous Catholic convert of the twenty-first century—Homer Simpson. Yes, that's right, I mean the beer-guzzling, overweight, vulgar, and incompetent resident of Springfield. I can see the beginnings of your dismissive, head-shaking smile right now. But before you skip this introduction and move on to supposed more substantial fare, I ask only that you allow me to explain my rationale.

Generation X: The Times Changed

I write as a Catholic born in 1968. Unlike the other contributors to this book, with respect to Vatican II, I am decidedly "post." Clearing the fog from my own early religious upbringing for a moment, I have vague memories of attending Mass while singing the folk standard, "They Will Know We Are Christians by Our Love." I still can picture a poster on the door of my parish church encouraging people to receive the Eucharist in their hands. Embarrassingly, to this day, the only thing I recall from my First Communion is wearing my brother's disco-inspired, second-hand leisure suit. I also remember planning an end-of-the-year CCD prayer service during which one girl asked the volunteer teacher if we could play Led Zepplin's "Stairway to Heaven." He politely said he'd consider it. Suffice it to say that this was a far cry from the Catholic ghetto where my mom grew up outside Detroit, Michigan in the fifties and early sixties.[1]

Politically, the two primary U.S. presidents of my youth were Jimmy Carter and Ronald Reagan. Unfortunately, despite all that he's done, I connect Carter with the Iran hostage crisis (1979–1981); and when I think of Reagan I can hear him saying, "Mr. Gorbachev, tear down this wall" (1987). Through it all the Cold War and the threat of nuclear annihilation loomed over us. The pope during all of these years was John Paul II.

Culturally, at least for a brief period of time, my brothers and I had the coolest house on the block due to the Atari Ping Pong video game we got for Christmas one year. For better or worse, I was there in 1981 when MTV first reached the airwaves. Not only did "Video Kill the Radio Star," but eventually television as we knew it changed.

All of these reminiscences place me in a group where I don't ordinarily place myself, but in which I am still a member in good standing—Generation X.

Though every generation or age defies stereotypes, let me offer several that position mine in contrast to the baby boomer and "Greatest Generation" which preceded it. To the consternation of their elders, Generation X'ers look upon institutions, church or otherwise, with a certain degree of suspicion. Rather than accept authority, we question it. Given the breakdown of so many things once held sacred, especially the Church and family, Generation X privileges personal experience. Subjective truth trumps objective realities. Ambiguity, diversity, pluralism, choice aren't bewildering; they're just the way things are. Technology, rather than something to be avoided, became the lifeblood of connection for many of us born during the years of the early sixties to the early eighties. One other thing to note—and this can't be overstated—is that Generation X takes popular culture seriously. We were birthed into it. What may have been difficult for the preceding generations to buy into, we were hooked on from the beginning. The music, the clothes, the artists, the television programs, the movies, all hold great meaning and substance for us, or so we told our parents.

Catholicism and the Simpsons

Speaking of popular culture, a television show that defines this generation, and even has carried over into Generation Y, is "The Simpsons." First appearing as brief segments on FOX's *The Tracy Ullman Show*, the Simpsons landed their own time slot in 1990 and have been going strong ever since, becoming America's longest running sitcom. Miss Sunday Mass . . . maybe a venial (if we still even use that word) sin. Miss the Sunday night airing of the Simpsons, even if you were forbidden by your parents to watch it, a mortal sin for sure!

As the show's audience has matured and changed over the years, I would contend that the appeal of certain characters has also changed. In the beginning, the "Eat my shorts" refrain of Bart—a rebel without a cause if there ever was one—resonated with countless adolescents unsure of themselves. In subsequent years, however, Homer has emerged as an "everyman" of sorts, voicing the cares and concerns of countless viewers. Though it might not be believed as possible, one of the areas that the Simpsons has treated humorously, seriously, and respectfully, over the years is religion.

You name the religious or spiritual topic—image of God, prayer, countless moral dilemmas, heaven and hell, the Bible, religion and science, Evangelical Christians (Ned Flanders), Judaism (Krusty the Clown); Hinduism (Apu), Buddhism (Richard Gere)—there's a Simpsons episode that deals with it.[2]

Of all the Simpsons episodes I've watched, none has been more meaningful and substantive and funnier than "The Father, the Son, and the Holy Guest Star," which first aired on May 15, 2005. It is so good that if I were to ever be given the position of DRE (and this next statement could very well disqualify me from ever getting that job), I would make this program mandatory viewing for those in the RCIA and, of course, those of us who are cradle Catholics. For me it bridges what it meant, what it means, and what it should mean to be Catholic. In essence the episode captures what *Reclaiming Catholicism* is all about: appreciating what has preceded us in faith, critically assessing the shortcomings of the Catholic traditions we should let go of, but also highlighting the practices we should retain—and realizing that this must be done in a constructive and creative way that serves to enhance our Catholic faith and identity.

The episode begins innocently enough with the announcement of a medieval festival at Springfield Elementary. I don't know if the writers meant to connect one of the programs dealing with Catholicism with a reference to the Middle Ages, but I don't think it was happenstance. To the chagrin of many, Blessed Pope John XXIII's words about the Church have yet to be realized: "We are not on earth to guard a museum, but to cultivate a flourishing garden of life."

Bring on the Characters

For the festival, Lisa, Bart's sister, is appointed queen; Martin, the schoolboy genius, is named king; while Bart, contrary to his expectations, is assigned the role of the village cooper rather than that of a chivalrous knight in shining armor. Principal Skinner arbitrarily decides that Groundskeeper Willie is to be the village idiot. Sibling rivalry gets the best of Bart who promises that he'll get even with Lisa for this grade-school humiliation. Before he can take any action, however, Willie—who rightfully hates his role—has already plotted and achieved his revenge on Springfield Elementary by releasing hundreds of rats when an oversized pie was cut into pieces. Some dessert! Suspicion immediately falls upon Bart and, without any due process, he is expelled.

Thankfully, there is a school that will take the troublemaker (who happens in this case to be innocent), and that is St. Jerome's Catholic School. Striking the fear of God into his son, Homer points out that "There you don't just get bad grades. You go straight to hell!" Perhaps it is a fault of mine, but as a teacher at a Catholic high school, I'm more apt to love a person to heaven than scare them out of hell. Fear and "Catholic guilt" do have their advantages of course—just usually not with the students of today.

On his first day at St. Jerome's, Bart's negative attitude and Nintendo playing ways immediately get him sent out into the hall where he is made to stand with his arms outstretched like Jesus on the cross. The person who metes out this punishment is a stereotypic woman religious, Sister Thomasina.[3] Not only is she angry, she is glad that rulers have given way to yardsticks. This gives her more reach to rap the knuckles of her students. Sadly, this caricature has lasted for far too long, perpetuated both by those outside and inside the Church.

I laughed, though, at the scene in which Bart reenters her class. Sister Thomasina is leading the class in a math lesson from the book, *The Word Problems of Our Lord*. She prefaces her lesson with the example: "Billy and Joseph start their penance at the same time. If each swear word brings a thousand years in hell..." Looks like the Simpsons re-introduced indulgences before Pope Benedict XVI did.

Having known several women religious in college and graduate school, all I can say is that they defy their popular "Nunzilla" presentations. Nuns are principals and professors, doctors and nurses, social activists and psychologists, spiritual directors and missionaries. The hospitals and schools they founded and staffed have educated countless generations of Catholics. Thankfully, this book bears witness through the stories of Srs. Madaleva Wolf and Mary Luke Tobin of the lasting contribution made by women religious to the Catholic Church and American society.

"Catholics Rock"

While out in the hall, Bart meets FBI (Foreign Born Irish) Father Sean (voiced by Irish actor Liam Neeson). After pleading his case, Bart is handed a copy of the *Lives of the Saints Comics* by Father Sean, who tells him that lots of church types were once "rotten wee buggers." After that, Bart's first day is a whirlwind introduction to the Catholic tradition. Later, at dinner with his family, Bart excitedly talks about his experience at Mass (Father Sean quoted Eminem!) and how he won the class art contest by drawing the bloodiest portrayal of St. Joan of Arc's burning at the stake. Much to the alarm of Marge, his mother, Bart finishes by exclaiming, "Catholics rock!"

Though we don't always communicate our Catholic tradition well and in the most positive light, the renowned priest and sociologist, Andrew Greeley has repeated this refrain time and time again: The appeal of the Catholic tradition is found in its stories. He says that "If we get you in the early years of your life and we fill your head with all of the Catholic stories, then it's very hard for you to stop being Catholic. Catholics are Catholics because they like being Catholic. They like the stories—Christmas, Easter, May Crowning, the souls in purgatory, the saints, the angels, the mother of Jesus. These are enormously powerful religious images."[4] Bart experienced it first hand and loved it.

The challenge for my generation, though, is how these Catholic practices and devotions can be reclaimed and practiced in ways that honor the teachings of the Second Vatican Council, especially with regard to such key issues as an openness to the world; the reformability of the Church; renewed attention to scripture; the practice of collegiality at all levels of the Church; an appreciation of diversity within the

Church (unity, yes; uniformity, no); the active role of the laity; reaffir-
mation of religious freedom; desire for better ecumenical relations with
non-Catholics and dialogue with other faiths; and working for a more
just world.[5] Rather than striving to make traditional Catholic devotions
ends in themselves (and using the practice of them to identify a person
as a "good" or "bad" Catholic), we need to approach these traditions
with a view to determining whether and how they unite us with Jesus
and the larger believing community of which we are a part.

When Bart says he'll say a Rosary for his mother and begins grace
with "*In nomine Patris, et Filii, et Spiritus Sancti,*" Marge has had
enough. She sends Homer over to St. Jerome's to pull Bart out of the
school. Walking up the steps, Homer attests to the longstanding belief in Catholic education by saying: "I'm sick of you teaching my son
your time-tested values." Before he can add anything else, though, he
is stopped in his tracks. It's the smell of pancakes. Hearing about the
monthly Pancake Dinner, he declares it a miracle that breakfast has
been transformed into dinner. Like his son Bart, Homer is hooked.
And—to top everything—after dinner he joins in some Bingo games.

In the course of the evening, he's introduced to one of the more
positive portrayals of the Sacrament of Reconciliation I've seen on network television (although on this show it is termed the Sacrament of
Penance and takes place in a confessional, aka "the box"). Homer begins with a magical "get out of jail" understanding of the sacrament
only to arrive at the end with a far more mature realization of what it
means. When told by Father Sean that he can't absolve Homer's sins
unless he's Catholic, Homer hesitates, then asks, "How do I join?" To
this Father Sean replies, "It begins by looking inside yourself and ends
with bread and wine." Who can refuse such an invitation?

Homer is being let into one of the great secrets of Catholicism,
one we don't celebrate or practice enough—our sense of community.
There in the parish hall, much like the parish cafeteria I was in this
evening for a Lenten fish fry, Homer sees a motley group of persons
united by food and faith—very eucharistic, very sacramental (the ordinary communicating the sacred), in the best sense of the term. What
is drawing Homer to the Catholic faith is its earthiness (In this episode
Marge has a dream that becomes a nightmare. At the conversion of
her husband and son, she looks on from Protestant heaven over at
Catholic heaven, where Jesus has "gone native," partying alongside
Bart, Homer, and motley crews of Italian and Irish Catholics.), its holiness, its lived stories. The political and theological polarization that

besets the Church today—one is either liberal or conservative, progressive or traditional—is absent at St. Jerome's. It's just Catholics sitting down at tables enjoying a good meal and fellowship together. And to think we assumed there was nothing to learn from the Simpsons.

Past to Present to Future

One of the things that drew me to this project is a real desire to understand and appreciate the Church's lived experience prior to the Second Vatican Council. Granted, I have a firm commitment to the reforms of the council, but I also recognize that I need to appreciate what came before me in the faith. *Ressourcement* (a return to the sources) and *aggiornamento* (updating or renewal), two words that characterize the substance of Vatican II, aren't opposed to one another but complementary. In order to go forward we must be mindful of the past. Likewise, if the past is to have any relevance, its spiritual wisdom must be integrated into the lived experience of believers. Catholicism, then, is never "either/or" but always "both/and." When balanced well, then, Catholicism is a *living* tradition.

I think you'll be shocked to know that one of the words used in the Simpsons episode is *transubstantiation*. When was the last time you heard that on television, EWTN programming excluded? In his catechism class Homer is asked what the word is which describes the bread and wine becoming the body and blood of Christ. Homer doesn't question this teaching of the Catholic Church on the real presence of Christ in the Eucharist but proclaims it to his catechism class. It must be admitted, however, that he had the answer written on his forearm. If only he had had a copy of the *Baltimore Catechism*!

Here I admit the need for greater *religious literacy*—knowledge of the basic doctrines, practices, and stories of our religious tradition—among my generation of Catholics. Part of the frustration within Catholicism today is our inability to use a shared language (not that all of that language before was good). If we don't have a shared vocabulary of faith, inevitably conversations are frustrated, and evangelizing opportunities are thwarted. One of the purposes of this project is to foster a shared sense of the Catholic tradition and a desire to know more about it.

Given my use of the Simpsons throughout this article, as opposed to quotations from the *Catechism of the Catholic Church*, it's clear that the invitation to a more substantial knowledge, understanding, and appreciation of the faith is going to take different forms depending on the group you're trying to reach. I'm sure that with his love of beer, Homer is a regular at the Theology on Tap series in his home diocese of Springfield. Which leads me to point out that one thing the Catholic tradition has over all the other religious traditions (except for maybe Judaism) is our ability to laugh at and with ourselves. It's time again to use it to our advantage. It's time to "reclaim Catholicism."

The next time I'm at Mass, during the sign of peace I'm going to look around the church and see if I find Homer Simpson there. As I extend my hand to him and wish him peace, I'm also going to thank him for converting to Catholicism. D'oh!

In addition to Homer, I must also thank several other persons. First, co-editor Tom Groome brought invaluable perspective and experience to the project. If there is a model of what it means to "reclaim Catholicism" it is he. Second, the contributors are in a class unto themselves. Their generosity of time and talent is much appreciated. The success of the book is largely due to their reflections. Third, Robert Ellsberg, our editor at Orbis Books, must be thanked for his acceptance of and support for the project. Finally, for providing me the time, space, and encouragement needed to complete this project, I offer thanks to my family—June, Cara, Brendan, and Nora.

Notes

1. An excellent article on the musings of another post–Vatican II Catholic is John J. Markey's "The Making of a Post–Vatican II Theologian," *America* (July 16, 1994).

2. See *The Gospel According to the Simpsons: The Spiritual Life of the World's Most Animated Family*, by Mark I. Pinsky (Louisville: Westminster John Knox Press, 2001, revised 2007).

3. I remember well from my days of growing up as a kid a song released in 1977 entitled, "They don't make nun names like that no more" by Tommy Sharp and the Sharptones.

4. Quote taken from an interview with Andrew Greeley on the weekly television news program, *Religion & Ethics Newsweekly*, May 10, 2002, Episode #536.

5. Avery Dulles has summarized these teachings nicely in the booklet *Vatican II and the Extraordinary Synod: An Overview* (Collegeville: The Liturgical Press, 1986).

I

PERSPECTIVES

1

Reclaiming Our Past and Moving Forward

A Pervasive Faith

JAMES D. DAVIDSON

It was 1941 in Great Barrington, Massachusetts. Mary Louise Fitzpatrick, a 100 percent Irish Catholic, was engaged to James Daglish Davidson, a white Anglo-Saxon Protestant (his father was a Scottish Presbyterian and his mother an English Anglican). Because Louise and Jim were of different faiths, they could not be married at the main altar in Louise's home parish (their wedding took place in the rectory), and they had to sign an agreement that their children would be raised Catholic.

Jim and Louise had two sons. I was born in 1942, as Dad was going off to World War II. My brother was born in 1946, when Dad returned from the war. Our mother's side of the family far outnumbered our father's side, so our Irish Catholic relatives had more to do with the way we were raised than did our Scottish and English Protestant relatives. Thus, our last name is Scottish, but culturally we are more Irish Catholic.

The Catholicism I Grew Up In

My Irish Catholic relatives were working-class people. None of them had ever gone to college, but they all expected their kids (my generation) to go. The men were the breadwinners, working in blue-collar

3

jobs or trying to start their own businesses. The women were what are now called "stay-at-home moms." The families' very modest incomes were spent on basics, like buying homes and saving for the kids' education. There weren't many vacations.

Religious prejudice and discrimination (anti-Catholicism) had created social and cultural barriers between the nation's religious elites and Catholic immigrants in the 1920s, 1930s, and 1940s. Although these barriers persisted into the 1950s, cracks were appearing in the walls that divided Protestants and Catholics. My Aunt Margaret could not get a job teaching in the public schools in the 1940s because she was Catholic, yet by the 1950s many of the teachers were Catholic.

The Church made no bones about its cultural distinctiveness. In a society that stressed democracy, the Church defended its hierarchical structure. Whereas the Protestant majority emphasized the authority of the Bible, the Church focused on papal infallibility and "tradition." While Protestant churches conducted their worship services in English, the Catholic Mass was conducted in Latin. Despite criticism from other faiths, the Church insisted that Mary was the Mother of God.

The Church also separated itself socially from the larger society. With good reason, it saw American society as hostile to its values and interests. Viewing itself as "the one true Church," it encouraged its members to participate in Catholic groups and discouraged them from joining non-Catholic organizations. The result was that Catholics' social circles included a very high percentage of other Catholics. Even when Catholics had non-Catholic friends—as I did in my public high school—we often participated in different social groups. My friends Milt—a Congregationalist—and Corky—a Jew—could belong to DeMolay (an international youth organization), but I could not, because of its ties to Freemasonry.

The Church served the social as well as the spiritual needs of its people. Ethnic parishes and celebrations (such as St. Patrick's Day parades) offered them ways of perpetuating their ethnic identities as they adapted to American society. Dioceses and religious orders provided a vast network of Catholic schools, which were like steps on an up-escalator into the middle class. Schools were also were places where Catholics found careers and spouses, and contexts in which the faith was transmitted across generations (the Catholic colleges my brother and I attended provided most of these benefits). The Church also offered Catholics age-related sacraments (such as First Communion,

Confirmation, Marriage, and Last Rites) at every stage in people's personal and family lives.

As a result, the Church was important to my whole family. It influenced everything my Catholic relatives did. It affected the décor in their homes (a crucifix hung on the wall in almost every room, pictures of Mary and/or Jesus were on the tops of the dressers in all the bedrooms). The Church shaped the family calendar (Are any of the kids serving morning Mass this week? Remember, Thursday is a holy day, so we've got to go to Mass). It established a rhythm (getting on your knees to say your prayers morning and night) for each day. It affected people's eating habits (no meat on Fridays, no food or drink of any kind between midnight Saturday and Communion on Sunday morning). It dominated Catholics' conversations (discussions of the pastor's idiosyncrasies were a favorite pastime). It also made others aware of one's religious affiliation (only Catholics put ashes on their foreheads and gave up cigarettes and chocolate for Lent).

My Catholic relatives believed there was a close relationship between their faith and the Church. The faith included the core Christian tenets such as belief in a personal God, the incarnation, and the resurrection, along with specifically Catholic beliefs having to do with Christ's real presence in the sacraments (especially the Eucharist), Mary, and concern for the poor. The Church was the religious institution that stretched from the Vatican to the diocese to the local parish and around the world. It was where the sacraments and devotional practices such as Benediction and novenas took place, and where the kids went for CCD. Like most other Catholics in the 1950s, my elders thought the faith and the Church were inseparable. The faith was lodged in the Church, and the Catholic Church was the fullest expression of the Christian faith.

There was an abundance of priests and a distinct culture of clericalism. Clergy and laity alike believed that priests were set apart by ordination and holier than lay people. They also believed that priests had more authority and played a more active role in the formulation and implementation of church teachings. Ordinary Catholics were to learn church teachings, incorporate them into their lives, and pass them on to their children. This top-down model of church life, with its emphasis on the teaching authority of the magisterium and the laity's obligation to obey, produced extraordinarily high levels of doctrinal and behavioral consensus. The lines for confession on Saturday were long.

Almost everyone went to Mass every Sunday. I don't remember adults openly disagreeing with church teachings.

Moving Forward (or What to Bring with Us)

Things sure have changed! Catholics who are my age or younger are now firmly entrenched in the upper-middle class and are considered part of the nation's cultural mainstream. We no longer see the Church as a refuge. The Church has a more positive view of modern society, and—with the exception of a few noteworthy flashpoints (e.g., abortion, capital punishment)—church leaders urge Catholics to adapt to the prevailing culture. The Church no longer affects Catholics' daily lives, conversations, and social networks the way it used to. Religious obligation has given way to a tendency for Catholics to view belief and practice as matters of choice. Obedience has receded into the background, as more and more parents teach their kids to think for themselves. Participation in the sacraments has declined, and disagreements over doctrine have increased. Fewer men are going into the priesthood, and lay people expect to be actively involved in parish and diocesan decisions.

Today's Catholics have little or no interest in returning to the social circumstances of the 1950s. They prefer being educated, white collar, prosperous, and integrated into the larger society. And, given these conditions, they believe that they are good and talented people who ought to have a say in all aspects of church life, including the selection of their pastors and decisions about parish finances. For the most part, they want to implement Vatican II's vision for the Church and its place in the world.

Older Catholics have been quite willing to let go of some things that were taken for granted in the 1950s but which we now know were wrong-headed or excessive, such as the Church's antipathy toward other religious traditions and its tendency to treat women and minorities as second-class citizens. They also have shown their willingness to embrace many new ideas, such as conducting the Mass in the vernacular and having the priest face the people at Mass. But many older Catholics also worry that, in our rush to modernize the Church, we may have thrown out some elements of our heritage that should be cornerstones of our future. They wonder if some traditional concepts and practices could be updated and contribute to the renewal that Pope John XXIII longed for when he convened Vatican II in 1962.

Younger Catholics—who have had no personal experience with 1950s Catholicism—have found it even easier to accept new ideas and to reject the most parochial, exclusionary, and unjust parts of traditional Catholic culture. But many young people also have heard inspiring stories about the 1950s or have seen admirable traits among older Catholics who were products of that era. They wonder if some of the traditions they have heard about should be reemphasized or revised in some way; if the things that fostered the religious pride and loyalty they see in their parents and grandparents could be reintroduced in some form; whether some of the ways in which the Church was useful to old immigrants might also be of help to new ones; and if there is something that could be done to bridge the gap between faith (being spiritual) and Church (being religious).

This book is for Catholics of all ages who have such questions and yearnings. It challenges liberal Catholics to find ways in which the best elements of 1950s Catholic culture can become the best elements of modern Catholic culture. It challenges conservative Catholics to adapt traditional ways to current conditions. It challenges all Catholics to imagine how reclaiming our past can be an important step in moving forward.

2

Becoming a Theologian

Ressourcement, *Personal and Ecclesial*

FRANCINE CARDMAN

Crossing the Bridge

My strongest early memories of Catholicism are of my Italian grandmother's hands. At any small, quiet moment—sitting in the kitchen, walking to the grocery store, riding the subway, standing on the back steps and enjoying the sunshine—her hand would reach for the rosary beads strategically positioned in the pocket of her apron, her "housecoat," her robe, even, much later in life, her mink coat. Her hands kneaded and baked bread, too, bread that nourished my childhood; bread that followed me to college in care packages, the first of which included a bread knife and cutting board that I still have; bread that one day I came to recognize as eucharistic.

Less clear are memories of my Polish grandmother's more ambiguous relationship to the Church: her steadfast church-going, the Infant of Prague statue and his several sets of vestments, my puzzlement about why she didn't go to Communion, the missing piece of information eventually supplied: she was divorced and remarried. My instinctive sense as a small child that something was amiss became a conviction that her exclusion from the Eucharist was unfair. I knew she was Catholic; why didn't the Church?

Growing up on suburban Long Island in the 1950s, I didn't know that my generation of Catholics would walk across the bridge our parents were building from the immigrant church of their parents and grandparents to the middle-class, American Catholicism that would help elect John F. Kennedy president in 1960. Perhaps also representative of my baby-boomer Catholic cohort, I attended public schools, a decision in which my mother prevailed by virtue of the contrast between the local elementary school's average class size of eighteen and the thirty-plus at St. Boniface parish school. As public school students we were released early each Wednesday afternoon to attend catechism class. I was acutely aware that we were second-class Catholics, not really as Catholic as the parochial school kids we had to sit behind on occasions when we all attended Mass together—even for First Communion and Confirmation. I didn't think that was fair, either.

I progressed through Baltimore Catechisms 1 and 2, cheerfully memorizing everything: the prayers, the strange words, the questions and answers on God, Trinity, incarnation, redemption, Church, grace, sacraments, the Ten Commandments, and the Mass. But information isn't knowledge, much less understanding. The hapless young priest who taught ninth grade CCD had only the seminary version of catechism answers to my increasingly dissatisfied questioning. When he insisted that the evolutionary theory I was learning in biology class was at odds with the Church's teaching on the single origin of human life (monogenism), I began to wonder how intelligent people—my father, for instance, or my high school Latin teacher—could be Catholic.

Then came Vatican II. I didn't know, of course, what a watershed it would be not only for the Church but also for me. I read about it in the *New York Times* and in *Time* magazine, where John XXIII was on the cover as Man of the Year in 1962. The council was an interesting but distant event and I couldn't imagine it would make much difference.

Becoming a Theologian

For most of my first year at college I simply didn't go to church, an advance beyond my late–high school practice of pretending to go to Sunday Mass, when I would silently roll our VW down the hill, pop the clutch to avoid making too much noise while starting the engine, drop by the church to pick up a bulletin, and head down to the beach to watch the wind on the water.

Then things began to change. I took a course on the New Testament taught by a former priest thoroughly versed in both the historical-critical method and Vatican II. It was a revelation of its own. I met faculty, students, and families from the town who were Catholics of this new sort, along with ecumenically-minded Protestants eager to interact with them. One Sunday, I'm not sure why, I went to the Newman Club liturgy in the Friends Meeting House on campus. Soon community and liturgy along with my studies were drawing me toward faith and, more slowly, toward understanding. A young Catholic math professor and an older (*much* older, it seemed then) professor of French formed a group to discuss Teilhard de Chardin's *The Divine Milieu*, which opened a window on creation and the possible coherence of faith and science. We read Edward Schillebeeckx's *Christ the Sacrament of the Encounter with God*, which reached back to the experience behind those abstract and unenlightening catechism answers and invited an organic appropriation of Catholic sacramental imagination. I acquired a copy of Walter Abbott's translation of *The Documents of Vatican II* that I still have, its red paperback cover flaking and its pages disintegrating. The rest is history: mine.

What I was discovering was a way of being Catholic that was integrated with the intellectual life; that valued participation, collaboration, and subsidiarity; that engaged the world and culture, promoted peace and development, understood the political dimensions of faith, and worked for justice. As I studied the history of the early Church—an entirely new world I knew almost nothing about—I found there the wellspring of the new but old Church that Vatican II was calling into being. I had to know more.

And so I went to graduate school to study historical theology and "patristics." I delved into the early sources and at the same time discovered the Catholic scholars who had been retrieving and reappropriating them in the decades before Vatican II, preparing the ground for renewal. The word "*ressourcement*" was unknown to me then, but that's what I was doing, too, as I entered into a far more expansive tradition than the Catholicism of my childhood. I admired how Henri de Lubac rehabilitated the unfairly condemned third-century theologian Origen by recovering his extensive biblical scholarship. Jean Danielou's reappropriation of the biblical typologies that structured early Christian liturgy and his interpretation of the history of salvation gave me a feel for the sources and dynamics of contemporary liturgical reform. I welcomed too his re-introduction of Gregory of Nyssa's mystical theology to Westerners suspended in the rigid medium of scholasticism, making available again a spirituality informed by Eastern Christianity's more generous assessment of the human capacity to grow freely in the love and knowledge of God.[1]

From Yves Congar I learned that to do theology well one had to remember a longer tradition than post-Tridentine Catholicism and be aware of a larger Christian community than the Roman Catholic or Orthodox churches. Taking history seriously and carrying *ressourcement* beyond the patristic era, Congar's painstaking work on tradition, lay people in the church, reform, and ecumenism convinced me that this kind of theological study was essential for finding a way through differences within Catholicism and among Christians. Introduced with some reluctance to Karl Rahner's often incomprehensible theological investigations, I began to grasp how Catholic doctrine could be articulated in a framework more in touch with Thomas than with neo-Thomism and could find in the human and historical dimensions of life the grace that permeates nature and opens beyond it.[2]

Later I would learn how costly the work of these theologians had been to them personally. Through the 1940s and 1950s each had come under suspicion from the Holy Office. Congar, de Lubac, Danielou, and de Chardin were silenced, the latter until his untimely death in 1955. As preparations for Vatican II were under way, Rahner was on the verge of being investigated and Schillebeeckx was embroiled in controversy. Then John XXIII appointed all but Schillebeeckx *periti* (theological experts) to assist the council's work and Schillebeeckx was soon giving lectures to large groups of bishops eager to learn about the "new theology" (*Nouvelle Théologie*) informing the council's discussions and documents. The rest is history: ours.

Past as Prologue

Looking back at the council and the post-conciliar years that formed me as a Catholic and a theologian, I can see the convergence of personal and ecclesial *ressourcement*. I can see, too, the ways in which this return to the sources for the sake of *aggiornamento*, bringing the church up to date in order to engage "the joys and hopes, the griefs and the anxieties of the people of this age" (*Gaudium et Spes* 1), has both succeeded and faltered and is itself now in need of renewal. When I wonder where that renewal will come from, I ponder the patient endurance of those theologians who helped the council find the words for its vision of a Church renewed in service of God's mission to the world. Like my grandmothers, they were faithful, even when wounded by the Church. Like my grandmothers, prayer was the work of their hands, whether holding rosary beads or writing theology. In time, I hope, the strength of their witness will show us the way to the future by calling us to continue along the path taken by the council—through a past that makes all things new.

Notes

1. Henri De Lubac's and Jean Danielou's reappropriation of patristic sources is reflected in the more biblical and patristic rhetoric of Vatican II, especially in foundational documents such as *Lumen Gentium* (church) and *Sacrosanctam Concilium* (liturgy). Henri de Lubac, *History and Spirit: The Understanding of Scripture according to Origen*, trans. Anne Englund Nash (San Francisco: Ignatius Press, 2007). De Lubac wrote several books on Teilhard de Chardin, e.g., *Teilhard Explained*, trans. Anthony Buono (New York: Paulist Press, 1968). Jean Danielou, *The Bible and the Liturgy* (Notre Dame, IN: University of Notre Dame Press, 1956). His selection of Gregory of Nyssa's writing is *From Glory to Glory: Texts from Gregory of Nyssa's Mystical Writings* (New York: Scribner, 1961).

2. Yves Congar and Karl Rahner helped shaped the theological outlook of the council through a more relational understanding of revelation and an appreciation of the human and historical dimensions of the Church and its mission in the world. Yves Congar, *Tradition and Traditions: An Historical and a Theological Essay* (New York: Macmillan, 1967); *Lay People in the Church: A Study for a Theology of Laity*, trans. Donald Attwater, 2nd rev. ed. (Westminster, MD: Newman Press, 1965); *Divided Christendom: A Catholic Study of the Problem of Reunion* (London: G. Bles, 1939). Karl Rahner, *Theological Investigations*, 23 vols., 1961–1992 (various publishers).

3

Studying the Bible, Then and Now

DIANNE BERGANT, C.S.A.

Way Back When

On November 18, 1965, Pope Paul VI solemnly promulgated Vatican II's Dogmatic Constitution on Divine Revelation. For many people, this document seemed to cause a shift in previously unrecognized tectonic plates that existed deep within the religious psyche of the Roman Catholic spirit. These people regarded the shift as a kind of tsunami wave that would sweep away all previous approaches to biblical study. However, that is not quite what happened. Unlike some changes that did indeed sweep away earlier devotional practices, this document opened the floodgates that had been holding back waters of renewal, waters that had been building up for more than twenty years, waters that were invigorating rather than destructive.

Biblical study was given new impetus on September 30, 1943 when Pius XII issued *Divino Afflante Spiritu*. In this document, the Holy Father encouraged the use of critical interpretive approaches for opening up the riches of the biblical tradition. Protestants had developed and employed these methods since the sixteenth century when Luther insisted that *sola scriptura*, scripture alone, should be the norm of theology. It seems that the Catholic Church had three hundred years of development to cover if it was to catch up with other Christian denominations. However, once again, appearances can be deceiving.

Many Catholic theologians had already been exploring new ways of reading the Bible. Chief among them was a French Dominican, Marie-Joseph Lagrange (1855–1938). He eventually came to be known as "the father of the Catholic Biblical Movement." Though censored by church officials during his lifetime, he achieved a delicate balance between fidelity to church authority and intellectual integrity. It was people like him who laid the foundation of biblical scholarship in the Catholic Church.

Back Then

Even before Vatican II, insights gained through the use of critical methods of interpretation had begun to appear in catechetical resources. An Austrian-born Jesuit by the name of Johannes Hofinger immediately comes to mind. His influence in biblical-based religious education cannot be overestimated. Women religious who were responsible for the education of children in parochial schools as well as for religious education programs flocked to his conferences and read his books. The old Bible History stories were replaced by the fruits of critical scholarship. The Sadlier textbook I used for seventh grade featured the Old Testament. Thus, an entire generation of religion teachers and students were well prepared for the direction set by the Vatican document.

Women religious laid the groundwork for biblical renewal, but they were still not accepted in graduate programs of biblical study. The prime example of this was Kathryn Sullivan, R.S.C.J. She became a biblical scholar despite the fact that she was denied entry into a biblical program. After earning a doctorate in history, she taught herself Hebrew and Greek and studied scripture privately. She was the first female member of the Catholic Biblical Association. She even became its vice president. However, as a woman she was not allowed to proceed to its presidency. She taught scripture both here and abroad, she wrote and translated the writings of others, and she was a founding member of the *Catholic Biblical Quarterly* as well as *The Bible Today*.

And Now

Today biblical scholars and teachers stand on the shoulders of those who went before us. They were the ones who explored new possibilities, who ventured into new areas, who suffered "the slings and arrows of outrageous fortune." We may sometimes feel that the church moves very slowly along the path of change and renewal, but the history of biblical interpretation since the time of the Reformation challenges this perspective. The official approach to scripture may have been couched in strict Catholic theological teaching, but pastoral needs of people prompted many individuals to investigate new ways of opening the riches of the biblical tradition. At several moments in history, biblical renewal flowers forth. Were this not so, the Catholic Biblical Movement associated with Marie-Joseph Lagrange, O.P., would not have come to life, the biblical catechetical ministry of Johannes Hofinger, S.J., would not have taken root, and the passion for scripture of Kathryn Sullivan, R.S.C.J., would not have enkindled a similar fire in the minds and hearts of others.

Though at one time Catholic biblical scholars were far behind their Protestant counterparts, they now stand toe-to-toe with all biblical scholars. And what of the people in the pew? Many who were opened to new insights before the council enrolled in graduate programs and became the teachers who brought the fruits of study to the rest of the Church. Graduate programs were now accessible to both men and women. And all of this occurred during the lifetime of many of us who spanned the pre- and post-Vatican II years.

Who's Who

Many people who spanned those years have set the directions taken by biblical study today. Some have continued to investigate cultural aspects of the ancient worlds that produced the scriptures. Bruce Malina (Creighton University) and Carolyn Osiek, R.S.C.J. (Brite Divinity School) have opened up the meaning of various social customs and values, thus helping us understand ancient people and why they thought and acted as they did. Other scholars are interested in methods of interpretation. Elisabeth Schüssler Fiorenza (Harvard Divinity School) is renowned for her development of feminist critical methods of interpretation, while Fernando Segovia (Vanderbilt University) investigates post-colonial approaches. Finally, there are those who devoted themselves to biblical theology and spirituality. The work of Carroll Stuhlmueller, C.P. (1923–1994) and of Sandra Schneiders, I.H.M., come immediately to mind. And there is a legion of other great Catholic scholars who paved the way of biblical scholarship and renewal, people like John McKenzie, S.J., Josephine Massyngberde

Ford, Raymond Brown, S.S., Joseph Fitzmyer, S.J., Pheme Perkins, Philip King, Richard Dillon, George MacRae, S.J., and many more.

All of these scholars have influenced the Church through their teaching, lecturing, and writing. While many of these names might be unfamiliar to the person in the pew, they are well known to those who stand in the pulpit or behind a lectern. They were all nurtured in the pre-Vatican II church, and they all stepped forward when the Vatican Council called for a deeper knowledge of and appreciation for the word of God. Several of them were educated in and now teach at graduate schools not associated with the Catholic Church. This in no way suggests alienation from the Church. Instead, it is evidence of the close association that exists between all Christian churches that value serious study of the scriptures. We all use the same critical methods of interpretation, and we all learn from each other.

What's What

Current Roman Catholic biblical study appears to be taking an interesting turn. It seems to be trying to recapture aspects of interpretation that were lost in previous generations. During the sixteenth century the reformers accused the officials of the Roman Church of reading biblical passages in ways that provided legitimacy to current church practices. This was the reason the reformers turned to the meaning intended by the original biblical authors, arguing that these ancient authors were speaking to issues that concerned their own communities and, therefore, their teachings could not be used to support later church teaching. Though the Catholic Church continued to interpret various biblical passages through its own theological lens, once it adopted critical interpretive approaches, it too shifted its focus from possible present meanings to those of the past.

This shift to the past proved to be a very good one, for it prevented people from twisting the meaning of a passage in order to produce whatever meaning they sought—proof texting. However, this historical approach often cut the passage off from the believing community of the present. The Bible certainly originated and was developed within past communities. Nevertheless, as the word of God, it belongs to present communities. So, while it may be important to ask: "What might this passage from Luke's Gospel have meant for the early Christians?" one must also ask: "And what might it mean for us today?"

The recent Synod of Bishops, "The Word of God in the Life and Mission of the Church," addressed this very topic. The bishops were concerned with ways of bringing the richness of the biblical tradition developed over these past several decades more deeply into the lives of the Catholic people of God. The synod applauded the advances that have been made, and it suggested new ways of furthering the development already achieved.

When I look back over the forty years during which I have been involved in biblical ministry, I am amazed at all the changes I have experienced and shared. From teaching Bible stories to children to directing future priests and pastoral ministers in the critical analysis of the biblical text; from conducting summer school catechism classes to earning a doctorate in scripture; from being handed a seventh grade textbook that featured the Old Testament to serving as president of the Catholic Biblical Association. Who says that the Church does not change? Or, that it changes too slowly? True, none of this would have happened had not there been women and men before me who followed the promptings of their hearts and committed themselves to the word of God.

We must be inspired by them and do as much in our own time.

4

Jesus

A Change in Emphasis

LUKE TIMOTHY JOHNSON

It is fairly common these days to hear from proponents of historical Jesus research that creedal Christianity has neglected the humanity of Jesus. Among post–Vatican II Catholics also, it is sometimes claimed that the Tridentine church so emphasized the divinity of Christ that Jesus disappeared into the Holy Trinity. Mary had to serve as the prime mediator between humans and God, as expressed in the common slogan, *ad Jesum per Mariam* ("To Jesus through Mary"). In contrast, it is claimed, the Second Vatican Council helped recover the human Jesus for ordinary Christians.

There is some truth to these assertions, but only some. They exaggerate by making an either/or out of a situation that is better viewed as both/and. The difference in the attention given to Jesus by Catholics before and after the Second Vatican Council is a matter of emphasis. Certainly, the aftermath of the council brought a helpful, even an essential dimension to the ordinary Catholic's appreciation of Jesus. But present-day Catholics also have much to learn from preconciliar practices of piety centered on the humanity of Jesus.

The difference in emphasis can be stated succinctly. Before the Second Vatican Council, Catholic piety toward Jesus focused on his love toward humans and fellowship with humans as demonstrated above all by the circumstances of his birth and the manner of his death. After the council, Catholic piety toward Jesus is directed above all to the character of his ministry, with special emphasis on his words and deeds.

The two foci of earlier piety fit with the emphasis of the Creed, which does not say anything about Jesus' ministry, but speaks only of his being born of the Virgin Mary and his suffering under Pontius Pilate. Throughout the medieval and post-Reformation periods, Catholic mystics devoted their meditation to the mystery of God's presence in an infant child—a form of humility that was consistently compared to Christ's presence in the humble matter of the eucharistic bread and wine; such reflections are found in the mystics Mechtild and Hadjewich as well as in Francis and Bonaventure. They were given physical expression (incarnation) in countless artistic expressions of the infancy gospels, and prayer at the crèche during the Christmas season.

Even more consistent was the focus on Christ's passion, often in minute and excruciating detail, as in the visions of Julian of Norwich and the poetry of Richard Rolle of Hampole. The humanity of Jesus was at the center also of Thomas à Kempis's *Imitation of Christ*, and of the great work it influenced, the *Spiritual Exercises* of Ignatius of Loyola.

God's Love in Human Form

The basis of such meditation, it should be noted, was the narratives of the canonical gospels, which were heard by the mystics in liturgical proclamation—thus the natural connection to the Eucharist—and read in private. The yield of such meditation was awe and appreciation for the love of God demonstrated through Christ's profound and utter sharing of the human condition, a sense of gratitude for the grace given through such love, and a commitment by the mystic to follow more closely in the same path of humble poverty and obedience. Such was the import of the distinctive devotion to the Sacred Heart of Jesus, which found in the symbol of the human heart the expression for God's love displayed in human character.

The same emphasis was found in the common practices of ordinary Catholics. The mysteries of the Rosary included, to be sure, the glorious events associated with Jesus' resurrection, exaltation, and sending of the Holy Spirit. But the two other sets of mysteries were devoted to the beginning and the end of the gospel story. The Joyful mysteries invited meditation on the humanity of Jesus in the annunciation, visitation, birth, presentation and finding in the temple—all derived from Luke's infancy account.

The sorrowful mysteries, in turn, followed Jesus through the passion narrative. Ordinary Catholics had an unusually rich repository of scriptural knowledge for this aspect of Jesus' humanity, for all during the season of Lent, the stations of the Cross—composed out of both Old and New Testament passages —provided a slow and solemn meditative performance of Jesus' last moments. During Holy Week, furthermore, all four passion narratives of the gospels were proclaimed liturgically, and the ceremonies of Palm Sunday, Maundy Thursday, and Good Friday brought the mysteries of Christ's passion to vivid realistic expression.

Although the focus of piety concerning Jesus was narrow before the Second Vatican Council, it was correspondingly deep. It was based in the reading of scripture and given embodiment by the liturgical practices of the church. Emphasis was less on knowledge about Jesus than on the sapiential imitation of Jesus; less on his deeds and words than on his character; less about information than about transformation.

Vatican II's Change of Focus

The change of focus after Vatican II came about as a result of two factors: the extension of biblical knowledge more widely among Catholics as a result of scholarly translation and popularization, and the development (not coincidentally) of liberation theology. Liberation theology distinguished itself from its predecessors by its steadfast attention to the political dimensions of the Good News, as found particularly in the portrayal of Jesus in the Gospel of Luke: Christian life should be one of strenuous effort to change unjust social structures and systems to ones more responsive to human need and more enhancing of human dignity. Luke's prophetic Jesus, who came to proclaim good news to the poor and liberation to the oppressed, is the model to be followed. Here, the focus is less on Jesus' human character that is to be imitated than on his vision for God's rule, emphasizing this world rather than the next.

Liberation theology both arose from and helped stimulate further attention to the Jesus of the gospels and his public ministry. Catholics, who had always felt themselves disadvantaged with respect to biblical knowledge compared to their Protestant friends, were eager to join in Bible study and find out all they could about the mission of the historical Jesus. As a result of the many opportunities offered them and their own enthusiasm for learning, Catholics today can be said to have far better knowledge of the full range of information about Jesus (both biblical and extra-biblical).

Catholic biblical scholars and many Catholic lay people also find themselves fascinated with historical Jesus research, explicitly or implicitly preferring the Jesus capable of being reconstructed by means of historical study to the Jesus portrayed in the gospels and proclaimed in the life of the Church. Even Catholics who have little acquaintance with liberation theology find themselves thinking about the significance of Jesus in terms of the transformation of human politics toward God's reign rather than in terms of eternal salvation.

Both Jesus of History and Christ of Faith

It is all to the good, I think, that Catholics have learned about Jesus' earthly ministry through their engagement with the New Testament. It is a positive enhancement of their discipleship to imitate the historical Jesus who embraced the poor and homeless, drove out evil spirits from the oppressed, touched the untouchable, and challenged the value system of the world. The fruits of such imitation of Jesus are seen in the many ministries of Catholics among the poor and outcast, not for the purpose of conversion, but simply for justice to be done. Indeed, even John Paul II, who was not a great fan of liberation theology, recognized the value of a piety focused on imitating Jesus' ministry and added to the Rosary new mysteries that invite meditation on aspects of his enactment of God's rule through his words and deeds.

It would be unfortunate, however, if the earlier forms of Jesus piety were displaced and forgotten, especially when they are so deeply embedded in the Creed and in the liturgical practice of the church. The deepest and most important level of Jesus' humanity, after all, does not reside in his words and deeds, but in the manner in which he participated in our shared human existence, shared it from humble and impoverished birth to obedient and shameful death, shared it with a human character marked by absolute obedience to God and absolute dedication to the needs of others. By so sharing he both showed us a new way of being human in the world and revealed the face of God in human form. If the older forms of piety are forgotten, then attention to Jesus' ministry threatens to become superficial and a form of false hope; but if the newer emphasis builds on and expands the deep tracks of the older piety toward the Christ of our faith, then devotion to Jesus within the Church grows wider without losing depth.

5

The Church

Catholicism Before and After Vatican II

RICHARD P. McBRIEN

Many self-described "traditional" or "orthodox" Catholics have been urging for a long while that we should make every effort to restore the Catholicism of the pre–Vatican II period—a time when, in their minds, the Church was more truly "Catholic" than it is today. As I have frequently pointed out in my various writings and lectures, a good number of such Catholics were not even alive in the years preceding the Second Vatican Council (1962–1965). They never experienced pre-conciliar Catholicism first-hand, as I did and as did countless other Catholics who are now over the age of sixty.

I have also pointed out, with tongue in cheek, that if these self-styled "orthodox" Catholics really want to go back to those pre-conciliar days, they will only get more priests like me! I am, after all, a product of pre–Vatican II Catholicism. I was baptized a Catholic soon after I was born in 1936, was taught by my mother my first prayers and the sign of the cross as a very young child, studied the *Baltimore Catechism* under the guidance of the parish nuns, served Mass as an altar boy, attended Catholic junior high and then the local high-school seminary on my way to studying for the priesthood. I was ordained in February 1962, just over eight months before Pope John XXIII formally convened the council.

I am, therefore, totally a product of the pre–Vatican II Church: born, educated, trained, spiritually formed, and ordained a priest in that Church. Perhaps for that reason, I have little patience with those who did not personally experience pre–Vatican II Catholicism or who "converted" to Catholicism some years after Vatican II, but who sometimes pontificate (excuse the word) on why the Catholic Church needs to go back to that time in order to save itself from itself.

Needless to say, there is much about the pre–Vatican II Church and the broad Catholic tradition it embodied that was and still is pastorally positive and spiritually enriching for those of us who directly experienced it and were profoundly shaped by it. Pre-conciliar Catholicism can and should serve as the wellspring of spiritual growth and wisdom for Catholics today.

But there were also elements of pre–Vatican II Catholicism that had to be jettisoned or at least significantly transformed, and the council served the Church well in doing both. In what remains of this brief personal narrative, I will focus first on those elements of pre-conciliar Catholicism that should not be lost, but refurbished and renewed, and then on those aspects of pre-conciliar Catholicism that should not be restored.

The Abiding Assets of the Pre–Vatican II Church

The Catholic Church of the 1930s, 1940s, and 1950s celebrated ("administered" was the more commonly used verb) the seven sacraments, and the Church of today still does. The Eucharist (more often referred to then as both the Mass and Holy Communion) was at the center of the Church's sacramental life, and it remains so today. Baptism made possible for (mostly) infants and (some) adults alike entrance into full membership in the Church, with all the attendant benefits and obligations. (To be sure, there was also an emphasis in baptismal catechesis on the "washing away" of the stains of original sin, but an explanation of this is beyond the scope of this piece.)

First Communion, preceded unfortunately as it is still today by first confession, marked young Catholics' passage into the fullness of spiritual citizenship in the Church, just as Confirmation would mark their passage into the beginnings of spiritual maturity.

There were, then as now, other sacramental milestones in a Catholic's life in that pre–Vatican II period: Marriage (for most),

Ordination (for a relative few), and Extreme Unction for the dying (this sacrament is now called the Anointing of the Sick to make it clear that it is also for the seriously ill, even the chronically ill who are not yet on the threshold of death).

Acknowledgment of one's sins and a recognition of the need for repentance, a firm purpose of amendment, and absolution were the basic elements of what was then popularly known as "Confession" (now the sacrament of Reconciliation). What has changed is not the absence of sin or the need for divine forgiveness mediated through the Church, but the format or venue in which this spiritual transaction occurs. In the pre-conciliar Church, it happened in a darkened confessional box; in the post–Vatican II Church, it happens in a reconciliation room, in a face-to-face exchange with the priest-confessor.

When the sexual-abuse crisis in the Catholic priesthood reached its ugly nadir in January 2002 with the shocking investigative series of articles in *The Boston Globe*, I pointed out on national television and in various interviews with the print media that this scandal was not at all confined to Boston, that it was national and even international in scope. And so it was, and is.

I also described it as being the most dangerous crisis to confront the Catholic Church in the United States in its entire history and the universal Church since the Reformation of the sixteenth century. In truth, the sexual-abuse scandal had placed a dagger at the throat of the Church by putting at fundamental risk the Church's most precious asset: its sacramental life. That sacramental life was, and still is, the principal reason why people enter and remain in the Catholic Church.

The Church's sacraments provide opportunities to ritualize, celebrate, and work our way through life's most joyful and most sorrowful experiences: the birth of children or grandchildren, their first taste of the Lord's Body and Blood in Holy Communion, their first stirrings of spiritual maturity in Confirmation, their falling in love and committing themselves to another person in a life-long union, their experience of guilt and their felt need for forgiveness, their encounter with serious illness, whether of a loved one or of themselves, and finally the loss of a loved one in death.

These are among the abiding riches of Catholicism, both before and after Vatican II, and they need to be creatively retrieved, preserved, and enriched. Like the wheat of the gospels, they continue to grow among us, but also with the weeds, in danger always of being uprooted with those weeds and thrown into the fire (Mt 13:24–30).

The "Weeds" of Pre–Vatican II Catholicism

Recent attempts to reignite interest in indulgences, auricular confession, and the Latin Mass have been motivated, whether overtly or
not, by some deeply felt need to restore one of the most characteristic
features of pre-conciliar Catholicism, namely, unchallenged and un-
challengeable clerical authority.

Some priests in the late 1960s and early 1970s had voiced complaints about the changes wrought by the Second Vatican Council, because they had too-hastily concluded that there was no longer any significant place for them in the life of the Church. The council had
welcomed the laity into ministries formerly reserved exclusively to the
clergy, even allowing lay persons into the sanctuary, not only to read
portions of the scriptures assigned for the day's Mass but even to distribute Holy Communion.

After the council most members of the congregation received Communion, not only in the hand but also, and more significantly, without
first going to confession—an obligation that many pre-conciliar
Catholics had assumed they had even if not in the state of mortal sin.

Indulgences, which are the remission of punishment still due to
sins that have already been forgiven, are a spiritual benefit that only the
pope or a diocesan bishop can grant. It should be noted, however, that
one of the conditions for the reception of a plenary indulgence, or the
full remission of punishment in purgatory, is that the prospective recipient go to confession—a sacrament that only a priest can administer.

And the Latin Mass as well is something that only the priest can
perform, without lay involvement. He alone knows what Latin words
to recite and how to conduct the required rituals, and he alone has the
power to do both.

A letter-writer to *The New York Times* in early 2009, writing in response to the brief controversy over indulgences, may have put her finger on the nub of the issue: "The salutary benefit [of these changes]
may be to buttress waning clerical authority…"

Vatican II's Renewal of the Church

In the end, what the Second Vatican Council did was to sustain
and enhance the abiding spiritual assets of Catholicism, especially its
sacraments, while planting the seeds of transformation and new life. In

the process the council challenged many conventional assumptions about the nature and mission of the Church: that the Church is equivalent to the hierarchy, that the laity have no active role to play in the Church, that the pope alone is in charge of the universal Church, that the mission of the Church is limited to the preaching of the word and the priestly administration of the sacraments, that only Catholics are in the Body of Christ, that all Catholics are "Roman" Catholics, and that any form of worship with non-Catholic Christians is always forbidden.

More than three years before the opening of Vatican II in October 1962, Pope John XXIII began referring to the coming council as "a new Pentecost," that is, a new outpouring of the Holy Spirit upon the Church. More than a decade later, Cardinal Leo Josef Suenens, primate of Belgium and one of the council's leading figures, tried to keep alive John XXIII's dream in his own book, *A New Pentecost?* The book's epilogue began with the words: "The Spirit remains at the heart of the Church, directing us toward the future. We should like to have a glimpse of that future, so as to read better the signs of the time. But that is not essential: our hope for the future is not based on statistics and charts. It derives entirely from faith in the Spirit, who is with the Church as it moves into the future."

The first Pentecost has sometimes been referred to as the "birthday of the Church." In reigniting the fires of the original Pentecost, the Second Vatican Council also brought about a genuine rebirth of the Church in our own time.

All of us continue to draw from that new life and from the wisdom which it so abundantly yields.

6

The Mass

Heaven on Earth

John F. Baldovin, S.J.

The Mass (now more commonly called the Eucharist) is at the center of Catholic faith and practice. It is the celebration of what God has done for us in Jesus Christ. We experience Christ in the Mass in a number of ways, but especially through the proclamation of the word of God and through his presence in the transformed bread and wine. In these essentials there is no difference at all between the pre–Vatican II and the post–Vatican II Mass.

On the other hand, the experience of the Mass was indeed very different prior to the council. In this essay I will attempt to provide a portrait of many of the distinctive features of the pre–Vatican II Mass, especially as I experienced it as a young man in the 1950s and early 1960s.

The Mass Code

The Mass was enshrined in an elaborate code but one that you could decipher. The first clue was color. As you entered a church you could always see the tabernacle on a pedestal right in the middle of the altar. The tabernacle containing the reserved sacrament was covered by a veil that corresponded to the feast or season. Like vestments on the statue of the Infant of Prague (at least in my parish church) the veil would be changed with some frequency. If the Mass were being cele-brated for someone who had died, then the veil (and the vestments that the priest wore) would be black. This was often the case with weekday Masses. There were even several different white veils depend-ing on the degree of solemnity. In other words, you didn't need to be an expert to be able to figure out what or whom in particular was being celebrated on a given day.

On weekdays the celebration of the Mass followed an elaborate code that depended on the Church's liturgical calendar and on the fre-quent Requiems (or Masses for the Dead). The name "Requiem" came from the first word of the Latin entrance chant, or Introit, of the Mass. In the Middle Ages individual liturgies got their names from this entrance chant, so that when someone referred to "Quasimodo" Sun-day, for example, you knew they were speaking of the Sunday in the Octave of Easter. Requiems often bumped minor saint's days in the parish calendar. Depending on the monetary offering that had been made by the donors, these Masses followed a pattern one also experi-enced in Sunday Mass. They were Low Masses, High Masses, or Solemn High Masses. Low Masses were rather perfunctory affairs with no singing at all. At the altar the priest was assisted by two servers, usually young boys. These Masses would last around twenty-five min-utes. A High Mass included chants such as the Preface of the Eucharis-tic Prayer sung by the priest as well as chants, for example the Gloria, sung by the congregation. Most elaborate were the Solemn High Masses in which three priests took the roles of priest celebrant, dea-con, and subdeacon. These Masses were surrounded by an elaborate choreography and usually a larger number of altar servers. High Masses and Solemn Masses also used incense at several points—at the entrance, at the proclamation of the gospel, and at the offertory.

Another feature of the Mass that was more characteristic of the pre-Vatican II liturgy than of the present one was the use of bells at the "Holy, Holy, Holy" and during the institution narrative. A server would ring a bell as the priest ended the preface and again after he pro-nounced the words of consecration over the bread and over the wine while the priest genuflected, raised the host or chalice, and genuflected again. I first understood the function of these bells when I saw men in an Italian mountain town put out their cigarettes on the church steps and come inside the church to "see the consecration" after the Sanc-tus bell had been rung.

There were other features that gave context and texture to the celebration of Mass. Up until the mid 1950s Catholics fasted from midnight if they were to receive Holy Communion. (That eucharistic fast was gradually reduced to three hours and then to one.) One of the consequences was that evening Masses were unheard of. With the exception of Holy Thursday, the Easter Vigil, and Midnight Mass for Christmas, Mass was something that happened in the morning. Another aspect that gave texture to the Mass was its surrounding atmosphere of silence. Much of what the priest did at the altar, like the Canon (or Eucharistic Prayer), was done silently. In the course of the 1950s and early 1960s, the dialogue Mass was introduced in the United States. Despite the fact that the Mass was couched in silence, the congregation now responded to the Latin invitations of the priest. Congregations learned simple Gregorian chants, like the Gloria of the Mass of the Angels, to participate in the Latin chants that would once have been the preserve of the choir. The entirety of the Mass was in Latin of course, but on Sundays the two readings (Epistle and Gospel) were read in English before the priest preached his sermon.

Together but Unequal

Everyone knew that the Mass consisted of two (unequal) parts. The first part was called the Mass of the Catechumens (equivalent to our Liturgy of the Word). The name came from the fact that in the ancient Church, unbaptized catechumens were allowed to remain at Mass until the beginning of the Creed or the Prayers of the Faithful. (The Prayers of the Faithful had actually fallen into disuse from around the end of the fifth century and were restored after Vatican II.) On Sundays one did not commit a mortal sin if she or he arrived at Mass before the end of the Mass of the Catechumens. From this one can surmise that the Liturgy of the Word was not deemed as important or essential as the next part. As with every part, the Mass of the Catechumens was accompanied by an elaborate choreography. The priest moved from the foot of the altar at the beginning of the Mass and then to the center. If a long version of the hymn, *Gloria in excelsis Deo*, were sung, he would sit on a *sedilia* (bench) after he had recited it while the choir sang it. He would return to the center of the altar for the Collect (or Opening Prayer) and then move to his right to read the Epistle. This was the name of the first reading as it normally came from one of the Pauline or other letters in the New Testament. After the epistle reading a server moved the altar missal to the left (or north) side of the altar from which the Gospel was read. The popular understanding was that the Gospel early on was proclaimed to the unevangelized North.

The Mass of the Faithful started with the Offertory, a series of ritual preparations, prayers and gestures by the priest, and ended with the final blessing, which oddly enough came after the dismissal "*Ite missa est*" (Go, the Mass is ended) that gave the Mass its most popular name. The Mass of the Faithful, i.e., the part reserved to the baptized, consisted of the Offertory, the Canon of the Mass, preparatory rites for Communion (like the Our Father), Holy Communion and the Post-Communion rites.

The relation between the Mass and the reception of Holy Communion was a rather curious one. Most of the time people received Holy Communion in the form of hosts that had been reserved in the tabernacle. (Reception of the Precious Blood was a practice restored by Vatican II after about a thousand years.) Everyone received Communion kneeling and the host was placed by the priest on the communicant's tongue. This was accompanied by a rushed formula whispered in Latin. Communicants normally knelt at a communion rail, which separated the sanctuary from the nave of the church. The rail was normally covered by a cloth at communion time and an altar server held a plate (or paten) under the chin of the communicant to prevent the spilling of fragments of the host. I have suggested the the relation between Communion and the Mass was curious because the reception of Holy Communion did not necessarily occur at the time of Communion at the Mass. Often enough, especially on weekdays when time was of the essence, a priest who was not celebrating the Mass would come out the sacristy after the consecration, go to an auxiliary tabernacle, and begin to distribute Holy Communion while the celebrating priest was continuing with the Mass.

The Mass ended with the dismissal but other prayers had been added. Before he left the altar the priest recited the Last Gospel (the Prologue to St. John's Gospel). At the foot of the altar he recited the "Hail, Holy Queen" and several other prayers—all added by Pope Leo XIII in the late nineteenth century for the conversion of Russia from Orthodoxy.

The ritual of the Mass that I have just described remained fairly stable from the high Middle Ages until Vatican II. Its longevity as a ritual alone tells us that it had much to recommend it. In the first place, as the church historian John Bossy has remarked, people knew that the most important thing that could possibly happen in the world—the presence of the God Man among us and his activity in saving the world—was actualized every time the Mass was said. They may not have been able to articulate all of the theological or doctrinal aspects of this reality, but the solemnity of the Mass itself, its obscure language, haunting chant, and atmosphere of silence and reverence all pointed to this reality.

At the same time, of course, Vatican II and the subsequent liturgical reform, backed by a great deal of historical scholarship since the Renaissance, sought to reform the liturgy and restore a number of features that had been lost in the course of the centuries: the use of an intelligible language, the varied ministries that characterized the ancient liturgy, the priest praying aloud, a much richer fare of readings from holy scripture, a weekday lectionary, more readings from the Old Testament, the Prayers of the Faithful, the connection between the Mass and receiving Holy Communion, the reception of Communion under both kinds. The post-conciliar reform also introduced some features that were new, like the variety of eucharistic prayers that we enjoy today and the ability to choose suitable liturgical music as a substitute for the chants printed in the Roman Missal.

I suggested at the outset that the Mass we celebrate today does not differ in essentials from the Eucharist as it has been celebrated throughout the centuries. Clearly we have experienced great gains in the pasty forty-plus years of liturgical reform and just as clearly there are aspects of the older Mass, such as its solemnity and reverential silence, that we can benefit from retrieving today.

7

The Humbling of the Priesthood

Donald Cozzens

Men of Awesome Power

The smell of beeswax candles and freshly starched surplices lingered in the servers' sacristy as four sleep-deprived boys assigned to the 6:30 morning Mass took scarce comfort from the morning cold. Moments later, vested in black cassocks and white surplices, we went studiously about our duties. Cruets of wine and water and a starched finger towel were placed on the credence table and the altar candles were lighted. As instructed, we checked in the floor length mirror to see that our surplices were on straight. We were ready. Then, with the solemnity of the Swiss Guard, we led the priest to the foot of the altar and the sacred, mystical ritual unfolded. *Introibo ad altare Dei...* More than half a century later, I can say that serving Mass shaped my Catholic imagination, gave me a sense of the sacred, and set me on the path that led to ordination.

When the late Bishop Kenneth Untener was asked why he became a priest, he liked to reply: "It wasn't my idea." Well, I have an idea why I'm a priest today. Not a clear idea, of course. I still shake my head in wonder at the mystery of the grace, destiny, and freedom that seem to be the essential ingredients for what Catholics call a "vocation." It was my idea to become a priest—and it wasn't my idea to become a priest. But beeswax, starch, and an amorphous sense of the sacred had their place in my pre-adolescent longing to be a priest one day.

Looking back to my altar-boy days, the priests I knew weren't par-ticularly gifted men. There was a certain aura about them, however—a quality hard to name. A handful were clearly bright and talented. One became a bishop; another, a seminary rector. To my young and inexperienced eyes, they were each men of mystery who daily touched the hem of the divine. They offered Mass, forgave sins, baptized, mar-ried, and buried. No senator, judge, or physician quite captured the imagination of Catholics then as did the parish priest. When my par-ents spoke of Doc Scullen, the pastor of Holy Name parish during the Depression and World War II years, it was with a note of affection. It was more than the respect commonly shown to clergy—it seemed to me they *revered* this man. They said Doc Scullen knew every parish-ioner by name and that he somehow found a way to get help for fam-ilies in trouble. My parents' pastor and the parish priests of my youth stirred something inside me. I wanted to be one of them.

Most pre-Vatican II Catholics in the steel-town of Cleveland be-longed to the working class and it seemed to many that priests con-stituted a kind of spiritual nobility. And the bishop, a personage who visited each year for Confirmation, seemed to be royalty—a kind of prince. He merited, after all, the un-American title "Excellency" and was treated with unparalleled deference. Didn't a Catholic fortunate enough to meet a bishop drop to one knee and kiss his ring? And wasn't a family, honored with a visit from the parish priest, always on its best behavior? What we now decry as clericalism, the nadir of cler-ical culture, was yet to be named. The status of bishops and priests, their private and often secret world of privilege and exemption, ap-peared to offend few Catholic sensibilities. To the contrary: it seemed the clergy's due.

But it was the priest, not the bishop, who anchored and directed the life of a parish. And for pre–Vatican II Catholics, the parish *was* the church. It was the parish, not the diocesan headquarters we know as the chancery or Catholic Center, that provided a sense of belonging. Especially for Catholics living in cities, the parish gave people the so-cial security, if you will, of a village, where geography and common worship forged identity and community. And in this ecclesial village, the pastor was the unquestioned leader and, therefore, a man of con-siderable power. Priests who clothed their power and status in pastoral kindness won the loyalty—and often the love—of their parishioners. Still, the priest remained a man of power, and to the eyes of believing Catholics, a truly awesome power.

The religious world of pre-conciliar Catholics rested on three cornerstones: adherence to the doctrines of the Church, a prayer life fostered by the sacraments and parish devotions, and a moral life in harmony with the commandments of God and the laws of the Church. In other words, the practicing Catholic's inner life was sustained by doctrine, devotion, and morality. In shorthand—*believe, behave, and be saved*. For most, behaving was the hard part, especially when it came to sex. From this perspective, a Catholic's interior life was reduced to the condition of his or her soul—one was in the state of grace or in the state of mortal sin. Die in the state of grace, and you were saved; die in the state of mortal sin, and you were lost. The great, singular prize was salvation—to merit eternal life with God and the communion of saints in heaven. For the believer whose understanding of religion was, to a great extent, moral living, the priest was the human broker of salvation. He alone possessed the power to absolve from sin.

The power of absolution was trumped only by the priest's power to celebrate the sacrifice of the Mass—to change bread and wine into the body and blood of Christ. Not only could the priest make one right with God through absolution, the priest made it possible to do more than touch the hem of the divine—he made it possible to receive Holy Communion, to be mysteriously, unspeakably close to God. "My God, what a life! And it is yours, oh priest of Jesus Christ" (Henri Lacordaire).

The Humbling of the Priesthood

Post-Vatican II priests are leaning into cold, humbling winds that their pre–Vatican II brothers were mostly spared. Consider the following realities and issues: an aging, dwindling priest corps, a drastic drop in the number of seminarians, the questioning of mandatory celibacy for diocesan priests, conflicting theologies over who is suited for the priesthood by gender and sexual orientation, and parents dissuading their sons from even thinking about life as a priest. Nothing, however, has buffeted and humbled the priesthood as the shocking, staggering sexual betrayal of children and adolescents by a significant number of clergy and the corresponding cover-up of the abuse by many bishops. The fallout from the clergy abuse scandals for priests and bishops—and for the church in general—is difficult to exaggerate. Moreover, unless church leaders are committed to identifying and correcting the systemic and institutional factors at play in the abuse scandals, for example, the secrecy and divisiveness of clericalism, the priest-hood will continue to flounder.

From a spiritual perspective, a humbled priesthood is a good thing. One of the great contributions of the council was its emphasis on the Church as the pilgrim people of God and on the fact that all the baptized, in terms of spiritual dignity, were equal members of the Church. Only in a metaphorical sense, then, is the priest a man set apart. He is ordained to be the pastoral leader of the parish commu-nity, but not the only leader. His ministry as preacher, sacramental minister, and servant-leader remains essential to the health and vi-brancy of the Church. But the priest is not the only one anointed by the Spirit with gifts and talents for the good of the Church. Finding his place alongside the deacon, the lay ecclesial minister, the vowed re-ligious, and the many untitled ministers in his parish will be an on-going challenge for the priest of the post-conciliar Church.

There are, of course, other challenges facing the post-conciliar priest. Engaging with and relating to educated, thinking, believing Catholic women is a daunting challenge for large numbers of priests. Many don't quite know what to do with the articulate, well-read women of their parish even as they admit that a Church that does not hear the word of God preached in the voice of women remains skewed and handicapped. At the same time, priests sense that the power dif-ferential between laity and clergy has changed. Catholics have come to imagine God differently in the post–Vatican II church. They no longer seem to be afraid of God's wrath—at least in the sense of spending an eternity in hell for missing Mass on Sunday. Pastors have known for some time now what recent surveys have made clear: more than two-thirds of Catholics don't celebrate Sunday Mass every week. For the majority of the faithful who fall into this category, there is little need for a pastor in the sense that Doc Scullen was pastor to the people of my home parish. Rather, they tend to see their parish priest more as a chaplain—someone on the margins of their lives, someone they can call upon for baptisms, weddings, and funerals. It's not this way, of course, in many of our healthy, vibrant parishes, but the mindset holds, I'm convinced, for large numbers of Catholics.

Holding On to the Sacred

It began for me with beeswax candles and starched surplices, with stained glass windows, with sisters who smelled of Ivory soap and unruffled priests who appeared to be genuinely happy men. Growing up as an altar boy in the village I knew as Holy Name parish gave me a priceless gift—a sense of the sacred. And without a fundamental sense of the sacred, a sense of the hidden presence of God, Catholicism loses its savor. That's why the sacraments—especially the Eucharist—are central to the life of Catholic faith. But the presence of the Spirit, the unbidden touch of the sacred, can't be restricted to the sacramental life of the Church. At least from time to time, Catholics discover the presence of God in their homes, their workplaces, in shopping malls, in sprawling cities, in the silence of the woods, in the beauty of nature. They experience the sacred in our great cathedrals and churches and in hospices and soup kitchens. The college students I teach speak of finding a sense of the sacred on their service trips to Honduras and Guatemala and in their weekly trips into the city to feed the homeless. Still, I suspect a sense of the sacred, a sense of God's presence, remains more elusive in technology-driven, financially obssessed first-world countries like our own.

Having, by God's grace, a sense of the Holy, priests should by their very presence foster a sense of the sacred, a sense of mystery. Perhaps as much by the integrity of their lives as by their preaching and ministry, priests should prompt people to wonder at the hidden presence of the divine. The best priests I knew as a boy did this. The best priests I know today do this. The ones who mask their humanity behind the persona of the priest, the ones who never seem to be quite real, never foster a sense of the sacred.

The cold, humbling winds continue to blow and today's priests lean steadfastly into them. In these days without sun, no one thinks priests can walk on water, but the One who did stands with them. That should be enough.

8

Catholics among Southern Neighbors in the 1950s

JEFFREY GROS, F.S.C.

It was an exciting time to grow up Catholic in the United States during the 1940s and 1950s, especially in the South. Memphis, Tennessee, is often called the Buckle of the Bible Belt because the majority of black and white Christians are evangelicals, Baptists, and Pentecostals. Catholics were among the earliest settlers on these Chickasaw Bluffs; the Spaniards came to Fortaleza San Fernando of 1767. Yet, after the religious revivals of the nineteenth century and the population decimation in the 1870s from the yellow fever epidemic—and before recent Hispanic immigration—Protestants came to make up nearly 90 percent of the population in the region.

In these recollections, I focus on three themes: (1) living as a member of the Catholic minority in the South in the 1950s and 1960s, (2) living with non-Catholic neighbors, and (3) the stirrings of renewal and change in the post–World War II Church.

Southern Catholics

Catholic identity was never a great problem for those of us who lived in this minority situation. There were two Catholic families on my block. Our neighbors across the way produced a son, a few years my senior, who went on to become a professor of English in southern

California. We knew well the anti-Catholicism of entrenched nativism. For that reason, Catholics bonded together even across ethnic lines. All of our schools had Protestant and Jewish students from Catholic kindergarten through Catholic college. Otherwise it would have been impossible to provide the Catholic education that was so important for us in interpreting our faith to those around us who were ignorant or prejudiced. Even to this day, religion is not a taboo subject in the South. In fact, especially in the African American community, religious language and imagery are prominent aspects of communication in everyday speech.

We also realized that we were resented by some sectors, and knew very well the difference between Christian denominations: Episcopal, Presbyterian, Disciples, Methodists, and others, all of whom held onto their prejudices. During the 1960 John F. Kennedy election one only had to look at the marquee of every white Baptist church to realize for whom "God" was calling the flock to vote, though neither candidate nor church affiliation were mentioned by name. My father, a staunch Republican, finally voted Democrat, largely out of revulsion for the bigotry of the campaign as it played out in Memphis.

In the tight-knit Catholic community, we transcended ethnic lines to pull together as one community. The public tensions between Irish, Italian, Lebanese, German, and Polish, so characteristic of Catholicism in locales where the Church dominated demographically, were muted in response to a Protestant majority. Of course, my parents had negative attitudes about Italians as they did about Greeks, Jews, and blacks, but these were muted in church circles, and—for the most part—in business. The Greek, Jew, and Italian were among the best insurance agents in the firm over which my father presided, since they "worked" their own ethnic groups well. Segregation meant that black agents would have been unknown in a white firm.

My father had New Orleans roots, so his Catholicism was more Mediterranean than Irish. He was very active with the schools and parish, but had a healthy objectivity about clergy. We knew the Franciscans were good for confession, the Dominicans good for the intellectual heritage. He went away to the Jesuits for retreat, and would have worked to build a retreat house in our diocese had the bishop of the time not been so anti-religious, with a special aversion for Jesuits.

Dad would scheme with the pastor, who was a master of the annulment for failed marriages, to subvert the bishop's regulations controlling what the parish could build or how its money could be spent.

On the other hand, he had no illusions about Monsignor Merlin Kearney's openness to lay leadership. The two required consultors were brought in on New Year's Eve to sign the annual mandated financial reports, which were never given to them to read. And Kearney brought them in at different times, with names covered. Yet, they would often end up in the club for a drink later in the day, assessing the parish in their own way. The pastor often got more support than he deserved and more expertise than his style was open to. Commitments to the Church were substantive, but bishops and priests were not taken naively as the experts they often put themselves forward as being.

Living with Our Neighbors

From first grade to graduate school, I attended only Catholic institutions. However, I was never in a classroom without Protestant and often Jewish fellow students through high school, until I entered a religious formation program with the Christian Brothers. Our grade school and high school always had non-Catholic teachers, though the bishop protested in the 1950s when Christian Brothers High School in Memphis hired a Protestant to teach sociology. It was a private school of which the bishop had not been overly supportive in any event. So, as with his protest in 1962 when the Brothers integrated the school, the bishop's observations were respectfully taken into account, and filed appropriately. The Christian Brothers' High School (and, after 1953, College—now University) was known as a "temple of tolerance" since the 1930s. It had a separate "ethics" program for non-Catholic students who preferred to opt out of religion classes, though many, especially the Episcopalian and Methodist students, chose to take these courses.

We grew up knowing Protestants who were more devout Christians than many of our Catholic friends. Many non-Catholic teachers knew and appreciated the Christian tradition better than some of our Catholic professors and even some religious. We were well aware of the difference between the Eucharist-centered piety of our Episcopal friends and the fundamentalism and occasional bigotry of our Baptist playmates. We felt more affinity with our Methodist friends who invited us to Sunday evening church where they often showed movies, than with our Evangelical neighbors who tried to convert us to their way of being Christian. Because we had to interpret our religion on the playground, we were grateful for the resources of our catechism classes.

As I noted before, my father had his ethnic and racial prejudices, but his insurance agency included two types of Presbyterian, one liberal and one Evangelical; two types of Episcopalians, one for the doctors and the other for the business executives; an Orthodox Jew; a Greek Orthodox; and Italian and Irish Catholics. For all his negative attitudes about the Italians and Greeks, my father tolerated their styles to tap into their communities.

My first Orthodox Divine Liturgy was at the wedding of Nick Capadalis, where, as an amazed ten-year-old, I admired the glorious iconography and the ceremonial crowning of the couple. In my family there was great respect for Ike Loscov because he was the most successful of the agents in the office. He would read *The Night Before Christmas* for us each year and "do" Santa Claus after our retiring. He and Dad would lobby together at national conventions for each other's dietary requirements: kosher food and fish on Friday, for example. At Dad's funeral, Ike stood outside the cathedral with his head covered, while his wife Berta sat in the last pew being less Orthodox-observant.

When the Second Vatican Council came along and affirmed religious freedom, it was a great relief. Paul Blanshard's *Protestants and Other Americans United for the Separation of Church and State* was well known in Memphis, and at another level of society the Ku Klux Klan was active. For Catholics living in a pluralistic environment, like the southern United States, where collaboration was a daily part of life and where we were in one another's churches and synagogues on a routine basis, the council's proclamation of ecumenism and interreligious outreach as central to Catholic identity came as a vindication of our experience.

While we had no theology to support it, we knew that there was a real if imperfect communion among fellow Christians whose faith was deep, with dedication rooted in a common gospel and commitment to a common Christian intellectual tradition. In practice, we often felt more affinity for religious Jews than for the Evangelical Protestant majority which often had the same prejudices toward both of our communities.

My parents had been active in the National Conference of Christians and Jews, even though the bishop wrote letters forbidding priests to go to the banquets that honored a Catholic each year, with Jewish and Protestant counterparts. Routinely Monsignor Kearney would receive episcopal reprimands when a picture of him with a rabbi, Protestant minister, or Orthodox priest would appear in the newspaper. Monsignor Kearney taught us by his example that it was easier to be forgiven than to be refused permission by asking.

Exciting Horizons Opening

For a Catholic studying in the 1950s, it was an exciting time. In college we were enriched by the superb literary revival represented by the Catholic English authors: Chesterton, Belloc, Dawson, Greene, and Waugh; and the French: Bernanos, Claudel, Péguy, Mauriac, and Bloy. The philosophy of Jaques Maritain and Etienne Gilson, the historical consciousness brought to the tradition by *The Development of Doctrine* of John Henry Newman, the historical study of liturgy, and the early inklings of Bernard Lonergan's work, all helped us to see and appreciate our Catholic faith, the handing on of the catechetical heritage of our order, and the interdisciplinary character of Catholic learning in a whole new light.

As a biologist I was excited by Teilhard de Chardin. I embraced the new, post-Sputnik biology that emerged in the early 1960s and was appearing in new high school texts. Likewise, the liturgical and biblical renewal of catechetics, with which the De LaSalle Brothers were involved through St. Mary's Press before the council, was exciting. When the new work of the council finally emerged in the mid1960s in theology and catechetics, we were primed to receive and transmit it, as we had been with the new biology before it.

Yes, we who grew up in the years before Vatican II have much for which to be grateful. Now we trust in the Spirit's continued action in the Church, nurtured for centuries, coming to new fruition in the council, and leading us now into new horizons.

9

Our Ancestors Would Be Incredulous

Vatican II and the Religious Other

MARY C. BOYS, S.N.J.M.

In September 2005 I participated in a conference at the Gregorian University in Rome commemorating the fortieth anniversary of *Nostra Aetate*, one of Vatican II's most significant documents. This international gathering included Buddhist scholars from Sri Lanka, Japan, and Turkey; Hindu scholars from India and the United States; and Muslim scholars from Lebanon, Scotland, Egypt, and Malaysia. Jewish and Christian scholars from Europe, Israel, and North America completed the roster of participants. Before the Second Vatican Council—the first council to refer positively to other religions—such an assembly would have been unimaginable.[1] Our respective ancestors would be incredulous.

Certainly, few Catholics before Vatican II could have envisioned the breadth and depth of interreligious exchange over the past forty years as symbolized by that conference. In the past, polemic and disparagement generally characterized the Church's attitude toward the religious other. The classic formulation was "outside the Catholic Church there is no salvation" (*Extra ecclesiam nulla salus*). This formulation, dating back to Cyprian of Carthage (d. 258) and Fulgentius of Ruspe (468–533), was promulgated for the whole Church by the Council of Florence (1438–1442):

> The Holy Roman church firmly believes, professes and preaches that "no one remaining outside the Catholic Church,

not only pagans," but also "Jews, heretics or schismatics, can become partakers of eternal life; but they will go to the 'eternal fire prepared for the devil and his angels' (Matt 25:41), unless before the end of their life they are received into it . . . For union with the body of the Church is of so great importance that the sacraments of the church are helpful to salvation only for those remaining in it; and fasts, almsgiving, other works of piety, and the exercises of a militant Christian life bear eternal rewards for them alone."[2]

Theologians sought to ameliorate the harshness of this decree by speaking of the salvific power of "implicit faith," which many of us educated in the pre–Vatican II church understood in terms such as "baptism of desire," "baptism of blood," and "invincible ignorance." These terms enabled Catholics to recognize that circumstances often prevented persons from being baptized in the Church. Nonetheless, many Catholics believed that "non-Catholics" would go to hell (or, in the case of unbaptized infants, to limbo). Yet in the pre-conciliar days, relatively few North American Catholics interacted with Buddhists, Muslims, or Hindus. What we did hear on a consistent basis, particularly in liturgical settings, was a denigration of Judaism.[3] This was especially evident in the prayers of Good Friday.

The Perfidious Jews

The Good Friday services of my childhood were austere: the altar and sanctuary devoid of adornment, the statues covered, the organ silent, and the presider clothed in black vestments. After the reading of the Gospel and the sermon, a series of prayers was solemnly recited according to ancient tradition in which the church prayed for all people on the day in which Jesus died for all. The prayers (in Latin, of course, so we followed in our missals) were dramatically intoned. "Let us pray," the presider said at the beginning of each intercession, then invited the congregation to kneel in silent prayer. After this contemplative moment, we were invited to stand. The prayer (for the church, for the pope, for government officials, for Jews and pagans) followed. For the Jews, however, the drama of the kneeling and rising was dispensed with because they had insulted Christ by bending their knees in mocking him.[4] Before 1955 the prayer was worded as follows:

> Let us pray also for the perfidious Jews: that Almighty God may remove the veil from their hearts; so that they too may acknowledge Jesus Christ our Lord.

> Almighty and eternal God, who dost not exclude from thy mercy even Jewish faithlessness: hear our prayers, which we offer for the blindness of that people; that acknowledging the light of thy Truth, which is Christ, they may be delivered from their darkness. Through the same Lord Jesus Christ, who lives and reigns with thee in the unity of the Holy Spirit, God, for ever and ever. Amen.

Some modifications were made to this prayer. In 1955 Pope Pius XII restored the kneeling/standing rubric to make the prayer for the Jews consistent with the other prayers. In 1962 Pope John XXIII removed the Latin *perfidies*, translated above as "perfidious" and then as "faithlessness."

The Jews, "First to Hear the Word of God"

Even the removal of "perfidious" did not ameliorate the negative depiction of Jews as blind and living in darkness. Such a representation did not accord with Vatican II, particularly section four of *Nostra Aetate*, which refers to Jews as a people whom God holds "most dear." Accordingly, a new prayer for Jews was composed. Since 1970 we have been praying in a strikingly different manner and tone:

> Let us pray for the Jewish people, the first to hear the word of God, that they may continue to grow in the love of his name and in faithfulness to his covenant.

> Almighty and eternal God, long ago you gave your promise to Abraham and his posterity. Listen to your Church as we pray that the people you first made your own may arrive at the fullness of redemption. We ask this through Christ our Lord. Amen.

According to longstanding church tradition, liturgy shapes theology.[5] Thus a revised prayer is significant in conveying the Church's realization that its posture toward the religious other—in this case, Jews—has changed. So, too, have attitudes toward other religious traditions; accordingly, the 1970 Good Friday prayers no longer refer to heretics, schismatics, and pagans, but to those who do not believe in Christ or in God. The modifications are reflected not only in a series of documents refining and expanding *Nostra Aetate*, but also in structural innovations: the establishment of the Pontifical Council for Interreligious Dialogue in 1964 and the Commission on Religious Relations with Jews in 1974.[6] Interreligious dialogue has become a serious endeavor, with a substantial literature and widespread involvement. Increasingly, it is being recognized as crucial if the diverse peoples of our world are to live in peace with one another.

Yet Vatican II's changed posture has not been accepted by all. One has only to survey the websites and blogs of various traditionalist Catholics to read their ferocious criticism. For example, in 1983 Archbishop Marcel Lefebvre, the founder of one of the most prominent groups, the Priestly Society of Saint Pius X, wrote an open letter to the pope that condemned his "support of collegiality, the revolutionary 'human rights,' the protestant mass and the free diffusion of heresies within the Church." The website continues: "The Pope seemed to sponsor this attitude with his scandalous visits to a Protestant temple and the Synagogue in Rome, his idolatrous acts in Togo and India, crowning the job with the ecumenical meeting of all religions at Assisi."[7]

While such traditionalist reactions to Vatican II represent only a small percentage of Catholics, the reality is that the council is still being interpreted.[8] Moreover, the complexity of interreligious dialogue means that disagreements are inevitable.[9] Yet, despite the tensions and difficulties, what Vatican II initiated by its recognition of the "ray of truth" in the religious other has shone new light on the mystery of faith. One had only to look at the faces of the participants at that 2005 conference in Rome to know that the Spirit of God was hovering in our midst.

Notes

1. This refers primarily to *Nostra Aetate*, 2: "The Catholic Church rejects nothing that is true and holy in these religions. She regards with sincere reverence those ways of conduct and of life, those precepts and teachings which, though differing in many aspects from the ones she holds and sets forth, nonetheless often reflect a ray of that Truth which enlightens all men." Similar expressions of this positive attitude toward other religious traditions may

be found in *Lumen Gentium*, 16–17; *Ad Gentes*, 3, 7–9, 11; and *Gaudium et Spes*, 22.

2. This text may be found in *The Christian Faith in the Doctrinal Documents of the Catholic Church*, rev. ed., ed. J. Neuner and J. Dupuis (New York: Alba House, 1982), #1005. For an excellent analysis of the context of this decree, see Jacques Dupuis, *Toward a Christian Theology of Religious Pluralism* (Maryknoll, NY: Orbis Books, 1997), 84–130.

3. For analysis of the church's relationship with Judaism, see my *Has God Only One Blessing? Judaism as a Source of Christian Self-Understanding* (New York/Mahwah, NJ: Paulist Press, 2000).

4. See T. Gilmartin, "Good Friday," *The Catholic Encyclopedia* (New York: Robert Appleton Company, 1909). Retrieved December 30, 2008 from New Advent: <http://www.newadvent.org/cathen/06643a.htm>.

5. I refer to the mid-fifth century formulation of Prosper of Aquitaine, "*lex orandi, lex credendi*," which more literally means that the law of prayer is equivalent to the law of belief. Liturgical theologians interpret this adage in various ways.

6. Various permutations in name and structure have occurred over the years. Pope Paul VI established the Secretariat for Non-Christians in 1964; it was renamed the Pontifical Council for Interreligious Dialogue in 1988. The Commission on Religious Relations with Jews is housed within the Pontifical Council for Promoting Christian Unity (originally the Secretariat for Promoting Christian Unity), which began as a preparatory commission for Vatican II.

7. From the website of the Priestly Society of Saint Pius X, retrieved December 29, 2008. <http://www.fsspx.org/eng/Society/cadreSociety/cadsociety.htm>. For analysis of traditionalist Catholicism in the United States, see Michael Cuneo, *The Smoke of Satan* (New York and Oxford: Oxford University Press, 1997). In 2007 Pope Benedict composed a Good Friday prayer for the Jews for the small number of Catholics who worship according to the Tridentine rite; for analysis, see my "Does the Catholic Church Have a Mission 'with' Jews or 'to' Jews," *Studies in Jewish-Christian Relations* 3/5 (2008). This is an e-journal: <http://escholarship.bc.edu/scjr/vol3/iss1/5/>.

8. See the fine book by Ormond Rush, *Still Interpreting Vatican II: Some Hermeneutical Principles* (New York/Mahwah, NJ: Paulist Press, 2004).

9. For an incisive analysis of theological issues and perspectives, see Paul Knitter, *Introducing Theologies of Religion* (Maryknoll, NY: Orbis Books, 2002).

10

The Pre–Vatican II Church and Women

SUSAN A. ROSS

For those of us Catholics who grew up in the pre–Vatican II church, the women we knew were most likely to fall into one of three categories: married women, nuns, and the Blessed Mother. I was born in 1950, and until my teens, all the women I knew were either married or nuns, apart from two single women who were college classmates and friends of my mother's. (The third option was already taken.) As I contemplated what I wanted to be when I grew up, the options seemed pretty clear: get married and have children, like my mother (I was one of six), and have a life filled with cooking, cleaning, chauffeuring, and the occasional bridge or golf game, or be a nun and have the opportunity to teach, travel, and live with other educated women. For me, the choice seemed pretty clear, especially if I wanted to have time to read, play the piano, and travel. Yes, there were those other issues, like celibacy, poverty, and—the one I worried most about—obedience; the chance of having a superior who might not understand you; or having to wear those habits in the hot summer. But such things seemed tolerable and I knew that I didn't want to be a housewife.

I was also fortunate during my high school years to study at a school run by a religious order of highly educated women—the Religious of the Sacred Heart. I had had the occasional experience of a less-educated and unhappy nun in the seven years of parochial school before and during the time I went to the "Convent," but for the most part, I came to know some very intelligent and caring women. As it turned out, Vatican II took place and the women's liberation movement began in earnest while I was in my teens, and I didn't become a nun after all. But in some very profound ways, the influence of those pre–Vatican II nuns still plays a big role in my life.

Options for Women

The recent film adaptation of the play *Doubt* offers some images of women's lives in the Church before Vatican II. There is Sister Aloysius, the main character, who clings stubbornly to the authoritarian world of Tridentine Catholicism; Sister James, younger and more open to the possibilities beginning to emerge from the council (the play and movie are set in 1964); and Mrs. Miller, the mother of the student whom Sister Aloysius suspects is being molested by Father Flynn, the pastor. All of these women operate within narrow confines. Sister Aloysius, the principal of the parish school, is in charge of the other nuns and the students but is ultimately subject to the authority of the pastor; Sister James is subject to her superior, Sister Aloysius; and Mrs. Miller is subject to the rage of her husband, who is physically and emotionally abusing his son, as well as to the racism of 1964 New York. They all know the limits of their situations and try to manage as best they can. From the vantage point of forty-five years later, it can seem that these women exist in a world of few choices—subject to male authority in one form or another. Yet even in this male-dominated world, Sister Aloysius is able to challenge Father Flynn and, despite her doubts, has a powerful effect on the lives of those around her.

I remember well the world of 1964 and have no desire to live in it today. In many ways, the opportunities for women then pale in comparison to what we see today. As a college senior in the early 1970s, I watched some of my classmates rejoice over their engagement rings and wondered what they planned to do with their lives after they had achieved their dream of marriage. But if we judge that world only by the standards of the early twenty-first century, we do an injustice to the many women who found creative ways of living their faith and their life in those years before the women's movement came into its own. There are indeed some things that might be worth remembering and retrieving from that world.

In the pre–Vatican II church, religious communities for women offered an alternative to the traditional path of marriage and children.

Some women, such as Sister Ann Ida Gannon, B.V.M., president of Mundelein College (now a part of Loyola University Chicago) from 1957 to 1975, gained their PhDs, served on educational and corporate boards, and were role models for young college women who aspired to live lives of challenge and contribution to their communities. While there were, of course, many nuns who were unhappy or even mean-spirited—and are still portrayed in popular culture as the "typical nun"—most of the nuns I knew combined a graciousness and a toughness that continues to inspire me.

Young women today have so many more opportunities than were ever even imaginable in the pre–Vatican II church. I recall my surprise not so many years ago when a young woman student told me that she had worked as a highway construction worker over the summer—a job, she said, that paid far better than retail or child care (jobs that I had had during my summer vacations). But there are other issues for women today that are pernicious: the idea that casual sex is a matter of course, or that we constantly need new (designer) clothes. I support and applaud the possibilities for women today in church and society, including those of being chancellor of a diocese or pastoral administrator of a parish, or—in other denominations—even ordination. Still, the discipline, graciousness, and toughness that the nuns of the pre–Vatican II church modeled for me are qualities worth retrieving. I see young women practicing these virtues in new, post–Vatican II ways: joining the volunteer organizations, such as the Jesuit Volunteer Corps, seeking work in social service agencies, or fighting domestic violence.

Old Virtues for a New Time

The discipline of religious life, in its best sense, is worth retrieving: regular time for prayer, meaningful work, and a community of like-minded people. In the current economic crisis (I write this in early 2009), we have recently been reminded by our new president that we need to live responsible lives. The nuns of the pre–Vatican II church lived in very constrained circumstances, but these conditions also forged a toughness that they passed on to their students: life was not easy, but we were privileged to have the community of the church and the school, and we had a responsibility to give back—to our families, our church, our communities. The discipline of a regulated life, with times for prayer, teaching, meals, and recreation was sometimes, no doubt, rigid and grim. But there is nevertheless a wisdom in sticking to a schedule and paying attention to how we spend our time that is well worth retrieving. And the graciousness that I encounter especially in the women religious I have known and continue to know, including Sister Ann Ida, a graciousness that is born out of a deep self-awareness that can come only from long hours of contemplative prayer and dedication to one's work, is something that all of us, men and women, corporate executives and health care aides alike, can hope to develop as well.

The things that are worth retrieving from the women religious of the pre–Vatican II church are not their habits, their uniformity, their harsh discipline meted out to children, but rather the virtues that lay at the heart of their vocation and that too often went unseen and unappreciated by the Church. The graciousness that, at its heart, was a loving acceptance of oneself and of God's grace; the discipline that was a mature way of living with one's weaknesses; and the toughness that came from seeing life's difficulties and refusing to be overcome by them—all of these were (and are) qualities that we need today more than ever.

11

Sin

"Don't Lose All That Old-Time Catholic Guilt"

CHARLES E. CURRAN

There was much activity in pre–Vatican II Catholic churches on Saturday afternoon and evening—not for eucharistic liturgies but for the sacrament of Penance (usually called "Confession"). Sin played a very significant role in Catholic life. All Catholics felt an obligation to go to confession at least once a year; devout Catholics went much more frequently; Catholic schoolchildren went at least monthly and often weekly. As a seminarian in Rome in the 1950s I can remember coming back to the seminary after a four-week vacation. When I told the confessor, "My last confession was four weeks ago," he said quite sternly, "Welcome back to the Church."

Through catechism classes and sermons Catholics were conscious of sin as an offense against the law of God. Mortal sin was a serious offense against the law of God which was understood to occur quite frequently and involved the loss of God's grace. The very word "mortal" comes from the Latin word *mors* meaning death. Thus, mortal sin brought about spiritual death and condemnation to hell. Venial sin involved a lesser offense against the law of God. The difference between moral and venial sin was based on the seriousness of the act itself. To prepare for confession the person made an examination of conscience to determine what sins had been committed. The contrite penitent then made a firm purpose of amendment to avoid such sins in the future and to live a better Christian life.

The strong emphasis on sin had the negative effect of creating a false sense of guilt (there are many stories about "Catholic guilt") and scrupulosity—the fear that one would commit sin no matter what one did.

From Law (or Act) to Relationship

Much has changed in the post–Vatican II understanding of sin and most of it, but not all, is for the better.

Sin is no longer understood primarily as an act against the law of God but as the violation of relationships. An important Vatican II development in understanding the moral life of the human person put greater emphasis on the person and the person's relationships. The Christian exists in relationship to God, neighbor, world, and self. Such an understanding of the human person results in a more relational understanding of mortal sin. Mortal sin involves the breaking of our relationship with God and affects all our other relationships. In light of this understanding of sin in relational terms, mortal sin is a much less frequent occurrence in Christian life.

We can learn much from an analysis of the human relationship of friendship. We all know from experience that friendships can be broken and this is a very serious and traumatic experience. But such breaking of friendships is comparatively rare and by definition cannot occur all that frequently. The same is true of our relationship of love and friendship with God. One cannot break this loving relationship five times a week or even once a week, once a month, or even once a year!

From looking at the external act alone you cannot tell whether the person has broken his or her relationship with God. There is an essential ambiguity about the human act looked at only in itself apart from the person. For example, in watching Tiger Woods and me play golf you might see just two shots—his missing a shot and my hitting a perfect one. You would be most foolhardy to conclude that I am a good golfer and he is not!

In fairness, however, the pre–Vatican II approach recognized that the act alone did not constitute a mortal sin. In addition to the act involving serious matter, two other conditions were required for mortal sin—advertence of the intellect and consent of the will. Often these conditions were described as clear knowledge and full consent.

These conditions indicated the importance of the interiority of the person involving the intellect and the will. Thus, the pre–Vatican II approach at its best did not put all its emphasis on the external act. But in reality the external act was often the only thing that was considered and the advertence of the intellect and consent of the will were assumed to be present.

Some theologians developed the newer and relational approach to mortal sin in light of the theory of the fundamental option. This somewhat complex theory recognizes two levels or aspects in every act—the categorical and the transcendental. The categorical is the concrete material act that is done, while the transcendental is the deeper unconscious relationship with God that is present in every act. However, even those who do not accept the theory of fundamental option still can understand mortal sin as the breaking of our relationship with God which ultimately affects our relationships with neighbor, world, and self.

There exists an intimate connection among all these relationships. The Christian tradition appeals often to the so-called last judgment scene in Matthew 25 which recognizes that our relationship with God is known and manifested in our relationships with our neighbor. "When I was hungry, naked, thirsty, and in prison you helped me." "But when, Lord, did we see you hungry, naked, thirsty, and in prison?" "When you did it to the least of these my sisters and brothers."

Sin cannot be identified only with the external act looked at in itself. For this reason some theologians do not call acts themselves sinful. External acts are right or wrong, but whether the wrong act is sinful cannot be determined from just observing the act alone.

Sin as Social

Post–Vatican II theology has developed a concept of social sin or sinful structures, which was not present before. Two reasons help to explain this new development. First, sin was primarily understood in its relationship to the confessional, but structures, institutions, and the ethos did not go to confession. Second, in the pre–Vatican II Church the social mission of the Church and the work for justice and peace were not seen as part of the saving and redeeming work of Jesus. Life in the world belonged to the realm of the natural as distinguished from the realm of the supernatural or of grace. Vatican II emphasized that faith, grace, and Jesus Christ had to affect our life in this world. The social mission of the Church was not simply the realm of the natural. A theological understanding of the mission of the Church in the world was thus open to the social understanding of sin and its role, an understanding that was then developed especially in liberation theology. Social sin affects the lives of all people who live in that milieu. Social sin involves the structures of institutionalized injustice, violence, greed, consumerism, exploitation of people and nature. Christians then are called to struggle against social sin and sinful structures through the help of God's love and grace in order to transform the world toward full justice for all.

While the post–Vatican II understanding of sin is theologically more sound than the pre–Vatican II approach, yet the danger exists of forgetting the reality of sin and not giving enough importance to sin and the human capacity for it on both personal and social levels.

Sin is present in all of us. Sin here refers especially to what pre–Vatican II theology called vices, which are the opposite of virtues. These are the dispositions and attitudes that affect the Christian person. Think, for example, of the sinful attitudes and dispositions such as selfishness, anger, intemperateness, lack of concern for others, consumerism, paying too much attention to those realities that are not most important, the lack of thoughtfulness, gratitude, and peace in our lives. The sinful attitudes and tendencies that are part of our person are analogous to the social sin and sinful structures that affect the life of society.

There is no possibility of growth in the Christian life if we are not conscious of the sinful attitudes that affect our multiple relationships with God, neighbor, world, and self. This growth is understood as conversion by which we move away from our sinfulness and grow in terms of the multiple relationships that constitute us as Christian persons. We have to become as aware of the need to stay in shape in our spiritual lives as we have become aware of the need to stay in shape in our physical lives. Many people today recognize the importance of an exercise regimen; gymnasiums and fitness centers abound in our cities; our streets and paths are filled with bikers, joggers, and walkers. Spiritual health requires that we recognize attitudes and dispositions that prevent our growth in our relationships and calls for us to overcome these obstacles.

To grow in our spiritual lives as persons and to strive to overcome the sinful structures in our milieu and society we first must become aware of our own personal sinfulness (in the sense explained above) and the sinful structures in our society. The pre–Vatican II and traditional practice of the examination of conscience is both helpful and necessary. We need to take the time to reflect and recognize our shortcomings and yes—our sins. What obstacles stand in the way of my right and loving relationships with God, neighbor, world, and self? What are the sinful structures in our society that need to be recognized and that our Christian faith requires us to struggle against?

12

From the Treasury of Vowed Women Religious

The Past Remembered, the Present Embraced

CHRISTINE VLADIMIROFF, O.S.B.

There are critical periods in a person's lifetime that cause one to look back and move through the rich memories of the past. Inherent in that journey backward is a temptation to romanticize life at another time. I belong to a unique generation of women religious. We entered young and impressionable. I was seventeen years old. We walked into the monastery and the door closed behind us and we were in the middle of pre–Vatican II religious life of the 1950s. It was a life untouched and removed from the world outside its walls. We spent ten-plus years in what sociologists would call a "total/closed institution" that would shape our identity. My generation would move on in the late 1960s and the 1970s to lead our communities through renewal with great debate and experimentation. We explored the implications of Vatican II mandates and the call to look at our life in the light of scripture, the signs of the times, and the charism of our founders. It was an exhilarating time of deep hope and promise. We now know that some new insights worked out well as we fashioned religious life for today. It is equally clear and evident today that we made some serious mistakes in the renewal of religious life. I will celebrate my golden jubilee of fifty years of monastic profession as a Benedictine sister this year. There is something to be learned from a journey back through time. It enables us to retrieve what was valuable and bring it forward in new ways. God is found in the present time, no matter how chaotic the times appear to be.

For me, the attraction to monastic life was transmitted by the Benedictine women who taught me in high school. They were the most educated, accomplished, joyous, caring women I had ever encountered. In my eyes they were competent and in charge of their lives and the institutions they administered; they had a sisterly care for each other. Their sense of belonging and commitment to the monastic enterprise gave meaning and purpose to their life in community. They seemed to energize a room by just walking into it. I wanted very much to be a part of their world.

Entering the community was crossing a threshold. I withdrew from the familiar and was stripped of what few markers I had that gave me personal identity. Putting on the habit of a postulant was the first step in becoming a sister. The separation from past life was total. Contact with family and friends was strictly limited. During the initial years there was no access to radio or newspapers. Letter writing was restricted and censored. Formation served as a time to undertake an interior journey to find your identity in the community. It tested your resolve to live an alternative lifestyle that would require total commitment to the new and abandonment of what had been. Identity was confirmed in the dailiness of life. A sense of community embraced you with both the joy and difficulty of living closely with others.

The life was marked by silence, prayer, study, and manual work. It was a life that was highly structured, with rigid boundaries established by rank in community. Each person had an assigned role. There were very clear expectations of how that role was to be carried out in community. Time was assigned for each activity and set the rhythm for the day. There was little room for choice or personal decision making. Your field of study was assigned to you with little or no consultation. Some customs and practices did not always make sense. Though adult women, we were at times treated as children, with no reward for initiative, creativity or responsibility—we were expected simply to be unquestioningly obedient. Those of us in initial formation managed to get into trouble by laughing uncontrollably at the wrong times at table, in chapel, in times of silence. We cried with our homesickness but knew how to console each other because this was our new family. We learned to depend on each other totally.

Prayer

In the silence of gathering outside of chapel for *statio,* long lines of habited figures moved in rank into the chapel for the Divine Office. The day began in choir with Lauds at 5:30 AM; the Little Hours interrupted our manual labor and/or study at mid-day and Vespers came at the end of the work day around 5 PM. Meals were an opportunity to take our turns serving each other by waiting tables. We ate most meals in silence unless it was a particularly important feast. Finally, the time for recreation came around and we sat and talked to each other in a large group until the bell rang for Compline. In silence the community moved once more to chapel. Night Silence or the Grand Silence followed and the day ended.

The very rhythm of the day and the chant of the prayers were constant reminders that we had chosen a way to seek God that demanded a deep spirituality to sustain us in our quest. The prayer and the silence stirred in us the desire to reach the holiness that we aspired to as we studied and read about the women who went before us. The psalms and the scriptures were slowly shaping our path to the God with whom we fell in love in those fervent days of formation. On feasts, the choir robes added to the solemnity and the Latin chant soared and we were carried by the joy of the festive celebration. Prayer was not a multiplication of actions or words or trips to the chapel but an ever deepening enveloping of our life in the presence of God.

Community

We dressed alike and so visually we witnessed for all to see that we were truly "sisters" and that our lives were intimately bound together. Whether we went out to college to study, to town to buy new shoes or on an errand, we never went alone. A sister companion went along. Our older sisters were kind and tried to ease any harshness the life might hold for the young sisters. They would share their memories of their initial days in community and we were socialized into our history through their stories of community. Our elders embodied the deep story of our charism and spirit. When we celebrated their jubilees, we knew that their fidelity would make possible our fidelity in the future.

Ministry

We were told that we were about God's work, and our obedience to assignments for ministry brought the grace we needed. In a hurting world we shaped institutions to reach the poor and the suffering. The Church in the United States founded the parochial system of schools, and the presence and work of religious sisters was needed as a labor force. Very often, with little or no preparation, we were placed as teachers in a classroom. Present-day professionalism would resist this; it was a practice that caused personal suffering for many.

We were not alone in a school; we had mentors and master teachers among us and we learned from each other. It was a common effort and a common goal that we shared as we staffed a school and lived community life in our parish residences. There were hard moments, and difficult pastors, but we learned to make our own happiness as we worked together in the ministry of education. We were assigned to mission houses in parishes throughout the diocese with a group of sisters not of our selection. We learned to live with each other; we learned to find our place in a new group as we were moved and assigned by the superior. These assignments broadened our experience and helped us learn to appreciate the gifts that others bring. Each sister had something to teach and if you let her into your life you would be richer for the experience. To this day we share the stories of those mission days and laughter comes easily as we remember another time.

For Our Time

The culture for women religious during the pre–Vatican II days was total and embraced every detail of life. There were protective barriers and behaviors that separated religious from the prevailing culture. The group was shaped by a strong tradition of values, hopes, and aspirations that knit the individuals into a living community. It is not possible or desirable to replicate that kind of isolation again. But we can deepen our grasp of the tradition and be formed by it and become holy women as our foremothers before us.

In the history of religious life we are at a defining point that holds promise and peril. It will take deliberate and intentional action on our part to create the future together with the best of the past and the freshness of life in the present. In our day we are to witness in the midst of the culture to a new way of life that gives glimpses of the reign of God alive in human community. The reality of religious life is that it is first and foremost a gift of God to the Church. Community is formed, lived, and sustained by people whose fidelity and integrity are manifest by their care for one another and their resolve to bring about God's reign on earth.

Whatever may be the future of vowed religious life for women, we can always learn from the faith and commitment of our foremothers who challenged their times as we must our times.

13

The Pre–Vatican II Parish

Haven in a Heartless World

James J. Bacik

What were Catholic parishes in the United States like in the decades before the Second Vatican Council opened in 1962? What were their greatest limitations and what can we learn from them in our ongoing effort to renew parish life?

Pre-conciliar Parish Life

Let us begin with a composite sketch of how one family experienced parish life in a Midwest city prior to the council. Bob and Kathy loved St. Catherine's parish, a mostly white, middle-class faith community that was the vital center of their religious and social lives. They taught their four children to have great respect for the pastor and the three associate priests who lived in the parish rectory and provided them with the Mass and other sacraments. The whole family usually attended the 9 AM Low Mass on Sunday, using their English translation missals to follow the priest, who said the Mass in Latin with his back to the people. Bob liked this Mass because it was brief—no hymns sung, no congregational responses, no greeting of peace, no partaking of the chalice. Now and then, Kathy and the kids attended the 11 AM High Mass to enjoy the beautiful hymns and Latin responses sung by the parish choir.

St. Catherine's parish provided the sacraments that structured the spiritual lives of the parishioners. Bob and Kathy had all their children baptized on Sunday afternoon, soon after their births—so soon that Kathy could not be present for the baptism of her two oldest. All of the children made their first confessions and communions in the second grade and were confirmed in the fourth grade. Once a month on a Saturday afternoon Kathy took the children to confess their sins privately to the priest in a confessional where they would be anonymous. The boys in the family began serving Mass in the fifth grade after learning all the proper responses in Latin. This opportunity was not open to the girls.

All the children attended the parish grade school for free, made possible by the sisters who taught all eight grades with very little financial remuneration. The boys played football, basketball, and softball for the parish grade-school teams, competing against other Catholic schools in the city. There were no opportunities for the girls to participate in sports other than as cheerleaders. The girls did have prominent roles in school plays and had the opportunity to be chosen to crown the Blessed Virgin Mary in the annual May Crowning.

Bob was involved in the Holy Name Society that sponsored the annual rally to give public witness to the Catholic faith and the monthly "communion breakfasts" that featured a guest speaker after the 11 AM Mass. Bob was also an active member of the St. Vincent de Paul Society that gave aid to the poor and needy. The pastor appointed him to a two-year term as a councilman responsible for approving the parish budget prepared by the pastor and the financial records kept by the parish bookkeeper. In all these roles, Bob had to learn how to get along with individuals who had very different backgrounds and viewpoints.

For Kathy, the parish was a source of stability and pride. She was confident that her children were getting a solid grounding in the faith from the parish grade school. It pleased her that the priests visited the classrooms regularly to have contact with the children and to offer religious instruction. The sisters were good teachers and did a great job of preparing the youngsters for first confession and Communion. As an active member of the Altar and Rosary Society, Kathy took great pride in making the church look clean and beautiful. Her social life was centered in the parish and included the monthly parties and dances she attended with Bob as well as the weekly bowling nights with her women friends in the parish league. She loved the devotional life of the parish: the ashes and palms; the blessing of throats and food; the special celebrations of Mary and the saints. Periodically, she took some of the children to the Thursday Sorrowful Mother Devotions and the Friday Stations of the Cross. She and Bob never missed the annual Parish Mission when a visiting priest (usually a Redemptorist or Paulist) would give a series of fiery sermons against the sins of drunkenness, sloth, and lust, combined with a plea for frequent confession. Kathy always felt a great sense of pride when priests from all over the diocese came for the annual Forty Hours Devotion that included Benediction in their beautiful church.

Other Parishes

Not all Catholic parishes before Vatican II were exactly like St. Catherine. Over half did not have a grade school and relied on CCD programs to instruct the youth in their Catholic faith. Predominantly Hispanic and black parishes had their own distinct customs. National parishes, comprising about 17 percent of Catholic parishes in 1960, were also committed to preserving ethnic customs and practices. Rural parishes had special celebrations, such as Rogation Days for fruitful harvests. Parishioners in recently founded suburban parishes relied less on the parish for their social activities. On the other hand, most Catholics of the period could identify with many of the values and attitudes of Bob and Kathy: their respect for priests; their love and loyalty for their parish; their appreciation of the Mass and other sacraments; their reliance on a rich devotional life for spiritual nourishment; and their strong sense of Catholic identity fostered by parish life.

Limitations

A theology of the parish that views the Church not as a static institution but as a dynamic event provides a basis for evaluating pre–Vatican II parishes. A parish is not simply a segment of the larger Church or the personal possession of a male, celibate clergy. It is, rather, the concrete actualization of the universal Church; the Body of Christ in action in a particular area; the people of God gathered for worship and mission; the pilgrim community wending its way though history.

From this theological perspective, we can recognize the severe limitations imposed on pre-conciliar parishes by the clericalism that gave so much power and responsibility to the clergy and constricted the contributions of the parishioners who were expected to "pay, pray and obey." We can also appreciate the great energy unleashed by the Vatican II reforms that have empowered baptized women and men to take a more significant role in the administrative, liturgical, and ministerial activities of parishes today.

Catholic Identity

In the pre-conciliar era, parishioners generally enjoyed a commonly held, clearly etched sense of Catholic identity that was a source of pride and solidarity, manifested, for example, in public rallies and the over 80 percent Catholic vote for John Kennedy in 1960. During the last half-century this form of Catholic identity has gradually faded, for various reasons: the demise of the Catholic subculture; greater awareness of pluralism in the Catholic community; religious education programs that stress open discussion more than clear content; progress in the ecumenical movement; the clergy sex-abuse scandal; and sharp disputes over the best public policies to combat abortion.

Many Catholics today, especially among the younger generations, are seeking a thicker, more secure sense of Catholic identity. Nostalgic efforts to return to the pre-conciliar era, however, are doomed to failure precisely because of developments in society, culture, and the Church. Catholic identity has a history as it struggles to remain faithful to its long and rich tradition, guided by scripture and authoritative teaching, while at the same time adapting to changing historical and cultural conditions. We need to find pride and solidarity today in essentials: a sacramental sense disposed to find the infinite in the finite and divine grace in ordinary life; a fundamental respect for the whole Christian tradition; an appreciation of the Petrine ministry; a positive sense of human nature and the value of reason, philosophy, and science; an embrace of Mary and the communion of saints; and a commitment to the works of justice and peace.

Our great resource for forming a viable contemporary Catholic identity is the reformed liturgy celebrated each weekend in parishes around the country. The inherent socializing power of the Eucharist is enhanced by prayerful presiding, effective preaching, and uplifting music. Christian service projects that include theological reflection are a great way to help parishioners, especially young people, to develop a Catholic identity committed to concrete acts of charity and the cause of justice and peace.

Parish Loyalty

Parish loyalty was a prominent feature of Catholic life before the Second Vatican Council. Parishioners generally felt a sense of pride in their home parish. Boundaries were important and respected. Loyalty to their parish forced Catholics to interact with various types of people, including those who were different or disagreeable. Parishioners had to learn how to negotiate with others who held different views. In the contemporary world, loyalty of all types is greatly diminished. A significant number of young Catholics feel free to abandon their heritage and join other denominations that meet their needs. It is common for Catholics to shop around for a parish that appeals to them. It is easier to switch parishes than to battle polarization and manage pluralism.

Efforts to revive Catholic loyalty today should begin with fidelity to Christ as witnessed in the scriptures, church teaching, and the Christian tradition. The virtue of loyalty needs this rich soil in order to develop and flourish. Loyalty prompts Catholics to remain in the Church and to be part of the ongoing effort to make it a more credible sign of Christ and his teaching. Parishes that utilize the talents of parishioners and serve their spiritual needs will earn their loyalty over a period of time. Catholics who associate only with like-minded believers run the risk of settling for narrow perspectives and cramped attitudes. We all can grow spiritually by engaging with parishioners who express diverse viewpoints. The virtue of loyalty today prompts dialogue that seeks common ground and collaboration that serves the common good.

Parish Devotions

Recent developments in university parishes around the country suggest that a significant number of young Catholics are interested in reviving elements of the devotional life that was so important to immigrant Catholics. After Vatican II, pastors and religious educators put more emphasis on scripture and the liturgy as the solid ground for a viable contemporary spirituality and less emphasis on the traditional devotions. At university parishes today, however, it is not unusual for students to take the initiative in organizing various devotional practices: for example, having Benediction along with regular adoration of the Blessed Sacrament; reciting the Rosary in common; wearing medals and scapulars; participating in novenas; celebrating saints' days; and consecrating themselves to Mary. This significant development among collegians, even if limited and driven by diverse motives, suggests that parishes can meet a current spiritual need by retrieving elements of the rich devotional life of the past and placing those elements in a solid theological context. For instance, Benediction can be explicitly related to the eucharistic liturgy where we offer ourselves along with Christ as gift to the Father, and Marian devotions can emphasize Mary's role as model of the Church and exemplar of Christian discipleship. In this way, parishes can provide a richer devotional life that enhances a contemporary spirituality grounded in scripture and liturgy.

All across the United States today, we find vibrant Catholic parishes that witness to the wisdom of the Vatican II reforms, especially those that unleashed the energy and talents of baptized women and men in service to the Church and the world. As parishes continue to adapt to a rapidly changing world, we can learn important lessons from the pre-conciliar parishes that fostered a clear sense of Catholic identity, promoted parish loyalty, and celebrated a rich devotional life.

14

Catholic Teaching on Sexuality

From Romanticism to Reality

CHRISTINE E. GUDORF

The period after World War II (1941–1945) until the end of the Second Vatican Council (1962–1965) was a dynamic one for American Catholics. The immigration of Catholics to America peaked between 1880 and 1910, with immigrants settling in urban ethnic neighborhoods in the East and Midwest, where their children and grandchildren remained. With the return of soldiers from Europe and the Pacific between 1945 and 1947, urban Catholic families experienced dramatic shifts. Though church teaching on sexuality and the family had remained virtually unchanged since the Council of Trent ended in 1563—and was one of the few areas of Catholic teaching that would remain relatively untouched by Vatican II—the times themselves would reshape American Catholic families. Americans had savings because military production had kept employment high during the war, but there had been little consumer production to spend wages on. New highways and suburban housing accommodated millions of young people who had postponed marriage and/or children because of the war and were now ready to settle down into domesticity. Women left employment by the millions, spurred on by government campaigns encouraging them to give their jobs to returning servicemen. The baby boom began.

Catholic Romanticism

For Catholics, the postwar romanticization of marriage and motherhood in American society was completely congruent with church teaching and with the inherited folkways of the Catholic community. Church opposition to contraception had begun to fade in Protestant communities following the 1934 Lambeth Conference of Anglican bishops, but was still strong in the Catholic Church. Until well into the urban-to-suburban population shift, Catholic neighborhoods were characterized by tight-knit ethnic parishes in which many of the cultural attitudes brought from Europe, including those surrounding marriage and family, still endured. Marriage was largely understood as a contract to partner in complementary roles (male breadwinner and female homemaker) in raising a family, with marital sex primarily aimed at procreation; this understanding reflected traditional Catholic teaching. The pope during the forties and fifties was Pius XII, who responded to post-war nostalgia for "normalcy" with an enthusiastic romanticization of women as mothers, of large families, and of parents who sacrificed for such families. Take, for example, two of his many utterances:

> Now a woman's function, a woman's way, a woman's natural bent, is motherhood. Every woman is called to be a mother, a mother in a physical sense, or a mother in a sense more spiritual and more exalted, yet real, nonetheless.[1]

and

> A cradle consecrates the mother, more cradles sanctify her and glorify her in the eyes of her husband, her children, the Church and the nation.[2]

Pius XII reflected the attitudes of his day. Given the huge loss of life in Europe during World War II and the postponement or interruptions of family life for five to ten years, the European yearning for domesticity was understandable and accounts for some of Pius's romantic language. But he shared with his predecessors, and indeed with his successors, some very basic and traditional understandings of sex/gender: that women were made to be mothers and homemakers; that the headship of men in families called for loving submission by women and children; that men had primary responsibility for family support but that when women had to work outside the home they should receive equal pay and should stick to work in line with their nature (work calling for care and compassion, not judgment). The very sensibility of women, according to the popes, made them excellent mothers, teachers and protectors of the weak, but also made them easily seduced and deceived, so that they needed the protection of more rational men.[3]

Family First

While Pius XII spoke very little about sexuality, the roles of men and women in the family, and especially motherhood, were favorite topics. He instructed mothers on breastfeeding babies—bottles he considered a selfish convenience. Pius did not need to address sexuality—the rules regarding sexuality were universal and long-standing in the Church: there was to be no sex outside marriage, sex in marriage was for procreation, and procreation was to be unobstructed. Anything tending to produce sexual arousal was a near occasion of sin and to be avoided. The rules were drilled into Catholic youth in the parochial schools, often by nuns, whose numbers were stretched during the fifties and sixties to staff all the new suburban parochial schools in addition to the urban ones. Catholic writers and directors educated in these schools later poked fun at nuns as sexually repressed, citing, for example, such things as bans on patent leather shoes for girls because such shoes might reflect the girls' panties and arouse young boys. But the sisters were only passing on traditional wisdom in the Church: that sexual arousal should be avoided because it was dangerously difficult to control; that women had the power to arouse even when they were unconscious of it. Of course, the real practical danger of sex outside marriage was pregnancy. Nothing was more scandalous than a pregnant and unmarried Catholic girl. Such girls were forced to drop out of school; they were surreptitiously sent away (to relatives or homes for unwed mothers) and returned without babies.

During this period, Catholic families on average were larger than other groups. My mother had nine living children from twelve pregnancies in eleven years. Her sister had eight living children from ten pregnancies in fourteen years. Our families were considered medium-large in the Catholic milieu; truly large were families with a dozen or more children. One farm wife in our parish gave birth to and raised twenty-one children—and threw hay bales like a twenty-year-old. Public health and the science of medicine had advanced to a point that, combined with a prosperous economy that kept nutrition levels high, allowed birth rates never seen before. In past ages, pregnancy levels were often very high but the number of live births, especially the number of children surviving to adulthood, was much lower. In mid-twentieth-century America, almost all pregnancies produced live children and most of those children survived.

Nuns worked for a fraction of the cost for lay teachers, allowing low tuition in parish schools; tuition for second or third children was even less or nothing. Every night my parents quizzed each of us on *Baltimore Catechism* questions assigned in religion class; they led prayers before and after meals and at bedtime as well as weekly family Rosary. Fourth through eighth graders constituted the parish choir, ensuring regular attendance among our many relatives. During May, families were often ritualed-out, between attending the parish May procession, First Communions for their own children, and then First Communions for nieces and nephews at nearby parishes.

A New Day for Catholic Sex

For Catholic baby boomers raised with many siblings and numerous aunts, uncles, and cousins, the changes following the advent of the birth-control pill in the sixties were traumatic. Though slower to use the pill than other groups because of church rules, as the cost of rearing and educating children increased and the ability of a single wage-earner to support a family decreased, Catholic couples began ignoring the Vatican ban on contraception. By the nineties family gatherings had shrunk in size. My mother had four siblings, my father seven; I have eight, my husband four. But my eight siblings and I gave birth to an average of 2.4 children (augmented by several adoptions); my husband and his four siblings had an average of 2.0 children. As the last ethnic parishes disappear, and suburban ones turn greyer with baby boomers, parish life is more anonymous. There are not only fewer children to bind families into shared projects, but also fewer nuns and less parental time available, since most mothers work outside the home in order to afford parochial school tuition or even basic sustenance.

While fertility and domesticity raged among American Catholics of the 1950s and 1960s, no one spoke about sex. There was no sex education in the schools, Pre-Cana Conferences for the engaged taught every aspect of marriage other than sex, and few parents talked to their children about sex. Television and movies suggested but never depicted sex, and all TV couples slept in twin beds. Yet my generation grew up on stories of the frustrated longing of parents separated by war, and giggled tremendously at discovering parents kissing.

Only in the late sixties, as the pill began affecting fertility rates, Catholics and other Americans slowly began to talk both publicly and within families about sexuality. With these discussions inside and outside the Church, sexual practice began to change, even though most church teaching did not. By the seventies, the Church had begun to stress love rather than duty in marriage in response to the post-war romanticization of marriage and the home. I can still remember the embarrassment of my very undemonstrative mother-in-law at first being pulled onto her husband's lap, to the grins and applause of their married, much more demonstrative children. Contract language for marriage had largely disappeared by the time of Pope Paul VI. The council, too, had contributed to this shift by speaking of shared "parental" responsibilities in marriage, rather than separating maternal and paternal responsibilities. John Paul II entirely replaced the contract language of duties with the language of loving partners.

We can have hope that Catholics are growing into Vatican II's vision of marriage as "a covenant of life and love."

Notes

1. Pius XII, "Address to Italian Women," October 21, 1945, *AAS* 37 (1945): 287.

2. Pius XII, "Le vingt-cinquieme," July 26, 1955, *Osservatore Romano*, July 28, 1955; translation: *Papal Teachings: Woman in the Modern World* (Boston: Daughters of St. Paul, 1959), 37.

3. For numerous examples, see Christine E. Gudorf, *Catholic Social Teaching on Liberation Themes* (Washington, DC: University Press of America, 1980), especially 264–302 on Pope Pius XII.

15

The Afterlife

Death, Judgment, Purgatory, Heaven, Hell

ZACHARY HAYES, O.F.M.

In order to get some orientation for a consideration of changes that have taken place in the theological area known as eschatology ("the last things"), it might be useful to recall the way in which Christian art over the centuries has presented a vision of the afterlife in various paintings as well as in literature. I have in mind the great painting of the last judgment by Michelangelo in the Sistine Chapel and the work of many other artists with vivid imaginations over the ages. In literary form, there is the *Divine Comedy* of Dante (1265–1321) which includes the *Paradiso*, the *Purgatorio*, and the *Inferno*. In these examples one sees, reads, and thinks of the terrible chasm between the souls of the dead and God represented by the various levels of descent into hell. These artistic and literary representations were taken so seriously and literally that a number of theologians, well into the nineteenth century, actually calculated the degrees of heat at the different levels of the underworld; for, after all, not all those who have been lost deserve the same degree of punishment.

A New Perspective

This was, to a great extent, characteristic of Roman Catholicism's theological understanding of the afterlife until well into the modern period. But gradually, during the late nineteenth and early twentieth centuries, a stronger sense of the historical nature of Christian doctrine entered the picture. And, specifically from the perspective of critical historical biblical studies, it became possible to see the biblical language about the other world as largely metaphorical rather than as literally, physically descriptive. At the same time, from a more philosophical perspective, it became possible to see biblical eschatological language as a specific religious way of dealing with the history of human hope. The language of human hope is commonly language about a future, and biblical language of hope is language about a future seen from a specifically Judaeo-Christian perspective. Thus, the language of theological eschatology for Christians is seen as language about a mysterious future for human existence that transcends human history, but can be spoken about only in the language that human beings generate within their historical existence, since that is the only type of language available for human beings to use, even in the case of scripture. This insight in the twentieth century would lead to a rich understanding of the theology of hope as a form of the Christian theology of history.

Given this context, heaven and hell are seen by theology as metaphors for ultimate success or ultimate failure as the outcome of human history, both for the human individual and for the human community as a whole. Purgatory is seen primarily as a symbol of the need for further maturation, either in the experience of dying itself, or in the aftermath of death and prior to the experience of heaven. This teaching relates to the conviction that some people die in the state of grace, but they are still burdened with some degree of temporal punishment for sins already forgiven, or for venial sins that still remain unforgiven, and therefore they must undergo some sort of purgation either in death itself or after death before entering fully into the immediate presence of God. It was this idea that was presented in so much of Christian art, especially in the medieval and Renaissance periods. But, unfortunately, all too often, at least in the popular imagination, heaven, hell, and purgatory became a form of other-worldly geography.

It is interesting to think of these theological metaphors in relation to non-theological studies of human death and dying. From a clinical and psychological perspective, the work of Elizabeth Kübler-Ross has been of great significance. It has helped greatly to see the experience of death as a deeply human experience. The theological thought of the twentieth-century Jesuit theologian Karl Rahner was very influential in this context. He developed a deeply anthropological understanding of the process of human dying from a philosophical point of view. This, then, he related to a theological perspective. In such a context, death is seen not simply as something biological that happens from outside, but as a process in which the person is deeply engaged interiorly, and for which one prepares by the quality of life one has attempted to live throughout one's personal history.

This theological understanding seemed to be enacted before me in 1963 when I stood with other friends around the bed of a dying friar in Germany. We had carried out the entire ritual of the Church as customary at that time, a ritual in which the dying friar himself took part. When it was completed, he sat up in bed and called out: "This is the end of the following of Christ." With that, he lay back on the bed and never spoke another word. This was the first time I had ever experienced a human person dying. Seeing the very active way this man was involved in the process opened me to wonder about the mystery of human dying. What is really going on in a dying person? Much insight was offered to me later when I read about the clinical work of Kübler-Ross. And the work of Karl Rahner would lead me to a a deeper understanding of the theological language dealing with death and its aftermath, which is the concern of Christian eschatology.

An Emerging Consciousness

From the perspective of Christian eschatology, we can say that heaven is not a symbol of some pre-existing, physical place in some other-worldly geography. Rather, it is the symbol of the final, fulfilling relationship between God and creation envisioned by Christian faith. This has been realized in a pre-eminent sense in the case of Christ, whose life and tragic death led to his glorification in the resurrection and ascension. And it remains to be realized for the rest of humanity through subsequent history, both individual and collective. In the case of Christ, theologians speak of realized eschatology, since the goal that God has in mind for creation has been realized in the destiny of Christ. Insofar as that which has been realized in Christ anticipates the collective destiny of God's creation, which is still not realized in the whole of creation, there is a future dimension to eschatology.

Writing on this subject in one of his earlier books, Pope Benedict XVI states this in very compact language. Heaven exists because Jesus Christ has given human existence a place in the being of God. Heaven is primarily a personal relation which is always marked by its historical origin in the death and resurrection of Christ. As for the rest of humanity, we are in heaven to the degree that we are near Christ.[1]

As a religious tradition, Christianity is marked by a strong conviction concerning the importance of human freedom. The actual outcome of human history, both individually and collectively, is not predetermined by God alone. Rather, a goal is offered by God, but its realization is brought about by the action of human freedom in its way of relating to the goal that God freely holds open to it. Hell is a symbol for the possibility that a person may freely close himself or herself to the love and grace of God and choose an existence of total isolation rather than one of communion with God. As Rahner has formulated it, metaphors such as fire, worms, and darkness all point in the same direction, namely to: "...the possibility of man being finally lost and estranged from God in all the dimensions of his existence."[2]

The language about heaven, on the other hand, is language about the possibility of the positive outcome of human history in relation to God. It is language about the final, definitive relation of a loving union between a creature that is called to love by a God who, in the deepest sense, is the purest reality of loving being. This mystery is called to mind by symbolic language about the heavenly wedding feast and other such evocative metaphors. Because of the dying and rising of Jesus Christ, therefore, Christians live with the positive hope that our eternal future is to be wrapped forever in the embrace of a loving God in a way that transcends history.

Summarizing this all in very compact language, Hans Urs von Balthasar has written: "God is the Last Thing of the creature. Gained, He is its paradise; lost, He is its hell; as demanding, He is its judgment; as cleansing, He is its purgatory."

Notes

1. Joseph Ratzinger, *Eschatologie: Kleine Katholische Dogmatik*, IX (Regensburg, 1977), 190

2. Karl Rahner, *Encyclopedia of Theology: The Concise Sacramentum Mundi* (New York: Crossroad, 1975), 603.

II

PERSONALITIES

16

John Courtney Murray

Theologian of Religious Freedom

DAVID HOLLENBACH, S.J.

John Courtney Murray, S.J., was the most creative and influential United States theologian of the twentieth century. One of the clearest indicators of his influence was the appearance of his portrait on the cover of *Time* magazine on December 12, 1960. Murray's great contribution was to initiate a deep dialogue between the American experience of religious freedom and the long Catholic tradition's understanding of how the Christian community should relate to the social-political life of the surrounding society.

Background to Murray's Contribution

Murray played a major role at the Second Vatican Council as one of the principal drafters of the council's Declaration on Religious Freedom (*Dignitatis Humanae*). Appreciation of how Murray drew deeply on his profound knowledge of the pre–Vatican II traditions as he worked to shape the council itself can contribute much to our understanding of the council's continuing importance today.

Through the modern historical era up to the time of Pope John XXIII and the council, official Catholic teachings approached religious freedom with suspicion and even hostility. For example, in 1832 Pope Gregory XVI declared that the right to freedom of conscience is an "insanity" (*dileramentum*). In large part through Murray's influence, a dramatic shift in this position occurred at Vatican II, which declared that "The right to religious freedom has its foundation in the very dignity of the human person, as this dignity is known through the revealed word of God and by reason itself" (*Dignitatis Humanae*, 2). Why was such a shift necessary, and how did it occur?

Most Americans today find it hard even to imagine living in a society where freedom of religion is not protected. The First Amendment to the U.S. Constitution states that the government "shall make no law respecting an establishment of religion, or prohibiting the free exercise thereof." Thus, most Americans take their freedom of religious belief for granted and presume that other societies should have religious freedom as well.

Pre-conciliar Catholicism, however, feared this religious freedom for three reasons. First, the teaching office of the Church saw religious freedom as closely linked with the secularizing initiatives of the French revolution, which sought to confine Christian faith to the sacristy. This approach would exclude the Church from any influence in social and political life. Second, it was sometimes argued that religious freedom should be protected because there is supposedly no way to know whether any religious beliefs are actually true. This argument linked religious freedom with agnosticism and skepticism. Third, the modern human-rights movement sometimes assumed a highly individualistic understanding of the person. It presumed that religious freedom, and other human rights also, would be best defended by protecting individual privacy and leaving people alone. Such approaches to freedom were and remain in tension or conflict with Catholic tradition.

Murray's efforts to argue that the official Church's position on religious freedom should be changed from opposition to support was seen by some church officials in Rome as a capitulation to these secularizing, skeptical, and individualistic tendencies in modern Western culture. Thus in 1955, Murray was effectively forbidden to write further on the issue of religious freedom. But just four years later Pope John XXIII announced that he would convene the Second Vatican Council, opening the way for the revival and ultimate triumph of Murray's argument for religious freedom.

Use of Tradition in Arguing for Religious Freedom

Murray's understanding of religious freedom drew deeply on Catholic tradition while developing this tradition in new and creative directions. Murray's thinking had three dimensions.

First, his argument was explicitly theological. He called this dimension of his position the "primacy of the spiritual." The human person is a spiritual being whose spirit reaches beyond all earthly realities in its quest for meaning. Ultimately, this quest can be satisfied only by union with God, and it can be attained only through a free act of faith. As Augustine put it, "our hearts are restless till they rest in thee." The transcendence of the human spirit must never be subordinated to the control of earthly powers such as the government. The state is ultimately incompetent to tell men and women how they should relate to God. Efforts by a government to enforce religion would thus deny the primacy of the spiritual over the political. To give such power to the state would be to subordinate religious faith to politics. It would place both the person's relation to God and the Church itself under the thumb of the state. Theologically, this is totally unacceptable and Murray argues for religious freedom by resisting this subordination.

Second, this theological stance has a direct political consequence. It grounds Murray's argument that the state is essentially limited in power. In the long Catholic tradition, going back to the apostles' statement that "we must obey God rather than any human authority" (Acts 5:29, NRSV), to medieval investiture controversies in which the popes resisted attempts by princes to appoint bishops, the Church has stood firmly in opposition to unlimited state power. In Murray's own time this argument had particular force, for the Church was involved in a sustained struggle with the totalitarian Soviet state. The limited nature of the state is essential for the protection of the freedom of the Church, and it has as a direct consequence the freedom of society from any form of absolutist control by the government. This means that citizens should be free from state control in their religious belief, which grounds the civil right to religious freedom. Analogously, citizens should also be free in other, broader ranges of their social life. Thus Murray argued that religious freedom is linked with the full range of civil and political rights that are guaranteed by constitutional democracy. Religious freedom and human rights more generally are directly linked with each other. This linkage has made the Church after Vatican II one of the strongest voices for human rights on the world stage today. Murray's use of the tradition in new circumstances helped make this possible.

Finally, Murray's approach had both ethical and juridical or legal dimensions. Because the state is limited, its reach does not extend to the promotion of the full common good that should be achieved in society, but only to the most basic moral requirements of social life that Murray called public order. Public order includes genuinely moral values, such as public peace, justice, and those standards of public morality on which consensus exists in society. These minimal moral standards are the concern of the government. But working for the attainment of the fullness of virtue and the totality of the common good is the vocation of the Church, of families, and of the many educational and cultural bodies that form civil society. The state's moral role is more limited: the protection of the basic requirements of peace, justice, and human rights that make life in society possible at all. Murray appealed to St. Augustine's argument that the state is unlikely to succeed in efforts to promote good sexual mores through the force of coercive civil law. This is rather the task of the Church, the family, and other communities in civil society that can more directly encourage personal virtue. In the same way, it is the role of the Church and its members—not the role of the state—to promote Christian faith and a fruitful relation to God among the citizenry. Thus Murray provides a moral and juridical argument for religious freedom.

Murray drew deeply on nearly two thousand years of Christian tradition in making his argument for religious freedom. His work was both profoundly traditional and dramatically innovative. He maintained that the most difficult question faced by the bishops assembled at Vatican II was that of whether and how Christian doctrine could develop and change. Through his scholarly retrieval of resources from the tradition and his wise use of these resources to address the pressing problems facing the Church in his time, Murray showed the council fathers that such development was possible and also how it could occur in the domain of religious freedom. His interpretation of religious freedom rested neither on an individualistic understanding of the human person nor on a view that religion is an essentially private affair. Murray's contribution, therefore, set the Church free to make important contributions to justice and peace in society.

Continuing Challenges Today

The development of tradition to which Murray contributed has, of course, not come to an end. After the council and shortly before he died, Murray suggested that the understanding of freedom within the Church's own internal life was a matter in need of further investigation and development. This has surely proven to be the case, as the Church has grappled with questions of morality and theology ranging from reproduction and sexuality, to women's roles in the Church, to the relation of Christian faith to other religions. Murray's life work can serve as a model for all who seek to grapple with these issues today. His success in bringing about a development of the tradition is a sign of hope in our own time, and can contribute to a deepening of contemporary faith as well.

Life and Major Work

Murray was born on September 12, 1904, in New York City. He entered the Jesuit order in 1920 at the age of sixteen. He received his BA from Weston College in 1926 and an MA from Boston College in 1927. He then taught Latin and English literature for three years at the Ateneo de Manila in the Philippines. He studied theology at Woodstock College in Maryland from 1930 to 1934, was ordained to the priesthood on June 25, 1933, and went on to receive his doctorate in theology from the Gregorian University in 1937. He returned to teach theology at Woodstock, remaining a professor there until his death in 1967. In 1941 he became editor of *Theological Studies*, and he published many of his most influential articles in that journal. He was also the religion editor of *America* magazine for many years. In 1955 he was told by his Jesuit superiors in Rome that it would not be prudent for him to continue writing on the subject of religious freedom. In a dramatic reversal of this silencing, Murray was invited in 1963 to attend the Second Vatican Council as a theological advisor to the bishops. He died August 16, 1967, less than two years after the close of the council he had helped shape.

His best known book, *We Hold These Truths: Catholic Reflections on the American Proposition*, was first published in 1960 (it is still in print today: Lanham, MD: 2005, Rowman and Littlefield), the same year John F. Kennedy was elected president of the United States. The overlap of these two events was doubtless the occasion for his appearance on the cover of *Time* magazine that year. Other major contributions are in the collections of his articles edited by J. Leon Hooper, *Religious Liberty: Catholic Struggles with Pluralism* (Louisville, KY: Westminster/John Knox Press, 1993) and *Bridging the Sacred and the Secular* (Washington, DC: Georgetown University Press, 1994).

17

Leonard Feeney

In Memoriam

CARDINAL AVERY DULLES, S.J.

With the death of Leonard Feeney, at the age of eighty, on January 30, 1978, the United States lost one of its most colorful, talented, and devoted priests. The obituary notices, on the whole, tended to overlook the brilliance of his career and to concentrate only on the storm of doctrinal controversy associated with his name in the late 1940s and early 1950s.

I knew Father Feeney only slightly before the spring of 1946, at which time I settled in Cambridge, Massachusetts, for several months as I was completing my naval service and preparing to enter the Jesuit novitiate in August. I went to Cambridge in order to rejoin St. Benedict Center, a lively gathering place for Catholic students, which I had been instrumental in founding, together with Catherine Goddard Clarke, some five years earlier. Mrs. Clarke, a woman of charismatic charm and contagious enthusiasm, had run the Center almost unassisted until 1943, when she obtained the services of Leonard Feeney as spiritual director. Father Feeney was then at the height of his renown. As literary editor of *America*, he had become a prominent

As it appears here, Cardinal Dulles's contribution is an edited version of a piece (same title) he wrote on Father Leonard Feeney in *America* (February 25, 1978): 135–37.

poet and essayist, much in demand on the lecture circuit. He had preached on important occasions at St. Patrick's Cathedral and had broadcast a series of sermons on *The Catholic Hour*. But after arriving in Cambridge he soon decided to make St. Benedict Center his single, exclusive, and full-time apostolate.

By the time I returned in February 1946, the Center was teeming with activity. It was not simply a place where students could drop in for a cup of tea or a friendly chat, but also a bustling center of theological study and apostolic zeal. Equipped with an excellent Catholic library (with my own collection as part of the nucleus), the Center had set up interest groups of various kinds, most of which met in the evening on a weekly basis.

Thursday nights at St. Benedict Center were, in a special way, for Father Feeney. He gave a carefully planned course of lectures, beginning with the act of faith and then passing on to the sacraments. His leading idea in these lectures seemed to be the integration of nature and grace. Faith he viewed as a sacrifice in which the believer offers to God the most excellent gift of reason. For the sacrifice to be meaningful it was essential, in Father Feeney's estimation, to have a proper esteem for the value of reason. In these lectures he therefore taught us to love the senses, the imagination, the memory and all the faculties of the mind. So, too, when he came to the sacraments, he labored to instill into his hearers a deep appreciation of the elements used in the church's rituals—water, oil, bread, wine, and the like.

Not only was the doctrine solid; the oratory was superb. Never have I known a speaker with such a sense of collective psychology. Father Feeney would not come to his main point until he had satisfied himself that every member of the audience was disposed to understand and accept his message. With unbelievable vividness he would make the gospel episodes come alive: scenes of the rich young man, of Zacchaeus in the sycamore tree, and countless others. When he quoted from the letters of Paul, one had the impression that Paul himself was speaking. To this day, I imagine St. Paul with the features and voice of Leonard Feeney.

His main interest was in those who made the Center their principal occupation in life—those for whom it was a kind of family, school, and parish all rolled into one. For this group Father Feeney would make himself available every afternoon, hearing confessions and giving personal direction. Later in the afternoon he would emerge for tea and a social hour. Then at suppertime a group of us would generally pile into Catherine Clarke's decrepit sedan so that we could continue our discussions over hamburgers in a restaurant. In the company of Catherine Clarke and Leonard Feeney conversation was never known to lag.

No Salvation outside the Church?

Were there, at the time I was present, any signs of the coming cataclysm? I did notice, toward the end of my stay, that Leonard Feeney was becoming increasingly polemical. His attacks on materialism, skepticism, and agnosticism became sharper and more personal. He used bitter invective against Hume and Kant, Marx and Freud. At times he denounced the "liberal Catholics" who had failed to support Generalissimo Franco. Even Jacques Maritain was in his eyes infected by the poison of liberal culture. Father Feeney's attitude toward the Jews was ambivalent. He felt that they could not achieve their true vocation except in Christ, but that when they accepted this vocation they excelled all other Christians. In his lectures and conversation he made us savor the total Jewishness of Mary, of Jesus, and of Paul. He used to talk of a certain Jewish taxi driver in New York whom he had instructed in the faith and who had become, in Father Feeney's judgment, a true mystic.

On the question of salvation outside the church, Father Feeney had not as yet adopted any clear position. He was convinced that Catholics must not hesitate to present the full challenge of the gospel, which for him included the whole system of official dogma. He felt that too many tended, out of politeness and timidity, to evade the task of forthright witness. As long as any person was alive, Father Feeney used to say, we should urge the necessity of his accepting the fullness of the faith. But after death, the situation was different. We could confidently leave our loved ones to the unfathomable mercy of God, to which we could set no limits. "I would infinitely rather be judged by God," Father Feeney would say, "than by my closest friend." Hence the damnation of non-Catholics was not at that stage, as I recall, any part of the Feeney gospel.

How did Leonard Feeney later become a proponent of the rigid and almost Jansenistic position attributed to St. Benedict Center? I have no personal knowledge of what happened in the late 1940s. Perhaps Father Feeney was somewhat embittered by his encounters with the non-Catholic universities about him; perhaps he was fatigued by his arduous apostolate and overtaxed by his poor health; perhaps, also, he was led into doctrinal exaggerations by his own mercurial poetic temperament. Then again, he and others may have been somewhat intoxicated by the dramatic successes of the Center and too much isolated from opinions coming from outside their own narrow circle. It occurs to me also that the religious enthusiasm of some of Father Feeney's convert disciples may have led him further than he would have gone on his own. He was ferociously loyal to his followers, especially those who had gone out on a limb to defend what they understood as his own teaching. Thus, when several faculty members at Boston College were dismissed for their teaching on salvation, he backed them to the hilt. From that moment the developments leading to Father Feeney's excommunication and to the interdiction of the Center were all but inevitable.

For those who loved and admired Father Feeney it was painful to see illustrated newspaper articles about him on the Boston Common, flanked by burly bodyguards, shouting vulgar anti-Semitisms at the crowds before him. No doubt he did become angry and embittered in the early 1950s, but happily this was only a passing phase. St. Benedict Center, after it moved to Still River, Massachusetts, in January 1958, became a different kind of community, more in keeping with the Benedictine spirit to which Father Feeney himself had long been attracted. Thus it became possible for the major portion of the community, including Father Feeney himself, to be reconciled to the Catholic Church in 1974. Two years later two members of this community were ordained to the priesthood so that they could carry on Father Feeney's ministry to the "pious union of Benedictine Oblates" that has sprung forth from the St. Benedict Center. It would have been tragic if Leonard Feeney, the great apostle of salvation within the Church, had died an excommunicate.

Cursum consummavi, fidem servavi ("I have finished my course; I have kept the faith"): These words could serve as Leonard Feeney's epitaph. They express his overriding concern to resist any dilution of the Christian faith and to pass it on entire, as a precious heritage, to the generations yet to come. In an age of accommodation and uncertainty, he went to extremes in order to avoid the very appearance of compromise. With unstinting generosity he placed all his talents and energies in the service of the faith as he saw it.

18

Madeleva Wolff, C.S.C.

Woman of Faith and Vision

GAIL PORTER MANDELL

In late nineteenth- and early twentieth-century America, the Roman Catholic Church and the educational system it supported offered a way out of limited circumstances and up the social and economic ladder for thousands of young men and women, many the children of immigrants. One of them was Mary Evaline Wolff, who grew up in a tiny logging town in northwest Wisconsin. At age twenty-one, she joined the Congregation of the Sisters of the Holy Cross, and as Sister Madeleva became famous as a poet, essayist, scholar, and educator.

During her long career, she published twenty books, including thirteen volumes of religious poetry; founded a college for women in Salt Lake City; and for twenty-seven years served as president of Saint Mary's College, Notre Dame, Indiana. As noted in *The New York Times* (July 27, 1964), two days after her death at age seventy-seven, perhaps her greatest achievement was establishing the School of Sacred Theology at Saint Mary's, the first of its kind and, for more than a decade, the only institution in which women or lay men could earn advanced degrees in Catholic theology. The school prepared a generation of women to take an active part in the intellectual life of the Church.

Discovering Catholic Culture

Born May 24, 1887, Eva, as she was called, grew up longing for status and culture. August, her German-born father, was a harness-maker whose formal education had ended with the third grade; Lucy, her mother, a daughter of immigrants, was a farm girl who managed to earn a high school diploma and taught in a country school for a few years before her marriage. Both of Eva's parents stressed the importance of education not only for their two sons but also—unusual at the time—for their only daughter, sending all three children to the University of Wisconsin. When, after her first year there, Eva was accepted at Saint Mary's, a Catholic college for women, the entire family was thrilled, in spite of the strain on their finances. A faith-based education at a convent school run by a French order of nuns signified the height of gentility.

At Saint Mary's, Eva became part of an expanding system of Catholic education in the United States that extended from the earliest grades through graduate school. Supported by religious congregations, it was an educational system designed to promote orthodoxy of views and practice. Required theology and philosophy courses focused on Catholic doctrine, and strict rules enforced the moral teachings of the Church. At its best, Catholic education imparted a shared view of the world and a common frame of reference; at its worst, it demanded conformity at the cost of creativity and critical thinking. Strong-willed and spirited, Eva resisted the rules, many of which she considered "rather foolish."[1] Her education, however, opened unexpected worlds to her. She discovered contemporary Catholic literature, avidly reading the poetry of Francis Thompson, Coventry Patmore, Alice Meynell, and other representatives of the English Catholic Revival, and was soon writing her own verse. Poetry became for her a form of prayer, an overflowing of her deepening spiritual life and an expression of an abiding relationship with God first formed during these college years.

Like many Catholic girls' schools at the time, Saint Mary's was literally and figuratively one step away from the convent. The college shared its campus with the motherhouse of the Congregation, whose members numbered at the time more than a thousand women in the United States alone. Eva found a vibrant religious community of women of all ages, passionately devoted to the service of God through prayer and good works. In attending daily Mass and mandatory college-wide retreats, Eva tasted the prayer and silent meditation of convent life at its most rarefied. From her classmates at Saint Mary's, many from privileged backgrounds, she learned to speak, dress, and comport herself as the lady she longed to be. But by the end of her junior year, Eva knew that in spite of her "huge Merry Widow hat and smart clothes," her "absolute wish was to become a Sister of the Holy Cross."[2]

Soon after she joined the Holy Cross order and before she finished her college degree, young Sister Madeleva was assigned to teach high-school classes with only a day's notice. Thanks to the vision of her religious superiors as well as her own initiative, Madeleva eventually obtained a first-rate education, earning a master's degree from the University of Notre Dame and distinguishing herself as the first religious to receive a PhD from the University of California at Berkeley, where she wrote a dissertation on medieval Christian literature. During a year's sabbatical, she completed post-graduate work at Oxford, studying with C. S. Lewis and J. R .R. Tolkien.

Realizing in retrospect that her own precipitate entry into her professional life was the rule and not the exception among young nuns, Madeleva instigated the Sister Formation Movement. Combating the stereotype of sisters as uneducated, subservient handmaids, the Movement worked to ensure the professional preparation and improve the status of religious women in the Church. Throughout her life, Madeleva used her position and influence to help generations of young nuns obtain educations similar in quality to her own.

Madeleva's Vision for Catholic Education

As a scholar and an educator, Madeleva kept abreast of contemporary culture (she drew criticism for encouraging young nuns to read *Lord of the Flies* and *Animal Farm* as part of their spiritual formation), refusing to draw a line between "secular" and "sacred." She also drew regularly on Christian tradition for inspiration and validation of her sometimes controversial initiatives. "Our journey into the past is a journey into the future," she wrote.[3] She revised the general education program at Saint Mary's, using the trivium of the medieval university as a model; the result was an interdisciplinary course that integrated the study of logic, literature, and composition. She added a major program in Christian culture that drew on the ideas of English historian Christopher Dawson, who stressed the dynamic, formative role of medieval Christianity in the development of Western culture. In establishing the School of Sacred Theology at St. Mary's, Madeleva cited as precedent the ecclesiastical leadership of seventh-century St. Hilda, abbess of Whitby.

In her return to the roots of Christian tradition, Madeleva's innovations were, by definition, radical; by adapting tradition to the needs of contemporary women, Madeleva gave it a modern twist and renewed relevance. In her view, women educated with men in co-educational institutions were educated as men;[4] when, however, women were educated with and as women, their educations became their own, made to their measure. Like others at the time, Madeleva stressed the complementarities of males and females rather than their equality. She nevertheless favored expanded roles for women in society and in the Church, ironically using the past to justify these roles and the male hierarchy of the church to effect them. This approach expressed itself most obviously in her creation of the School of Sacred Theology.

In line with John Henry Cardinal Newman, Madeleva held that the curriculum of the Catholic college should center on the study of theology, as it had in the medieval university, and not on religious education, the norm at the time. Because Catholic universities and seminaries refused to admit lay people into their theology programs, nuns—who taught most of the religion classes in Catholic schools—were denied the academic preparation they needed. Demonstrating the wisdom of working within a system, Madeleva engaged sympathetic priests and bishops in the design of a graduate program in theology that the hierarchy could approve. Formally established in 1944, the School granted 76 doctoral and 354 master's degrees before it closed in 1970. Even though the curriculum, mandated by Rome, guaranteed a conservative approach, Madeleva understood that women learning theology with and as women would inevitably change the discipline itself. Within a few years, graduates of the school were teaching not only at Saint Mary's but in theology programs across the country.

A "One-World" Woman for Our Time

During her long tenure as president, Madeleva succeeded in making Saint Mary's a center of Catholic thought and culture. The times supported her success. Catholic identity was strong and distinctive. Famous converts such as philosopher Jacques Maritain, writer and theologian Thomas Merton, and social activist Dorothy Day added substance and excitement to the Catholic faith. Because most of the student body had been educated in Catholic secondary schools, they arrived prepared to appreciate the Christian art, music, and drama that Madeleva offered them and the wider community. She used her extensive contacts and personal friendships to bring noted Catholic intellectuals, writers, artists, and performers to campus, many as visiting scholars and artists in residence.

With an orientation she described as "one-world-mindedness," Madeleva also brought international students to campus from as many as thirty-eight different countries at a time. If the college could not fulfill the Christian obligation to go forth and teach all nations, she explained, Saint Mary's must "bring all nations to us."[5] She justified controversial decisions, such as the racial integration of the college in 1941, by calling on the authority of the gospels and finding priests to back her up. Well before Vatican II, she spoke out in favor of ecumenism, stating, "I'm eliminating the word 'Protestant' from my vocabulary because I believe we are all children of God."[6]

Madeleva's life illuminates a time when religious congregations and the schools they sustained were among the glories of the Church. She used her position as a spokesperson for Catholic education and a proponent of Christian culture to combat the insularity of the Church and growing secularism of her day. As an advocate for women's education, she inspires us to speak with and for the marginalized and disenfranchised of our own time. Cherishing tradition without clinging to it, she reminds us of the need of each era to interpret our heritage anew. Her rise to leadership in her congregation shows the extent to which the Church of her day not only attracted and supported but also encouraged and lifted up ambitious women of vision and faith. So may it always be and the Church be blessed in every generation by great prophetic women like Sister Madeleva Wolff.

Notes

1. Sister M. Madeleva Wolff, CSC, *My First Seventy Years* (New York: The Macmillan Company, 1959), 28.

2. Ibid., 32–33.

3. Ibid., 137.

4. Ibid., 127.

5. Gail Porter Mandell, *Madeleva: A Biography* (Albany: State University of New York, 1997), 172.

6. Ibid., 173.

19

Pierre Teilhard de Chardin

Communion with God through the Earth

John F. Haught

I first became acquainted with the writings of Pierre Teilhard de Chardin (1881–1955) soon after graduating from college in 1964. I was immediately swept away by the power and freshness of his thought. At that time I was studying in a Catholic seminary which I left soon afterwards in order to pursue a lay career in academic theology. My decision to take up theological studies was also a consequence of exposure to the writings of Karl Rahner, but, as I recall, it was mostly due to the excitement I had felt in my very limited acquaintance with Teilhard and the direction in which he demonstrated that creative Christian thought could move. A year after coming to Georgetown University in 1969, I saw the need for a course in science and religion which I taught to undergraduates for the next thirty-five years. Throughout this time and afterwards, even though I have sought intellectual support for relating theology to science in the work of many other religious thinkers as well (especially Bernard Lonergan, A. N. Whitehead, and Michael Polanyi), Teilhard has been my main inspiration. I am not as uncritical of his thought as I may have been when I was much younger, but I still draw upon the audacity of his efforts to understand Christian faith in the context of evolution and his conviction that acquaintance with science can help theology expand and deepen our understanding of God. Here I want to point out that even before I came across his writings, his bold ideas were already influencing some of the theological reflection that would make Vatican II such an important event in the history of the Church.

A Guide to Vatican II?

Gaudium et Spes, the Second Vatican Council's Pastoral Constitution on the Church in the Modern World (1965) is revolutionary for many reasons, not least for making the following two statements:

> 1. The human race has passed from a rather static concept of reality to a more dynamic, evolutionary one. In consequence there has arisen a new series of problems...calling for efforts of analysis and synthesis. (§5)

> 2. A hope related to the end of time does not diminish the importance of intervening duties but rather undergirds the acquittal of them with fresh incentives. (§21)

It is hard to read these words without seeing in them some of Teilhard's central ideas. Early in the twentieth century this controversial Jesuit geologist and innovative religious thinker had already expressed the very same sentiments as *Gaudium et Spes*—although more powerfully and emphatically—developing his ideas in numerous unpublished essays and in his major books, *The Human Phenomenon* and *The Divine Milieu*. During his own lifetime the Vatican had prevented Teilhard from publishing his reflections on evolution and Christian faith. In 1962 it even issued a *monitum* (admonition) about his writings to seminary professors and university presidents to "protect the minds, particularly of the youth, against the dangers presented by the works of Fr. Teilhard de Chardin and his followers." However, by 1965 Teilhard's bold integration of Christianity and modern science had become widely known and appreciated. And there can be little doubt that among the experts who drafted *Gaudium et Spes* there were at least some "followers" who had been exposed to Teilhard's "dangerous" ideas either directly or indirectly.

Presumably it was Teilhard's ideas on original sin that had seemed especially alarming earlier in the twentieth century. However, the Vatican's censoring of his work was motivated no less fundamentally by the fact that church officials and theologians at the time were still distrustful of evolution and the world-affirming religious ideas that Teilhard had expressed. Until the council most bishops and catechists alike would have found the two propositions excerpted above quite unsettling. And yet, by 1965—a mere ten years after Teilhard's death—the Church had come to adopt Teilhard's provocative claims as officially its own.

In order to appreciate *Gaudium et Spes* today, I believe it is essential to reflect seriously on Teilhard's main themes—now more than ever. Although chronologically the French Jesuit is pre-conciliar, in thought and sentiment he is in most respects a decidedly post-conciliar interpreter of Christian faith. After Vatican II we have yet to catch up with his revolutionary, nuanced, and deeply Christian synthesis of science and faith. Hence contemporary Catholic thought, in order to appropriate the theological reflection that lies behind the two passages I have highlighted from *Gaudium et Spes,* would do well to examine more closely than ever Teilhard's earlier prescriptions for the renewal of Christianity in a scientific and post-Darwinian age.

By and large, I believe, it has still failed to do so. And it does not help matters that Pope Benedict XVI (along with his former student Cardinal Christoph Schönborn of Vienna) has undeniably given the impression to many intellectuals that Catholicism these days is more tentative, and at times even grudging, in its embrace of evolutionary science than it was during the papacy of John Paul II. Nevertheless, Vatican II itself provides a firm theological sanction for undertaking the "analysis and synthesis" of what it means to be Catholic after Darwin and Einstein. Even now Teilhard's thought remains a vital resource for a constructive theology of nature in keeping with the spirit of both scientific discovery and the Second Vatican Council.

Christianity and the Unfinished Universe

According to Vatican II, the relatively recent migration of enlightened human consciousness from a static concept of reality to a "dynamic" and "evolutionary" one requires fresh "efforts of analysis and synthesis" on the part of Catholics, theologians, and the teaching Church. A good place to begin this analysis and synthesis is to go back and ask Teilhard what he meant when he made this same point, one that seemed unacceptable early in the twentieth century but one that Vatican II enthusiastically endorsed decades later.

To begin with, Teilhard would reply, a still evolving universe is an *unfinished* creation. This observation alone is theologically and ethically momentous. It means that the world is still coming into being, that the cosmos remains open to a future of ongoing creation "up ahead." The whole universe, along with earth and humanity, is perishable, of course, but it may still have a rich future in the meantime. That the universe is still being created allows Christians to observe that something of great importance has been going on in the universe since long before human beings arrived. And the hope that creation may continue into the future has wholesome implications for Christian ethics and eschatology, as the second excerpt suggests.

What then is going on in the universe, and why should Catholic thought be concerned about it? Here, in a nutshell, is how Teilhard would respond:

(a) Traditional Catholicism first came to expression at a time when everyone understood the universe to be essentially static and unchanging. As a result of modern science, however, Catholic thought today needs to understand that the *whole* universe, not just terrestrial life and human history, is in the process of becoming. Teilhard, I should note, was one of the first scientists in the last century to have observed that the entire cosmos—and not just the biological and human periods—is a still-unfolding story. Theology needs to become fully awakened to the fact that the universe is not just a stage for the human drama. Human existence must now be reconnected to the larger narrative of creation, as even St. Paul proposed (Romans 8:18–21) in Christianity's foundational phase.

The Pauline intuition, Teilhard would advise, must now be reconfigured in accordance with our latest scientific understanding of the world. Such theological reconstruction, I would argue, is what the council is encouraging when it points to the need for new "efforts of analysis and synthesis." In this project Teilhard's thought, in spite of whatever imperfections it may have, is more vital today than ever.

(b) On our own planet the cosmic process has already brought about the geosphere and the biosphere. So what's going on now? Because of developments in communication technology, commerce, engineering, and global politics it appears that the earth is now gradually weaving onto itself something like a brain, a "noosphere." Teilhard did not live to see the Internet, but his ideas clearly anticipated this and many other developments in planetary complexity. It is an exciting development in religious history that in Vatican II Catholic thought formally acknowledges that people of faith must realize their own lives are part of the ongoing, adventurous creation of the universe. The Christian exhortation to faith, hope, and love, Teilhard would add, is a unifying force essential to the future thriving of the earth and the universe that enfolds it.

(c) There is a discernible direction to cosmic process. Although biological evolution may seem at times to be a drunken stagger, the net movement of the universe has been in the direction of more and more physical complexity. The process has passed from the relatively simpler pre-atomic, atomic, and molecular stages to unicellular, multicellular, vertebrate, primate, and human forms of life. Overall, the long cosmic journey has come to expression in a measurable intensification of organized complexity. One can only wonder, then, where cosmic evolution will now carry its mysterious tendency to ongoing complexification.

The emerging noosphere appears to be actualizing just such an expectation. As Teilhard realized, however, at the present stage of its evolution the process is empty and doomed if it is not animated by love and "a great hope held in common." In this respect one of the objectives of Catholic theology must be to elevate awareness of how the life of faith, hope, and love can contribute to the ongoing creation of "more being" in God's universe.

(d) What does Teilhard mean by "more being"? During the course of the world's "evolution," as matter has become more complex in its organization, consciousness and spirit have intensified in a correspondingly impressive way. As visible matter has become more complex outwardly, the invisible "insideness" of things has become more vital, centered, conscious, and free. And, having reached the level of human consciousness, there is no reason to assume that this movement will now be suspended. In fact the universe is still being invited to become "more" by organizing itself inwardly and outwardly around an always new and higher Center. This Center is the very God who in Christ has become fully incarnate in the universe and who is still being clothed in the folds of an emergent creation.

(e) The incarnation of God in Christ continues to stir up the world. The entire cosmic story is even now being called irreversibly and everlastingly into the embrace of God. This is the ultimate reason why evolution, understood in both a cosmological and biological sense, takes place at all. Evolution now means that creation is still happening, and God is still creating the world, not *a retro*, from out of the past, but *ab ante*, from up ahead. All things are still being brought together in the Christ who is coming. As a fervent devotee of St. Paul, Teilhard suggests that what is *really* going on in cosmic process and biological evolution is that the "whole of creation" is groaning for the renewal wrought by God in Christ through the power of the Holy Spirit (Romans 8:22).

What Then Should We Be Doing with Our Lives?

Life's evolution and humanity's religious quest are recent chapters in the universe's long journey into the mystery of God. Cosmologically speaking, our religious hope is the blossoming of a persistent and ageless cosmic anticipation, a conscious opening up of the world to the future of creation. Through our hope and struggles the universe that gave birth to us still reaches out toward its unifying Center and Goal.

In view of these considerations, then, our second excerpt from *Gaudium et Spes* takes on a significance that would not have seemed obvious in a pre-evolutionary age. "A hope related to the end of time," the council declares, "does not diminish the importance of intervening duties but rather *undergirds* the acquittal of them with fresh incentives."

What does this mean? A Teilhardian interpretation would recognize here a belated response by the Church to the modern accusation that Christian hope is a kind of escapism that negates the value of action in the world. Marxists and other secular critics had long complained that the Church had failed to motivate people to participate fully in what Teilhard refers to as "building the earth." However, once we realize that the universe is a work in progress, then genuinely Christian hope orients our existence toward participation in the ongoing work of creation. Our hope for final fulfillment is not a reason for passivity here and now, but a "fresh incentive" to contribute our lives and labor to the great work of bringing the whole world to fulfillment in Christ.

20

Thomas Merton

Monk and Prophet for the World

THOMAS P. RAUSCH, S.J.

I first heard of Thomas Merton in 1959 when I was a freshman in college. I knew little about monasticism, still less about the Trappists, though I had heard something about the austerity of their lives. Still, I was interested. I read *The Seven Storey Mountain,* and remember how I was gripped by his narrative as he gradually discerned what he wanted to do with his life and began to move toward entering the Trappist monastery at Gethsemani. I read more of Merton in the next couple of years as I began my own formation as a Jesuit, though I remember thinking then that Merton seemed a little narrow; he wrote as though the monastic way was the only way to holiness.

That impression began to change in the turbulent mid-sixties. In the aftermath of the Second Vatican Council and the countercultural shifts that accompanied it—the hippy subculture with its celebration of psychedelic drugs, the sexual revolution, the civil rights movement, and energizing it all the controversy over the war in Viet Nam—I began reading a very different Merton. This monk who had once celebrated his escape from the world had become engaged;[1] everywhere he was part of the conversation.

The Monk

Who was this monk, Thomas Merton? The son of two artists who died while he was still young, Merton grew up on both sides of the Atlantic without stable relationships or a home to call his own. Brilliant but unsettled, he was brought back by his guardian to New York in disgrace after a wild year at Cambridge, which included fathering a child out of wedlock. Merton completed his education at Columbia University, became a Catholic in 1938, and entered the Trappist Order at Gethsemani on December 10, 1941, three days after the Japanese attack on Pearl Harbor.

Trappist life in those days was rigorous in the extreme and Gethsemani was one of the strictest houses in the order. The monks rose at 2:00 AM for the first office of the day and returned to choir six more times before Compline brought the day to a close. Life in the monastery was Spartan and regimented. The diet was vegetarian; no meat, fish, or eggs. The monks fasted during Advent and Lent. There were no mirrors, no private rooms, no privacy, period. The monks slept in their habits on straw mats in a common dormitory, each in a curtained off area or "cubic." Hygiene was primitive; they shaved once a week and showers were rare. The monastery was unheated. The winters were bitterly cold, the summers stifling. Incoming and outgoing mail was read by the prior or novice master.[2]

But Merton flourished. He thought he had left his persona as a writer behind him, but his abbot, Dom Frederick Dunne, encouraged him to write. His famous autobiography, *The Seven Storey Mountain*, appeared in 1948 and quickly became a best-seller. In one single day, ten thousand copies were ordered. Yet in it he complained about "this shadow, this double, this writer who had followed me into the cloister . . . And the worst of it is, he has my superiors on his side."[3] If Merton's early works were pious lives of the saints, celebrating the monastic life he had discovered, and some poetry, he continued to grow and to change. He came to recognize that he could become his true self only by owning the writer that he was. And his contemplation opened him up to the world beyond the monastery gates.

In a famous passage, he describes an experience in 1958 that marked a significant transition in his life: "In Louisville, at the corner of Fourth and Walnut, in the center of the shopping district, I was suddenly overwhelmed with the realization that I loved all those people, that they were mine and I theirs, that we could not be alien to one another even though we were total strangers. It was like waking from a dream of separateness, of spurious self-isolation in a special world, the world of renunciation and supposed holiness."[4]

The Contemplative Critic

In the years that followed, Merton's writings reached out to embrace the world. Rejecting the duality of his earlier works, he began to speak with a new voice. He wrote, "that I should be the contemporary of Auschwitz, Hiroshima, Viet Nam and the Watts riots are things about which I was not first consulted. Yet they are also events in which, whether I like it or not, I am deeply and personally involved."[5] In 1959 he wrote to Dorothy Day, who with Peter Maurin had founded the Catholic Worker, beginning a long relationship that was to lead to a number of articles expressing his anti-war stance and resulting in his being silenced for several years by the abbot general. When Pope John XXIII published his encyclical *Pacem in Terris* (1963), stressing personal responsibility rather than blind obedience to authority, Merton wrote the abbot general, saying, "It was a good thing that Pope John didn't have to get his encyclical through our censors."[6] Besides the threat of nuclear war, the civil rights movement and the struggle over the war in Viet Nam began increasingly to occupy Merton's attention. He became an unofficial pastor to the Catholic peace movement. When some suggested that he should leave the monastery to become fully involved in the protest, he resisted, though it cost him considerable anguish. As Michael Mott points out, to have left Gethsemani to win the approval of his friends would have been to give in to his false self that needed the approval of others.[7]

During and after the Second Vatican Council he wrote about the renewal of religious life and helped move his own community forward. The council had called religious to a twofold renewal: first, to a continuous return to the sources of Christian life and to the original inspiration of their institutes, and second, to adapt their religious life to the changed conditions of the times (*Perfectae Caritatis*, 2). Having served first as master of scholastics and then as master of novices for more than ten years, Merton had considerable personal experience. He observed that too many young religious entered the community with no sense of their own identity and thus found it difficult to live authentic lives as religious. He insisted that monks should be open to the world, not closed off from it, but as contemplatives rather than in the way of active religious. He argued that the monastic life was about discipleship, not religiosity and external observances, and thus the style of monastic life needed to be rethought.[8]

As the Trappists sought to rediscover their original vocation as contemplatives rather than as the penitential order they had become, the outward form of their life began to change. They dispensed with the traditional sign language and began to gather occasionally for recreation. Silence was still valued, but as an aid to contemplation, not an end in itself. They questioned the assumption that being a monk generally meant being a priest and did away with the rigid separation between choir monks and lay brothers. All the monks began to wear the same white habit. At Gethsemani the chapel was renovated, stripping away the faux gothic interior to uncover the original brick and replacing the church's tall spire with a simple bell tower characteristic of early Cistercian churches.

In many ways Merton was ahead of his Church. He had written about the desperate situation of African Americans as early as 1948 in *The Seven Storey Mountain* and published a number of essays in the 1960s addressing issues of black identity, the confusion of Christianity with Americanism, and the co-opting of the Black Power movement by sucking its leaders into government or academe.[9] He insisted that the way of non-violence must include an absolute refusal of evil, and could not succeed if separated from the pursuit of truth. His love for nature made him sensitive to ecological issues, and he questioned the reliance on chemical fertilizers and insecticides used on the monastery grounds after finding dead birds in the woods he so loved. The Church did not begin to speak out on the environment until Pope John Paul II's 1987 encyclical *Sollicitudo Rei Socialis*. With Merton's remarkable capacity for friendship, he entered into correspondence with representatives of other religions, beginning a dialogue that would become increasingly important in the new century. Most of all, he helped popularize the idea that contemplative prayer was not just the preserve of monks and mystics; even if a gift of grace, it represented a deepening of faith to the point where our direct union with God is realized and experienced.[10]

This marvelously human monk, who used to shout each morning at the king snake who inhabited the outhouse near his hermitage, "Are you in there, you bastard?" and who fell briefly in love with a young nurse two years before his untimely death, was truly a "spiritual master," a teacher for the ages.[11]

Notes

1. Thomas Merton, "Is the World a Problem?" in *Contemplation in a World of Action* (Notre Dame, IN: University of Notre Dame Press, 1998; first published in 1971), 141.

2. See Michael Mott, *The Seven Mountains of Thomas Merton* (Boston: Houghton Mifflin, 1984), 208–10.

3. Thomas Merton, *The Seven Storey Mountain* (New York: Harcourt, 1998), 448–49.

4. Thomas Merton, *Conjectures of a Guilty Bystander* (New York: Doubleday, 1989; first published in 1968), 156

5. Merton, "Is the World a Problem," 142.

6. Cited by Jim Forest, *Living with Wisdom: A Life of Thomas Merton* (Maryknoll, NY: Orbis Books, 1991), 146.

7. Mott, *The Seven Mountains*, 429.

8. See "The Monk in the Diaspora," *Blackfriars* 45 (1964): 290–302; "The Identity Crisis," 58–83 and "Openness and Cloister," 128–40 in *Contemplation in a World of Action*.

9. See Thomas Merton, *Faith and Violence* (Notre Dame, IN: University of Notre Dame Press, 1968).

10. *Contemplation in a World of Action*, 157.

11. From Merton's essay, "Day of a Stranger," cited by Laurence S. Cunningham in *Thomas Merton: Spiritual Master* (New York/Mahwah, NJ: Paulist Press, 1992), 220.

21

Virgil Michel and Godfrey Diekmann

"Full, Active, and Conscious Participation"

MARY COLLINS, O.S.B.

Virgil Michel (1890–1938) and Godfrey Diekmann (1908–2002), both monks of St. John's Abbey in Collegeville, Minnesota, also had in common their role as the first two editors of *Orate Fratres*, now *Worship*, the premier journal of the North American liturgical movement in both the pre- and post-Vatican II Council eras. The name of each Benedictine monk has subsequently been memorialized to honor their work. St. John's University at Collegeville hosts the Virgil Michel Ecumenical Chair in Rural Social Ministries. The North American Academy of Liturgy established the Godfrey Diekmann Award at the time of his death in 2002 to honor a significant national or international contributor to the liturgical renewal sanctioned and promoted by the 1963 Constitution on the Sacred Liturgy (*Sacrosanctum Concilium*). The different slants in the memorial awards point to the distinct emphases in their academic backgrounds, interests, and even their temperaments and life-spans.

Virgil Michel: Liturgy and Society

Michel's scholarly interest was community and society and their rapid disintegration in twentieth-century American culture. The interest led him to the study of philosophy and social thought as well as theol-

ogy. During a year allocated for academic work in Europe, Michel became aware of the liturgical movement spreading through Benedictine
abbeys in Germany and Belgium and he found opportunities to meet its
leaders. The recurrent emphasis in Belgium on Pope Pius X's vision that
a revitalized liturgy was the source of social and spiritual renewal spoke
to his own concerns. Upon his return to the United States he convinced
his abbot that St. John's could spread the vision through education. The
Liturgical Press was established in Collegeville in 1926, with Michel as
the founding editor of *Orate Fratres* and the Liturgical Press.

Michel's frequent writings consistently connect liturgical and social renewal, underlining the dignity of the community of the baptized
and their mission to contribute to social transformation through living
and promoting right relationships in society. This linking of liturgy
and life gave the pre-conciliar North American liturgical movement its
distinctive emphasis and its wide appeal to lay-based Catholic Action
groups. Throughout the 1940s and 1950s, groups like the Catholic
Rural Life Movement and the Christian Family Movement grounded
their apostolic efforts in the belief that the liturgy was indeed the true
source of the Christian spirit.

Michel's broad interests and his imaginative and competent educational leadership were both his gift and his burden. The Liturgical
Press responsibilities did not replace but accompanied his academic responsibilities as academic dean and professor at St. John's College, and
overwork eventually led to a breakdown in his health. The respite ministry he took up while recovering led to three years of service within
the Catholic Chippewa Indian communities in northern Minnesota.
Upon his return to St. John's, he resumed both his academic and editorial responsibilities with new energy. During this era, the young
Godfrey Diekmann was appointed his editorial assistant. Yet even with
help, Michel's zealous commitment to many matters academic and editorial continued to wear down his health. He died in 1938 at the early
age of forty-eight, leaving behind a significant legacy in shaping the
pastoral liturgical movement and Catholic commitment to social renewal. Unfortunately, in his short life he was unable to articulate fully
his emerging theological vision.

Godfrey Diekmann: The Living Liturgical Tradition

Godfrey Diekmann's academic interest was patristics, the study of
the early Christian writers of the first four or five centuries, most of

them bishops concerned with forming the young Church through sacrament and the biblical word. This study provided the link that grounded Diekmann in the liturgical, theological, and catechetical movements at the time he succeeded Michel in 1938 and so became responsible for editing *Orate Frates*. He remained in this post for the next twenty-five years, while continuing to teach college theology, up to the time preparations for the Second Vatican Council were unfolding in Rome.

The young Diekmann, like Michel, had first met leaders of the European liturgical movement in the 1930s while doing doctoral studies in the German abbey of Maria Laach. That abbey was the home of significant scholarly work on liturgy, including the publication of academic journals and books. Furthermore, Maria Laach was already renowned as a site for pastoral liturgical reflection and the promotion of the dialogue Mass with lay participation. There Diekmann witnessed firsthand the linking of scholarship and pastoral liturgy and the power of communal ritual to shape community identity.

As gregarious and spontaneous a personality as Michel had been reserved and serious, Diekmann—a big man with a big personality—became an inveterate public advocate of the pre-conciliar North American liturgical movement, successfully linking for laity and clergy alike patristic theology and the pastoral concerns of the liturgical renewal. He was also a beloved patristic professor at St. John's University and was often invited to lecture at many Catholic colleges and universities.

Diekmann was one of two American liturgists, the other being Frederick McManus, who received an appointment early in the 1960s to the pre-conciliar preparatory group responsible for drafting the text that would become the Constitution on the Sacred Liturgy of Vatican II. Diekmann continued as a consultant during the council and was subsequently named to the post-conciliar body, Consilium, charged by Pope Paul VI with the implementation of the Constitution on the Sacred Liturgy. As that work was in process, he was named a member of the Advisory Committee to the newly forming International Commission on English in the Liturgy (ICEL), the body established to begin the work of translating the Latin liturgy into English.

Godfrey Diekmann loved the prayer of the Church, enjoyed traveling to the early Christian sites of the Mediterranean world, thrived in collaborative work with other liturgical scholars and pastoral leaders, and never lost the early Collegeville integrative vision of a renewed liturgy as the source of spiritual and social renewal. Godfrey Diekmann's work for liturgical renewal spanned almost five decades, encompassing the pre-conciliar, conciliar, and post-conciliar eras. In each setting, his contribution consistently reflected his confidence in the wisdom of the early Church Fathers of the East and West that word and sacrament are the core of the Church's life of faith.

The Centrality of the Worshiping Community

Both these monks of St. John's Abbey, Virgil Michel and Godfrey Diekmann, made notable and unique contributions to the twentieth-century liturgical renewal in North America. Whether their insights have lasting impact is for the future to assess. At the turn of the new century, the vision of the magisterium for liturgical reform and renewal are focused elsewhere. Seventy years after Michel's death, for example, the centrality of the worshiping community as the place for both ecclesial renewal and social transformation and the catechesis to support this understanding of liturgy are receiving only modest attention from church leaders in North America. The magisterium, reflecting the concern voiced by Pope Benedict XVI, expresses fear that the post-conciliar implementation of the Constitution on the Sacred Liturgy has become earth-bound, horizontal in its orientation toward the affirmation of human and ecclesial community and disconnected from the transcendent mystery of Christ at the heart of liturgical celebration. Yet a careful reading of Michel's theology shows that his understanding of the mystery of Baptism as the source of the Christian life undergirded his confidence that the transformative power of the Holy Spirit was always already at work in every worshiping assembly. Good liturgy and good preaching would nurture what God had begun and would sustain.

Michel's early theological vision of the mystery of Baptism finds explicit expression in chapter one of the Constitution, most clearly in its declaration that full and active participation in the liturgy is the laity's the right and duty by reason of their Baptism (*Sacrosanctum Concilium*, 14) and that vital liturgical celebration is both source and summit of the Christian life (*Sacrosanctum Concilium*, 10). Magisterial leadership in the fifth decade after the council has refocused attention on other matters. First is the doctrinal integrity of translated text, rising from fear that less-than-literal translation of traditional liturgical texts from Latin into English will jeopardize the Catholic laity's accurate understanding of the Church's tradition of eucharistic and sacramental theology. Second is the concern for a sacramental theology that corrects a perceived North Atlantic ecclesial imbalance emphasizing the immanence more than the transcendence of grace in the Church's liturgical celebrations and its life.

The way forward in continuing liturgical reform and ecclesial and social renewal perhaps lies in the advance of an integrative liturgical theology, one able to explicate more fully both the nascent vision of Virgil Michel in the 1920s about the transformative power of a Catholic liturgical spirituality and Godfrey Diekmann's confidence in the spiritual wisdom of the early bishops, East and West. Revitalized homiletics and a renewed adult liturgical catechesis are needed to transform the religious imagination of Catholic people now living in a secularizing and globalizing world, just as the early Church Fathers were able to give a vision of a grace-filled world to their contemporaries.

I remember well a day trip I made with Godfrey and a New York priest from a Rome meeting to Assisi. After arriving, we began climbing the steep road up to Francis's hillside retreat, climbing because Godfrey said it would be wrong to take a cab if we were making a pilgrimage (although he had already had one heart attack.) To motivate us, he told how he had learned from his fellow Swiss students at Maria Laach years earlier that the way to climb was to keep going a step at a time, a step at a time. It was warm; we took our jackets off, but we were moving a step at a time. Suddenly Godfrey declared, "To hell with the Swiss! Let's sit down!" So we did.

If the liturgical movement has been anything, it has been a pilgrimage to more full, conscious, and active participation. This has required that persons like Godfrey Diekman and Virgil Michel, who despite resistance and difficulties, go "a step at a time." But the story also suggests that, when we need to do so for the long journey of liturgical renewal, we should sit down and rest up for the work that still remains.

Virgil Michel and the Liturgical Movement by Paul Marx, O.S.B. (Collegeville, MN: The Liturgical Press, 1957) provides a full-length narrative of its subject, as well as a comprehensive bibliography of Michel's published works. Kathleen Hughes, R.S.C.J., narrates Diekmann's liturgical journey in *The Monk's Tale: A Biography of Godfrey Diekmann, O.S.B.* (Collegeville: The Liturgical Press, 1991). It includes both a bibliography of his writing and a twenty-three page appendix on honors and awards conferred on him.

22

Fulton J. Sheen

"The Man with Hypnotic Eyes"

MARK MASSA, S.J.

If a random sample of U.S. citizens between 1952 and 1957 were asked to name one American Catholic they had heard of, a good bet would be that they would name Bishop Fulton Sheen. This man was, far and away, the most visible and most respected popularizer of Roman Catholic thought and practice in a culture in which Catholics still thought of themselves as "outsiders." Sheen's show, *Life Is Worth Living*, was the first mass-marketed religious program in the relatively new medium of television, and Sheen used that medium to bring sophisticated theological and philosophical concepts into the living rooms of millions of Americans every week. The American Research Bureau estimates that at the height of his popularity in the mid-1950s, Sheen's audience rating was 23.7—the highest ever recorded for anyone on TV in those pioneering years of television. Stories abounded at the time (and since) of New York cabbies leaving their motors running outside bars to run in and see as much of the program as they could without being ticketed, and of Jewish housewives handing over their children to babysitters so as not to be distracted from the "man with hypnotic eyes." In a real sense, Sheen invented the category of the "religious media superstar" decades before the phenomenon of televangelists at the end of the twentieth century. And Sheen remains, even today, the most successful exemplar of blending show business savvy with serious content in a primetime media context.[1]

With the Help of Angels

Sheen's immense success on TV was not a foregone conclusion by any means: he was scheduled in the "obituary slot" at 8 PM on Tuesday nights, opposite the hugely popular shows of "Uncle Miltie" (Milton Berle) and Frank Sinatra. For Sheen's opening show in a medium still new enough to cause general cultural excitement, the Adelphi Theater on 54th Street just off Broadway in New York City was besieged with many times the number of ticket requests than could be granted for its eleven hundred seats. The stage of the theater had been arranged to resemble a study, filled with books, and the only props were a statue of the Virgin Mary (soon to be christened "Our Lady of Television") and a blackboard that would serve as the site of the longest running gag on television during the 1950s: after Sheen had written on the board, the camera would then focus on his figure, while a stage hand (whom Sheen always referred to as "my little angel") erased the board for the next part of the "lesson." Even after dozens of shows, Sheen's remark about his angelic help always elicited laughter from his audience.[2]

Sheen offered rapt audiences twenty-eight minute presentations with titles like "Science, Relativity, and the Atomic Bomb," and "The Philosophy of Communism"—presentations that were ecumenical and non-dogmatic but unmistakably theological in character. While the titles and subject matter of Sheen's "lectures" might sound too intellectual to appeal to a wide prime-time audience, Sheen played his part broadly: he mixed serious scholastic philosophy with old shoe jokes and sight-gags on his blackboard, always punctuating his comments with references to his "little angel." Sheen's famous sign-off at the end of every telecast—"God love you"—would be heard for five seasons at the very beginning of television's national presence in American homes, and became an iconic byline for the "most widely viewed religious series in TV history."[3]

Perhaps his single most famous broadcast—certainly the one that drew the most press attention—was aired on February 24, 1953 and entitled "The Death of Stalin." Sheen delivered a hair-raising reading of the burial scene from William Shakespeare's *Julius Caesar*, with the names of Caesar, Cassius, Marc Antony, and Brutus replaced with the names of Stalin, Beria, Malenkov, and Vishinsky. "Stalin must one day come to judgment" Sheen intoned to a mesmerized audience at the height of Senator Joe McCarthy's anti-communist crusade, "and Stalin's spirit, ranging for revenge...shall come hot from hell, and shall cry 'Havoc!'" Several days later the Soviet dictator suffered a sudden stroke, and died a little over a week later, on March 5, 1953. Sheen's performance made front-page news across the nation in reports of the Russian leader's death.[4]

A Catholic Superstar

Pundits at the time noted the surprising irony that a Catholic bishop and scholastic philosopher, with no other props than a blackboard and a statue of the Virgin Mary, seemed to be just what America needed between 1952 and 1957. But many American Catholics were eager to interpret Sheen's popularity as evidence of a long-overdue acceptance of their own religious tradition by their fellow citizens as not only "respectable," but as offering important insights for all Americans, regardless of religious affiliation. This was something new and culturally significant in a nation where anti-Catholicism was labeled "America's oldest prejudice."[5]

Unlike media religious personalities both then and now, Sheen was a well educated scholar who brought considerable learning and a critical mind to his TV programs. Having earned doctorates in philosophy at the Catholic University of America in 1920, and at Belgium's University of Louvain (at which he was awarded the prestigious Mercier Prize for his dissertation, the first American ever so honored) in 1925, Sheen returned to teach philosophy at the Catholic University of America for twenty years before beginning his television career. His first scholarly book, entitled *God and Intelligence*, was an extended Catholic answer to the philosophical agnosticism of John Dewey, and much of his scholarly output before 1952 constituted a Catholic response to the perceived threat of Freudian psychoanalysis and to the soft religion of what would become known as "peace of mind" theology, popularized by Norman Vincent Peale's *The Power of Positive Thinking*.[6]

But, despite his impressive academic credentials, Sheen was hardly a stranger to publicity or to popular success before the premiere of his TV show. Sheen was already a celebrity "convert maker" by 1952, having brought into the Catholic Church the likes of Congresswoman and author-playwright Claire Booth Luce (wife of *Time/Life* mogul Henry Luce) and motor scion Henry Ford II. Further, Sheen had already achieved national media attention well before 1952 on *The*

Catholic Hour, a radio program that began in 1930 and was broadcast every Sunday evening at 6 PM. For over two decades, Sheen's voice could be heard in homes across the land on Sunday nights, making him perhaps the most famous preacher in the U.S., certainly the best known Catholic priest. Requests for transcripts of his radio talks bespoke an immense radio audience that listened to him, and more than 30 percent of the mail his radio broadcasts generated came from non-Catholics. Sheen would later reminisce that the most satisfying achievement of his radio career was both the improved image and reputation of the Catholic Church and the greater religious understanding between Protestants, Jews, and Catholics that it helped to foster. In recognition of his important role in representing Catholicism in the United States, Father Sheen was named a "Monsignor" in 1934 and consecrated auxiliary bishop of New York in 1951. Evangelist Billy Graham—himself no slouch on such matters—had by that time already dubbed him "one of the great preachers of our century."[7]

Public Catholicism

While Sheen's radio and television programs were clearly designed to be both entertaining and broadly ecumenical in tone, there remained something high toned and distinctly Catholic in them that separated Sheen's presentations from both Billy Graham's folksy style of evangelical revivalism, and Norman Vincent Peale's vague mix of psychology and spirituality widely dubbed "mind cure." Perhaps the best way to describe Sheen's media style is to apply to him David O'Brien's famous phrase of "Public Catholicism"—a resolutely social and corporate faith in which faith and reason were complementary and mutually-enforcing, so that "Catholic" philosophy and theology could appeal to everyone's common sense and reason, regardless of personal religious faith. Sheen offered a (rare) overt recognition of St. Thomas Aquinas, whose philosophy provided the intellectual groundwork for Sheen's radio and TV career, as it did for the entire intellectual enterprise of his style of pre-Vatican II Catholicism: "His works represent the greatest masterpiece in the realm of philosophy. His gigantic powers of intellect naturally led him to God. His first principle was: you cannot begin religion with faith; there must be a reason for faith, and a motive for belief."[8]

Sheen's own version of Catholic philosophy and theology—heavily dependent on St. Thomas and his modern interpreters—was replaced with newer approaches to the Catholic tradition of Christianity after reforms of the Second Vatican Council in the United States after 1965. To that extent, the explicit theological and philosophical content of Sheen's presentations on both radio and television now appear dated, and even old-fashioned. But Sheen's style of "Public Catholicism" set the benchmark for best practice by a religious media personality in the United States. In a real sense no media evangelist, either Catholic or Protestant, in the half century since his final TV show has come close to Sheen's broadly ecumenical appeal, his theological sophistication, and his optimistic trust that everyone in his audience, even the most theologically illiterate, would welcome presentations of sophisticated and timely religious ideas in clear and accessible ways. Surely our own time also would be well served by such convictions and good practice.

Peter John Sheen was born in El Paso City, Illinois, on May 8, 1895, and took his mother's maiden name ("Fulton ") only later in his life. He was educated at St. Paul Seminary in Minnesota and ordained a priest on September 20, 1919. After his graduate education in both the United States and Europe, he was invited back to the Catholic University of America, where he wrote the first of seventy-three books produced during his academic and pastoral career. He served as auxiliary bishop of the Archdiocese of New York from 1951 until 1965, and in 1966 was consecrated bishop of the diocese of Rochester, New York, which he served for three years. Sheen died on December 9, 1979, and is buried in the crypt of St. Patrick's Cathedral in New York City. His most important works are: *The Eternal Galilean* (New York: Popular Library, 1954 [1934]), *Life of Christ* (New York: McGraw-Hill, 1958), *Peace of Soul* (London: Burns and Oates, 1962 [1958]), and *Treasure in Clay: The Autobiography of Fulton J. Sheen* (San Francisco: Ignatius Press, 1993).

Notes

1. "Microphone Missionary," *Time* (April 14, 1952): 72. Tim Brooks and Earle Marsh, *The Complete Directory to Prime Time Network TV Shows* (New York: Ballantine, 1992), 512. Kathleen Riley Fields, "Bishop Fulton J. Sheen: An American Catholic Response to the Twentieth Century" (PhD dissertation, University of Notre Dame, 1988), 113–23.

2. "Microphone Missionary," 72.

3. For a sampling of the broadly theological but nonsectarian nature of his television broadcasts, see Fulton J. Sheen, *Life Is Worth Living: First Series* (New York: McGraw-Hill, 1953), "Science, Relativity and the Atomic Bomb," chapter 3, 19ff.; "The Philosophy of Communism," chapter 7, 62ff. All five seasons of the TV show were recorded, transcribed, and subsequeently published by McGraw-Hill as *Life Is Worth Living, First through Fifth Series.* For "the most widely viewed," see: Gretta Palmer, "Bishop Sheen on Television," *Catholic Digest* 17 (February 1953): 75–81, 75.

4. "The Death of Stalin," chapter 15, 157ff., in *Life Is Worth Living, First Series.* See also Brooks and Marsh, *The Complete Directory*, 512.

5. For various interpretations of the cultural meanings of Sheen's popularity, see Donald Meyer, *The Positive Thinkers: Religion as Pop Psychology from Mary Baker Eddy to Oral Roberts* (New York: Pantheon, 1980), 332ff.; William McLoughlin, *Revivals, Awakenings, and Reform* (Chicago: University of Chicago Press, 1979), 186ff.; Martin Marty, *Pilgrims in Their Own Land* (Boston: Little, Brown, 1984), 414ff.

6. On Sheen's education, see: D. E. Noonan, *Missionary with a Mike: The Bishop Sheen Story* (New York: Pageant Press, 1968), 4–6. For examples of Sheen's disdain for the kind of "peace of mind" theology popularized by Norman Vincent Peale, see Fulton J. Sheen, *Peace of Soul* (New York: McGraw-Hill, 1949), 7, 20, 69ff.

7. Fields, "Bishop Fulton J. Sheen," 113–23. Billy Graham quote in Jay Dolan, *The American Catholic Experience* (Garden City, NY: Doubleday, 1985), 393.

8. Val Adams, "The Bishop Looks at Television," *New York Times* (April 6, 1952). David O'Brien, *Public Catholicism* (New York: Macmillan, 1985). Fulton J. Sheen, *Life Is Worth Living, Second Series* (New York: McGraw-Hill, 1954), 153–54.

23

John Tracy Ellis

Historian and Priest

THOMAS J. SHELLEY

When Vatican II ended in 1965, Monsignor John Tracy Ellis, the leading historian of American Catholicism, was sixty years old, an age at which people do not readily change long-held convictions. Ellis lived another twenty-seven years and told an interviewer in 1989: "I have read about revolutions, taught about revolutions, but I never thought that I was going to live through one." He told the same interviewer that the Catholic Church in the United States was experiencing the most serious decline in its two-hundred year history.[1]

Despite this somber assessment of the state of the American Catholic Church a quarter-century after Vatican II, Ellis never wavered in his belief that Pope John XXIII's decision to convene the council was providential. Although he declined an invitation from Bishop Robert Tracy of Baton Rouge, Louisiana, to serve as a *peritus* and told Thomas Merton in 1961 that he expected little to come from the council, he followed the proceedings of Vatican II closely. His initial skepticism quickly turned to delight as he witnessed the bishops assert their independence of the Roman Curia during the first weeks of the opening session.

Ellis welcomed the results of the council, especially the introduction of a vernacular liturgy, the replacement of a desiccated neo-scholasticism with a more biblically oriented theology, the effort to reverse a century of relentless Roman centralization with a more collegial ecclesiology, and the attempt to open a dialogue with the modern world. The son of a devout Catholic mother and a non-practicing Methodist father, Ellis was gratified at the positive attitude of the council toward Protestant and Eastern Orthodox Christians. As an American Catholic he was proud of the role played by the American hierarchy and Father John Courtney Murray, S.J., in securing the approval of the Declaration on Religious Freedom. He hailed it as "a vindication of what had been the accepted American practice from the nation's earliest years." "In other words," he said, "an ecumenical council has put its seal of approval on the only system that American Catholics have ever known."[2]

Vatican II: Taking the Historians' Long View

The disarray and confusion that surfaced even before the conclusion of the council disturbed Ellis greatly. He voiced his concern at the questioning of the most fundamental Christian doctrines, the decline in Mass attendance in the United States, the departure from the ministry of large numbers of priests and religious, and the catastrophic decline in vocations. By 1968 he was speaking of a revolutionary crisis in the Church and two years later said that the American Catholic Church was passing through its darkest hour. However, unlike many of his contemporaries, Ellis did not become a "prophet of gloom and doom." He never regretted the work of the council or sought refuge in a nostalgic yearning for a return to the pre-Vatican II Church. He consistently displayed a critical but favorable attitude to the winds of change that the council had let loose in the Church. He liked to quote his favorite author, John Henry Newman, to the effect that "to live is to change, and to be perfect is to have changed often."

Ellis viewed the tumultuous decades that followed the council from the twin perspectives of a professional historian and a devout priest. As a historian he emphasized the necessity of situating the council within the context of the cultural upheavals that erupted virtually everywhere in Western society in the 1960s and 1970s, with the questioning of all authority accompanied by a revolution in sexual mores and a widening generation gap. "The Church can't help but be affected by it," he said. "She doesn't exist on Mars. She exists here." In the United States the situation was further exacerbated by the Vietnam War, the resistance to the civil rights movement, and the Watergate scandal.

As a church historian Ellis also attempted to place Vatican II within the context of the Church's long history and noted that ecumenical councils were often followed by periods of contentiousness and recrimination. In a series of lectures and articles he reminded American Catholics that the history of the Church had been characterized by recurring cycles of achievement, decline, and renewal. "*Mater Ecclesia* has been here before and she has seen and endured worse," he told a friend in 1968. "It is not the most positive of arguments for the *aggiornamento*," he added wryly, "but it helps to steady one's nerves."[3]

The ideological polarization and the hardening of positions that occurred among American Catholics in the wake of the council were deeply disturbing to Ellis. It cost him the friendship of two of his closest priest friends, who broke their ties with him because they regarded his advocacy of reform as a disservice to the Church. "A plague on both your houses," Ellis said more than once with reference to the extremists on both the right and the left. He regretted the loss of civility and charity among Catholics as they debated their differences. "Somewhere out there lies a *via media*, vague as it may be," he said wistfully, "and it is that *via media* that all of us, I think, must keep in mind."[4]

Ellis tried to practice what he preached with regard to theologians who questioned aspects of church teaching. "I would not agree with those who contend that a theologian should be judged solely by his peers and not by the magisterium," he told an English Catholic friend. "But I would hope and pray," he added, "that those who speak in the name of the magisterium would observe the accepted norms of procedure meant to protect individual human rights." Ellis sympathized with Edward Schillebeeckx but not with Hans Küng, who, he thought, had publicly defied the Holy See. With regard to the travails of his friend and colleague, Charles Curran, Ellis mused about the contrast between the Catholic University of America in the 1980s and the Catholic University of Louvain in the 1840s when the archbishop of Malines told the papal nuncio to bring his complaints about the university to him and not to Rome. Ellis often thought of his alma mater as a Louvain manqué.[5]

One of Ellis' greatest fears was that Paul VI and John Paul II would react to the crisis in the Church with a series of harsh condemnations like *Mirari Vos*, the Syllabus of Errors, *Pascendi*, and *Humani Generis*. For him, reform, not reaction, was the appropriate response to a revolutionary situation. He quoted with approval the statement of the Council of Latin American Bishops in July 1968 at Medellin that "the alternatives are not the status quo and change; rather they are violent change and peaceful change." Ellis added: "We are passing through a revolution that will force change whether we like it or not, and ecclesiastical history will not be kind to churchmen of whatever rank who do not show themselves sensitive to what is transpiring before their eyes."[6]

Although Ellis applauded the role of the American bishops at Vatican II, especially their support of religious freedom, he was disappointed at their hesitant and uncertain leadership in guiding the American Church through the post-conciliar period. He faulted them for their "lack of spiritual and intellectual gifts that the leadership of others demands in the community that is the Church." He went on to note that "in the case of most of these ecclesiastical personalities, theirs was an education that deadened initiative by its insistence on the routine of traditional procedures, and what is sadder to relate, a disconcertingly large number of them found in this pattern the comfort that is an accompaniment of conformity for mediocre or fretful minds."[7]

Keeping Hope Alive

Ellis detected a considerable improvement in the American hierarchy after the appointment of Archbishop Jean Jadot as the apostolic delegate to the United States in 1973. As for himself, he was aware that both Cardinal Patrick O'Boyle of Washington and Archbishop Joseph McGucken of San Francisco (where Ellis lived for twelve years while teaching at the Jesuit University of San Francisco) were uneasy about his presence in their dioceses. During a semester that Ellis spent in Rome in 1975 teaching at the North American College, he quipped that at last he had found a bishop who did not seem to be uncomfortable with his presence in his diocese.

American Catholic intellectual life was a lifelong concern for Ellis. A decade before the council, his article in *Thought*, "American Catholics and the Intellectual Life," caused a greater stir than his two-volume biography of Cardinal James Gibbons. When a number of Catholic colleges severed their ties with the Church after Vatican II, Ellis expressed little regret because he had long regarded the proliferation of small and academically weak Catholic colleges as a major reason for the lack of excellence in Catholic higher education.

Seminary education was another recurring theme in Ellis's writing. When he was told that more attention would be given to the pastoral formation of seminarians after the council, he reacted warily at the thought of how this might work out in practice. "They'll not be effective in the pastoral if they don't have something in their heads," he replied. "When you downgrade the intellectual, then the pastoral ministry suffers."[8]

One would get an incomplete picture of Ellis's reaction to Vatican II if one failed to take into account the fact that he viewed the council from the perspective of a devout priest as well as a historian. Although he was critical of the anti-intellectualism that pervaded his own seminary education, he was always grateful to the Sulpicians for the spiritual formation that he received at Divinity College (now Theological College) in Washington. To his dying day he was faithful to a daily routine of Mass, meditation, breviary, Rosary, and Stations of the Cross. When he spoke about Christ's promise to remain with his Church always, it was not pious boilerplate, but the expression of his own deeply held convictions. He was writing both as a historian and as a man of faith when he reminded American Catholics during the post-conciliar troubles that the religious revivals of the eleventh, sixteenth, and nineteenth centuries were "born out of the Church's tragedies in a way that could only suggest a mystery in her endurance, a survival that necessarily posited a hidden power over it all."[9]

Notes

1. *The Catholic Standard*, March 2, 1989.

2. John Tracy Ellis, "Contemporary American Catholicism in the Light of History," *The Critic* 24 (June–July 1966): 11–12.

3. Archives of the Catholic University of America: John Tracy Ellis Papers (hereafter ACUA: JTEP), Ellis to George A. Kelly, April 27, 1968.

4. ACUA: JTEP, Ellis to Kelly, October 21, 1976.

5. ACUA: JTEP, Ellis to Norman St. John-Stevas, January 8, 1980.

6. John Tracy Ellis, "Whence Did They Come, These Uncertain Priests of the 1960s," *American Ecclesiastical Review* 162 (1970): 146, 157–58.

7. John Tracy Ellis, "The Church in Revolt: The Tumultuous Sixties," *The Critic* 28 (January–February 1970): 18.

8. *The Mountain Echo*, March 3, 1977.

9. John Tracy Ellis, "The Future: Does It Need A Prologue?" *Catholic World* (October 1971): 26.

24

Father Charles E. Coughlin

"The Radio Priest"

MARY CHRISTINE ATHANS, B.V.M.

I never recall hearing Father Coughlin on the radio. I was quite young during the years when he was broadcasting. What I do remember is that my Irish grandmother adored him. "Ah, sure—if he's a good Irish Catholic priest, what he's sayin' can't be all that wrong!" My father, who had come from Greece at the age of fifteen, felt very differently. He would reply, quietly: "The dirty bum!" I knew that this radio priest was very controversial, but it wasn't until years later that I had the opportunity to explore his life, his personality, his theology, and his politics.

It has been said that in the 1930s and the early 1940s the only voice more recognizable on the radio than that of Father Charles E. Coughlin was that of President Franklin D. Roosevelt. People remember that you could walk down the street on a hot summer Sunday afternoon when all the windows were open in many a city—large or small—and never miss a word of his broadcast. Every radio in the neighborhood was tuned to his program. In the early Depression his voice inspired hope.

Who was this Catholic priest who burst upon the scene in the late 1920s? Charles Edward Coughlin was born on October 25, 1891, in Ontario, Canada, the only child of parents of Irish ancestry. He studied at St. Michael's College, Toronto, joined the Basilian Congregation, and was ordained to the priesthood in 1916. He taught at Assumption College in Windsor, Ontario, and frequently served in parishes in Detroit, Michigan, on weekends. Because of changes in the Basilian Congregation in Canada, he left the Basilians in 1923 and was incardinated into the Diocese of Detroit. In 1926, Bishop Michael J. Gallagher asked him to build a new parish to be named for the recently canonized Thérèse of Lisieux, known affectionately as "the Little Flower," in an obscure suburb of Detroit known as Royal Oak. To raise funds, Coughlin negotiated his first radio program which aired on October 17, 1926 over WJR in Detroit.

Coughlin's style of sermonizing changed with the Depression. He spoke more of sociopolitical issues and the frustrations of the people. He became an "authority" on communism and monetary issues. By 1930 CBS had picked up his program nationally and he had an estimated forty million listeners. Short-wave radio from Philadelphia carried his voice all over the world on *The Golden Hour of the Little Flower*. A devotee of Franklin Roosevelt, Coughlin became involved in the 1932 presidential campaign and coined expressions such as "The New Deal is Christ's Deal" and "Roosevelt or Ruin." After the election, however, President Roosevelt did not look to Coughlin for advice. Rejected, Coughlin became a rabid anti–New Dealer.

Crossing the Church/State Divide

In 1934, Coughlin founded the National Union for Social Justice, and in 1936 he started publishing his weekly newspaper, *Social Justice*. Deciding that it was imperative to oppose Roosevelt in the 1936 campaign, he joined with Gerald L. K. Smith (a Protestant minister and heir apparent to the recently assassinated Huey Long), and Dr. Francis P. Townsend (a physician and founder of a program for the elderly in California), to form the Union Party. They chose two colorless figures, Congressman William Lemke of North Dakota and Thomas O'Brien, district attorney of Boston, as their presidential and vice-presidential candidates. The campaign was dominated by Coughlin and Smith. At one point Coughlin overextended his theatrics, ripped off his Roman collar, and called FDR a liar and a betrayer. The Vatican was disturbed by this, but Bishop Gallagher supported Coughlin to the end. Roosevelt won by a landslide and Coughlin retired temporarily from the radio and public life. Despite complications with the

Vatican, Coughlin's supporters pleaded that he be allowed to return to the radio and he did so in 1938.

Promoting Anti-Semitism and Hitler?

In his earlier years, Coughlin had been open to other religious groups—inviting Catholics, Protestants, and Jews to join the National Union for Social Justice. However, by 1938 he had become increasingly anti-Semitic. He focused on what he perceived to be undue Jewish influence on FDR and even published chapters of the famous forged document *The Protocols of the Elders of Zion*, which accused Jews of an international plot to take over the world, in *Social Justice*. He sought scapegoats, and they were usually Jews. He pronounced Jewish names in exaggerated fashion. His radio speeches became more angry and vitriolic. He was labeled one of the "demagogues of the Depression." During this period he began to rely on the writings of an Irish theologian, Father Denis Fahey, C.S.Sp., who provided him with a theological rationale for his anti-Semitism.[1]

More than once, Hitler appeared on the cover of *Social Justice*. Coughlin exhibited sympathy for the German leader and described Nazism as "a defense mechanism against Communism" even after the United States entered World War II. In 1942 *Social Justice* had its mailing privileges revoked and President Roosevelt sent word to Archbishop Edward Mooney of Detroit that, if Coughlin were not curtailed, he would be indicted under the Espionage Act of 1917. Coughlin received the directive of his archbishop in a spirit of obedience, but confided to Fahey that it was related to "the almost universal ecclesiastical subservience to Franklin D. Roosevelt who is surrounded by high Masons and dominated by crafty Jews."[2]

The "radio priest" was silent on political issues after 1942 but continued as pastor of the Shrine of the Little Flower until his retirement in 1966. Although he wrote a few small volumes denouncing communism and questioning Vatican II, often with apocalyptic emphases, he lived mostly in seclusion. He died on October 27, 1979 in Birmingham, Michigan.

Religion and Politics: A Question That Remains

In his earlier years, Coughlin was clearly a "star" on the American scene and many Catholics were thrilled to have a young, attractive

Irish priest as their spokesman. He was often on the cover of magazines and newspapers. His popularity in those years could be compared to the television celebrity of Bishop Fulton Sheen in the post–World War II era. Coughlin is credited with popularizing the papal social encyclicals (*Rerum Novarum*, 1891, and *Quadragesimo Anno*, 1931) supporting the rights of working people. Unfortunately, it was later discovered that Coughlin's own financial dealings contradicted some of what he was saying.

The radically anti-Semitic words and actions of Coughlin's later years created suspicion and fear. It had after-effects for years to come and is one of the sad consequences of his legacy . In retrospect, I believe that the anti-Semitic attitudes of some Catholics, many of them Irish Catholics, even today might be traced to the ideas inculcated by Coughlin in the generation of the 1930s and 1940s and passed on to their children and grandchildren.

Coughlin was a priest and a politician. At times he seemed to be more the latter than the former. (The PBS special on "The Radio Priest" with actual film footage of his speeches is a vivid presentation of his radical stance.) Although some members of the Catholic hierarchy such as Cardinal George Mundelein of Chicago spoke out against his tirades, according to canon law only his own bishop could silence him. In an era when church-state relations were often a source of controversy, Catholics were often portrayed as subservient to the Vatican without real "freedom of speech." (Recall the accusation that if Democratic presidential nominee Al Smith were elected president in 1928 the pope would come to live in the White House!) This may account for the hesitancy of some bishops to criticize Coughlin. Ironically, it was Roosevelt's threat to indict "the radio priest" that gave Archbishop Mooney the impetus to "silence" Coughlin in the summer of 1942.

When the revised Code of Canon Law appeared in 1983 limiting the role of priests in politics, I wondered if the specter of Charles E. Coughlin was in the background. Even today, the political and social actions of priests, ministers, rabbis, and other religious professionals are often under scrutiny, especially at election time. To what degree should religious authority limit the activities of its leaders who seem to go beyond the bounds? Conversely, is it proper for religious authority to exercise control over its leaders when political and moral issues overlap?

Speaking up for the faith is to be commended as priests and laity have been empowered since Vatican II, but the danger of demagoguery—both overt and subtle—has not disappeared from the land.

The Catholic conviction that our faith must become "public" (in addition to being personal and private)—and therefore influence society—makes these questions even more complex. A study of Father Coughlin allows us to explore these challenges anew.

Notes

1. See Mary Christine Athans, *The Coughlin-Fahey Connection: Father Charles E. Coughlin, Father Denis Fahey, C.S.Sp., and Religious Anti-Semitism in the United States, 1938–1942* (New York: Peter Lang, 1991).

2. Ibid., 182.

25

Monsignor George Higgins
and Monsignor John Ryan
Public Intellectuals and Social Reformers

KENNETH R. HIMES, O.F.M.

An oft-cited claim about American Catholicism in the decades prior to Vatican II is that it was a sub-culture, set apart from the wider social life of the nation. Although legitimate in several ways, the claim is not applicable to the lives and ministries of John Ryan and George Higgins. Both of these priests were notable as public intellectuals who utilized the wisdom of the Roman Catholic tradition to address a range of social issues in American life, especially the situation of working-class people.

The historian Joseph McShane has written that World War I was the "midwife of American Catholic unity."[1] Prior to the war, the focus of episcopal energy was the diocese, and the experience of Church for most Catholics was the local parish. The war prompted bishops to think nationally and to act corporately in addressing social issues. The desire to support the wider war effort and the particular need to care for Catholics in the military led the bishops to organize the National Catholic War Council. With the war's end, that fledgling organization evolved into the National Catholic Welfare Council (NCWC), and Catholics had an institution to represent the Catholic community's views on issues of national concern. In 1919 the administrative board of the NCWC issued a Catholic program for social reform in the post-war era.

John Ryan: Advocate of a Living Wage

The author of the bishops' program for social reform was a Minnesota priest, John A. Ryan, who was the first director of the Social Action Department (SAD) within the NCWC. Ryan was a trained moral theologian, also well versed in economic affairs. From the inception of SAD until 1945 he was the key person in articulating the Catholic perspective on economic and social matters on behalf of the U.S. Catholic bishops.

During the 1920s Ryan identified three problems with the American economy: insufficient wages for most workers, excessive incomes for some capitalists, and the concentration of capital ownership in the hands of a few. His proposed solution was economic democracy that entailed social reform legislation and a new status for workers. Ryan and his colleagues at SAD struggled throughout the twenties to get a hearing for their views, but with the onset of the Great Depression and the election of Franklin Roosevelt in 1932 there was an openness to economic and social reforms that had been resisted earlier.

Ryan was a strong advocate for bold federal action and government programs to assist the working class and the poor. He earned the nickname "Right Reverend New Dealer" by those who opposed his support of Roosevelt's policies. Yet Ryan was skilled in his intellectual arguments that official Catholic social teaching, as found in the papal encyclicals *Rerum Novarum* and *Quadragesimo Anno*, was compatible with much of FDR's New Deal. There is little doubt that for more than twenty-five years Ryan was the most significant Catholic voice in building a bridge between Catholic social thought and public policy debates in the United States.

George Higgins and SAD

Shortly after completing his graduate studies at the Catholic University of America in 1944, George Higgins was invited to join the staff of SAD. An early assignment was to accompany John Ryan, who was seriously ill, home to St. Paul, Minnesota, where Ryan would die four months later. Higgins worked closely with Ryan's associates from the founding era of SAD and he fit in well, for he was well versed in Ryan's vision and policies.

Higgins had studied Ryan's theory of underconsumption. According to this theory, one of the major causes of the Great Depression was that the working class had insufficient incomes to enable their consumption patterns to offset the decline in the economic fortunes of the wealthy investment class. Promoting the cause of better wages for workers was a major focus of the policies favored by SAD during the years of Ryan and then Higgins.

Both Ryan and Higgins had a particular interest in labor unions. They saw organized labor as crucial in promoting better wages. Throughout the years after World War II, Higgins was the most prominent defender of labor unions and advocate for worker justice within the Catholic community. He authored annual Labor Day statements issued by the bishops' conference and wrote for the Catholic News Service a syndicated weekly column that addressed issues of economic justice.

Higgins also regularly attended union meetings and assemblies and served on various committees and task forces associated with labor organizations. He became an unofficial "chaplain" to many labor leaders as well as a wise advisor to Catholic public officials in the expanding federal government of the modern era. Though he was a man of firm convictions, he was open minded in his encounters with others. I was privileged to know Higgins personally and never heard him denigrate individuals even when he disagreed strongly with them. On more than one occasion he said to me, "He's wrong, but not completely wrong." The "not completely wrong" caveat was Higgins's acknowledgment that he could learn from those with whom he argued.

Higgins and Vatican II

In the late sixties Higgins became involved in the plight of farm workers who lived itinerant lives, working long days for low pay and few benefits. His advocacy of the United Farm Workers, a new kind of labor organization led by Cesar Chavez, led Higgins into policy debates about related issues of race and immigration. The farm worker issue also forced Higgins to confront some traditional labor leaders who opposed Chavez and sought to undercut his new movement.

As a result of his involvement as a *peritus* (advisor) to the American bishops at the Second Vatican Council (1962–1965), Higgins was prepared for his role with the farm workers. The experience of

Vatican II had given him a clear sense of the worldwide Church and put him into closer contact with the issues of poverty, work, and justice as these were viewed by people outside the prosperous United States. Higgins also read much of the theological literature that both prepared for and developed out of the council. This gave him a renewed sense of how the Church should serve people in a wide variety of cultures and societies.

In the years following the council, Higgins expanded his involvements in public life through the promotion of Christian-Jewish dialogue, racial justice, and fair treatment of immigrants. He also addressed issues of justice within the Church and the treatment of workers in church-related institutions. Holding fast to his convictions about the importance of organized labor, Higgins opposed the growing animus against labor during the "conservative revolution" of the 1980s.

In a "memoir" written shortly before his retirement from the bishops' conference in 1994, Higgins cited a quotation from John Ryan that he claimed as his own credo: "Effective labor unions are still by far the most powerful force in society for the protection of the laborer's rights and the improvement of his or her condition. No amount of employer benevolence, no diffusion of a sympathetic attitude on the part of the public, no increase of beneficial legislation, can adequately supply for the lack of organization among the workers themselves."[2]

Lessons for the Church Today

In his landmark encyclical *Rerum Novarum* ("Of New Things") written in 1891, Pope Leo XIII stated that the social question of the time was the plight of the worker in the new industrial age. In the United States the document inspired a young John Ryan to employ the resources of the Catholic community and its institutions to improve the situation of the working class. In 1931 another pope, Pius XI, added his support for social reform and inspired another generation of Catholic activists. Building on the example of priests like Ryan, George Higgins joined and eventually led those clerics who came to be known as "labor priests," men who were dedicated to seeing the Church take up the cause of workers and their right to organize.

For both Ryan and Higgins the ultimate goal was not to advance organized labor. Rather, they saw labor unions as the key to economic justice, and economic justice as essential to the gospel challenge to protect human dignity and promote human rights. In the example of these two men, both trained and formed within the pre-conciliar church, there are several lessons for our time.

The Church cannot simply be a sub-culture or self-enclosed social world; it does not exist for itself but for the wider society and world. The Church's mission cannot be understood as a message of religious salvation having no political or economic implications for life in society. Just as Ryan and Higgins were prepared to work with and support independent organizations like labor unions in the cause of the common good, so too the Church today may forge practical alliances with groups and institutions with whom the Church shares common ground in promoting human dignity and well-being, even when the fullness of the Church's mission differs from that of such associations.

Finally, Ryan and especially Higgins were each not only a public intellectual, but a certain kind of public intellectual—what has been called an "organic intellectual." By that phrase is meant an intellectual who is embedded in the lives and activities of people, engaged not only with ideas but also with the experiences out of which ideas are born and shaped.

A theologian or pastoral leader who is an organic intellectual will be engaged in doing practical theology, allowing the lived experience of individuals and communities to influence the questions posed to the tradition as well as the answers that are drawn from the interaction of experience and tradition. Theology and spirituality, if they are to be life-giving, must arise out of the ordinary world of human experience, helping people see the presence of God in the lived world and revealing God's concern that the world be guided by norms of justice and fairness.

Notes

1. Joseph McShane, *"Sufficiently Radical"*: *Catholicism, Progressivism, and the Bishops' Program of 1919* (Washington, DC: Catholic University Press, 1986), 62.

2. George Higgins (with William Bole), *Organized Labor and the Church* (New York/Mahwah, NJ: Paulist Press, 1993), 78.

26

Mary Perkins Ryan

Loyal and Prophetic Woman of the Church[1]

PADRAIC O'HARE

Mary Perkins Ryan was in the vanguard of the Liturgical-Catechetical Movement in the Catholic Church from the 1930s on. This was, and remains, a movement to render liturgy, above all the Eucharist, ever more humanly transforming—not merely rubrically impressive; a movement to render church-education more humanly transforming—not merely an affair, in the words of Joseph Andreas Jungmann, of "arid intellectualism." The Liturgical-Catechetical Movement insists now, as it always has, that eucharistic praying moves hearts at a deeper, more effective level than any other form of "educating," other forms being desirable and necessary but subordinate. And "transformative" means to be more free: liturgy and catechesis that helps us be more free, more free in ourselves, more free in Christ.

There is in these first words, already, a criticism of the predominant pattern of liturgy and church-education *in illo tempore* ("at that time"). Will I therefore succeed or fail in achieving the mandate of our editors, not only to be "critical," and "recognize shortcomings" of the pre-conciliar Church in the way I handle my subject, but to address the subject in such a way that the reader can also be helped to "retrieve spiritual wisdom from those days to ours." I think I have the formula. Describing Mary Ryan's work in the vanguard will dramatize what needed fixing in those days. Describing what sort of a Catholic, what sort of a human being, Mary Ryan was will enable the reader to "re-trieve spiritual wisdom" for our own time.

A Woman ahead of Her Time

Mary Ryan was born in April, 1912, and died in October, 1993. She was fifty years old when the Second Vatican Council convened. During her professional life she authored, co-authored, edited, or translated twenty-six books, the first of which, *At Your Ease In the Catholic Church* (1937), dealt with the relationship between liturgy and catechesis. This was three years before the first Liturgical Week in the United States, an event at which a twenty-five year old Mary[2] spoke; her topic was the lay person praying the prayer of the Hours, the rich and absorbing monastic prayer of the Church. Mary worked with Michael Mathis, C.S.C., one of the first wave of distinguished liturgical renewers at the University of Notre Dame's Liturgical Insti-tute, founded in 1947. And, over many creative years, Mary edited two exceptional journals, publications the pages of which featured a staggering array of topics of educational, pastoral, and theological concern and gave voice to an equally impressive range of the best peo-ple practicing and theorizing about these concerns (all of them gently but firmly and precisely edited by Mary). These were *The Living Light* and *Professional Approaches for Christian Educators* (*PACE*).

The twentieth-century Catechetical Movement in the United States had it roots principally in nineteenth- and early twentieth-cen-tury European movements of liturgical reform and renewal. Historians of liturgical reform trace its nineteenth-century origins to French Bene-dictines and to the Abbey of Solesmes. In 1918 Romano Guardini's study, *The Spirit of the Liturgy*, served to broaden zeal for liturgical re-newal. The United States liturgical pioneer, H. A. Reinhold, said of reading Guardini, ". . . the restrictions and commandments that had seemed to be the essence of Catholicism . . . vanished before the vision of Christ's Mystical Body and the incredible beauty of His Mystical Life among us through the sacraments and the mysteries."[3]

In the United States, a defining figure in the movement was the Benedictine monk, Virgil Michel (1890–1938). Michel translated the works of European liturgical reformers (for example Dom Lambert Beauduin's *Liturgy: The Life of the Church*, with its call to "democra-tize the liturgy"), and Michel pointed persuasively to the educational effects of liturgy and to its social consequences, its social demands.[4]

This is the backdrop and context of the greatest of Mary's contributions to reform and renewal, her contributions to constituting a renewed conciliar Catholic Church. Her own words, delivered to us during that heady time, precisely capture the essence of her passion, the needed reforms she promoted and embraced.

In Mary's Own Words

Mary's first words here are from the year 1963, when the Second Vatican Council was meeting. They appeared in the journal *Worship*. "A catechesis centered in the liturgy will...be completely realistic, leaving out of account none of the realities of human experience and, as such, will correspond to the best desires for reality, for vital experience, for meaningfulness in life."[5]

These are astounding words: church-education that emanates from rich immersion in liturgical acts must be real, must serve the real, must flood actual human experience with meaning and illumine ordinary experience. The remarks partake in the theological revolution that Vatican II sought to enshrine. They were prepared for by Newman's distinction between "the real" and the merely "notional" and by Blondel's "method of immanence," overcoming the dead letter "extrinsicism." They echo Rahner's insistence that we are already grasped in our experiences by the Divine, but we must be taught to pay attention, to listen, to hear. Pre-conciliar liturgical action and church-education were at least as concerned with conforming themselves to inherited dogmatic formulas as they were to outfitting Christians to follow Christ. As Mary's words reveal, the renewal was about illumining concrete, existential, and recurring human experiences in liturgical action and church-education, about relating these actions, this educating, to what Christ means for the ordinary events of our lives.

And the remarks show that Mary partook, as well, in the best educational thinking of the times, of any time. Educational practice should be humanly useful.

Note more of her words, from a presentation at the 1961 Liturgical Conference in Washington, D.C., words that predate the opening of the council by a year: "Today we are all inescapably on trial before our neighbors, before the world. We are called to witness not so much to the truth of Christianity as to its *values* [Mary's emphasis]...before a world that has generally lost hope in the ultimate worthwhileness of human life . . . in everything we do, we have to proclaim 'Christ in us, our hope and glory' to a world losing hope in humanity along with faith in God."[6]

These are words that more than hint at the intimate link between worship and action (action that is merciful, just, forgiving, and compassionate), a defining feature of what Mary and the other citizens of this vanguard bequeathed us.

So Mary's vision was a vision of liturgical-catechetical practice in a renewed Church, a vision suffused with incarnational theology, pragmatic education, and ethically demanding liturgy. In *How Firm a Foundation: Voices of the Early Liturgical Movement,* Kathleen Hughes says of Mary that she ". . . brought together liturgical and catechetical renewal . . ." into a ". . . national movement."[7]

A Controversial Bridge-Builder

In 1964, again during the Second Vatican Council, Mary published a highly controversial book, *Are Parochial Schools the Answer? Catholic Education in the Light of the Council.* In it Mary wrote: "In trying to provide a total Catholic education for as many of our young people as possible, we have been neglecting to provide anything like an adequate religious formation for all those not in Catholic schools, and we have been neglecting the religious formation of adults."[8] Gabriel Moran has written that Mary ". . . took an unmerciful verbal beating in the diocesan press and at various conferences that could hardly speak her name. 'That woman' or 'the housewife who wants to destroy the Catholic schools' were the typical forms of reference."[9]

This defining event in Mary's professional life, there can be no doubt, was linked to her passion for a catechesis that emerges from the richest of liturgical experiences, liturgical and catechetical renewal for all! Then, as now, a suspicious obsession with the priority of Catholic school ministry even to the extent of pauperizing broad parish ministerial action was in evidence.[10] The historian of Catholic religious education, Favette Veverke, captures how important were Mary's contribution and her passion for a multivalent liturgical-catechetical practice in the Church:

[Mary] questioned the adequacy and the justice of an educational strategy that ignored the vast number Catholics schools did not reach. Her argument helped to direct renewed attention, resources and personnel into other catechetical efforts such as CCD, CYO, youth ministry, and retreat movements for those outside of Catholic schools...Her critique raised consciousness and created a climate that would support the explosion of ministries such as the RCIA process, parish renewal programs, lay ministry training programs, support groups and adult Bible study."[11]

Prayer and Loyalty

Gabriel Moran characterizes Mary as "...one of the last links to a vital and rich Catholicism that antedated Vatican II...a bridge between an old time Catholicism and a still shaky new form."[12] But what does her life tote across the bridge? What can we retrieve of the "spiritual wisdom of those days" from this life? Here it is essential to have known the woman. And I did!

These are two features of the woman we may contemplate with benefit. First, Mary's theological speech emerged from praying; she was a person of deep and daily prayer. Second, in the most adverse of times, she was loyal to the Catholic Church. As Gabriel Moran says of her vanguard generation, now all gone, "The virtue I most identify with this generation of Catholics is loyalty."[13]

I do not mention her prayer life and Catholic loyalty as equivalent values. Retrieving the sapiential emphasis in theological speech (that wise theological speech comes from praying) seems to me essential to save the Church from theological obscurity and dogmatism, and even violence. Loyalty to the Church, on the other hand, loyalty to the Church even as a structure of power (though not because it is a structure of power), this seems to me a more ambiguous proposition. Still, there is little doubt that, as for Dorothy Day before her and Gustavo Gutierrez after her, for Mary speech and advocacy about God and the "things of God" required loyalty to the faith community as well. And this seems to be essentially tied to a sense of the length of the journey.

Of Mary and her vanguard compatriots Moran says, "Their commitment was to people and to the institution for the long journey."[14] In these challenging times for both liturgical and catechetical reform, we do well to learn from Mary the need for good prayer to sustain us in wise loyalty—over the long haul.

Notes

1. Elements of this essay are reworked from an essay I published at the time of Mary's death: "Mary Perkins Ryan (1912–1993) *Mulier Fortis*," *The Living Light* 30, no. 3 (Spring 1994).

2. As Dorothy Day was "Dorothy," Mary Ryan was "Mary" to all; the unorthodox usage here is the only mode of reference that feels comfortable.

3. Quoted in Ann Morrow Heekin, "Mary Perkins Ryan: Twentieth Century Religious Educator: Educating to a New Vision of the Church" (PhD dissertation, Fordham University, 2006), 20. I am indebted to Ann Morrow Heekin of Sacred Heart University in Connecticut for her splendid doctoral dissertation on Mary.

4. The characterization of Michel's work is in Heekin's "Mary Perkins Ryan," 24. Indeed, the history sketched and opinions noted in this and the previous paragraph are all those of Ann Morrow Heekin.

5. Mary Perkins Ryan, "The Focus of Catechetics," *Worship* 37 (March 1963): 240.

6. Mary Perkins Ryan, ""Witness to the World," an address given at the North American Liturgical Week in Washington, DC, in 1961; 65–66 in the *Proceedings*.

7. Kathleen Hughes, *How Firm a Foundation: Voices of the Early Liturgical Movement* (Chicago: Liturgical Training Publications, 1990), 219.

8. Quoted from Mary's book but in *Professional Approaches for Christian Educators* (May 1991): 283.

9. Gabriel Moran, "Loyal and Steadfast," *Professional Approaches for Christian Educators* (November 1994): 3.

10. I am not here criticizing the maintenance of a private Catholic secondary school system, at once fiscally independent of parishes and often remarkably prophetic.

11. Fayette Breaux Veverke, "Are Parochial Schools the Answer? Twenty Five Years Later," *Professional Approaches for Christian Educators* (May 1991): 284.

12. Moran, "Loyal and Steadfast," 3.

13. Ibid., 4.

14. Ibid.

27

Marie Augusta Neal, S.N.D. de Namur

Passionate Voice for Justice

Mary E. Hines

Early Years

When Helen Neal entered the Sisters of Notre Dame de Namur in 1943, not long after completing undergraduate work at Emmanuel College in Boston in 1942, the world was in the turmoil of war, but expectations for the life of a religious sister seemed pretty clearly defined. Like many active congregations of religious sisters of the time, the Sisters of Notre Dame engaged in the active apostolate of teaching while living a very cloistered life in community. While the Sisters of Notre Dame always had a central commitment to "the poor in the most abandoned places," the spirituality of the time tended to be privatistic, concerned with personal striving for "perfection." Spirituality focused on saving one's own soul, while apostolic activity in the world was kept separate from this. The less one had to do with the world the better! The Sisters of Notre Dame in Massachusetts ran numerous elementary schools, high schools, and Emmanuel College in Boston.

At first, Sister Marie Augusta's religious life followed the normal pattern of the time. She was assigned to teach high school, first in South Boston and then in Lawrence, Massachusetts, and at the same time completed a master's degree in sociology at Boston College. In 1953 she began teaching sociology at Emmanuel College, which remained her base until her retirement in 1991 and where she served three terms as chair of the Sociology Department. But the course of her religious life was far different from 1943 expectations. By the time of Sister Marie Augusta's death in 2004, religious life had changed dramatically. She was a major architect of that change.

The two major themes of her life, commitment to social justice and the need for renewal in religious life for women, coalesced to form the driving force of her life. Although Vatican II and the other social movements of the 1960s, especially civil rights and feminism, reinforced Sister Marie Augusta's commitment to these issues, its seeds were sown well before the council by her father, Thomas. She credits him with introducing her to Catholic social teaching by her exposure to the Catholic Action movement during her time as a student at Emmanuel and by the concern for the poor of the Sisters of Notre Dame.

Laying the Groundwork: The Priests' and Sisters' Surveys

Sister Marie Augusta received her doctorate in sociology from Harvard University in 1963, at a time when she was an unusual species in that rarified atmosphere, both as a woman and as a Roman Catholic sister. At Harvard she studied under Talcott Parsons, a prominent sociologist particularly influential in the 1960s. She tested his functional theories of social change empirically in her doctoral dissertation, which was published in 1965 under the title *Values and Interests in Social Change*. In it she surveyed a sample of priests from the archdiocese of Boston to determine if values or interests predominated in their attitudes to change, whether positive or negative. Significantly she found that, though in the early 1960s there was a considerable percentage of priests (mostly younger) open to change on the basis of their Christian values, those in positions of authority tended to fall into the "non-change on the basis of interest" category. Sister Marie Augusta suggested that as these priests grew older the numbers of value-change priests would increase and move into positions of authority. And this did happen—for a while. Coinciding as it did with Vatican Council II and its call for *aggiornamento*, or updating in the Catholic Church, her study attracted wide attention and set the agenda for much of her life's work. She is credited with developing what became known as the "Neal scale," a method for evaluating attitudes toward values and change. This early work was done in the era of mainframe computers and punch cards!

Not long after the priests' study she was asked to conduct a similar survey of attitudes to change among women religious. The first sisters' survey, conducted in 1966, was initiated by the Conference of Major Superiors of Women (CMSW, now Leadership Conference of Women Religious, or LCWR) to assess the responses of Catholic Sisters in the United States to the conciliar Decree on Renewal of Religious Life. Sister Marie Augusta was asked to direct the CMSW Research Committee and to design the survey instrument for the study. The results of this survey were distributed to the participating congregations and in many cases provided the foundation for the chapters of renewal held in the late 1960s and early 1970s. In 1982 the survey was replicated and extended to provide an assessment of the almost twenty years of post-Vatican II renewal of religious congregations of women. Results were published in *Catholic Sisters in Transition: From the 1960's to the 1980's*. The sisters' survey had an enormous influence on the renewal of religious life in the United States.

Themes of Her Lifetime: Social Justice

In 1970 Sister Marie Augusta was invited to South Africa by the South African Catholic Education Council to do a study of Catholic schools. Although the bishops had expected that she would study only white schools, she insisted that to do the research adequately she would need to study both black and white schools. On this same trip she also visited the sisters of Notre Dame in Brazil. These powerful experiences of institutionalized racism, poverty, and oppression outside the United States solidified her conviction that the privatistic spirituality of the past must give way to a biblically based spirituality that focused on alleviating the systemic causes of poverty and oppression.

Her students at Emmanuel from this time recall that from 1965 on she started her introductory sociology classes by asking the question, "Why are there poor people in a rich society like the United States?" and from the 1970s the question became, "Why is it that two thirds of the world is poor when we have the technologies sufficient to provide well for all but we do not?" No students of Sister Marie Augusta (or young Sisters of Notre Dame, who often helped compile survey results) escaped the exhortation to do critical social analysis and her insistence on the need for conscientization, or raising awareness of and opposition to oppressive social structures. The centrality of social justice to the mission of Emmanuel College remains a legacy of Sister Marie Augusta.

Like many prophets, Sister Marie Augusta's passionate advocacy for social justice tended to make the comfortable uncomfortable, and in those Cold War times she was often accused of being a communist. It must be acknowledged that because of her clarity about the needs of the world, Church, and religious life she could sometimes be impatient with those who didn't see things quite as clearly, or as quickly. She didn't view herself as a revolutionary, however. In an interview with the *Boston Globe* she said that she was a "faithful Catholic and a committed scholar who simply applied the teachings of the church to the world around her."

From the 1970s on Sister Marie Augusta was widely recognized and in much demand as speaker, author, and consultant. She was one of two religious members of the Massachusetts Governor's Commission on the status of women in the 1960s and visiting professor at University of California, Berkeley; Harvard Divinity School; and Boston College. She served as president of the Association for the Sociology of Religion and president of the Society for the Scientific Study of Religion, groundbreaking roles for a Catholic sister. Among her numerous honorary doctorates is one from the University of Notre Dame where her papers are archived. She published more than seventy articles and six books probing different aspects of justice, peace, and civil and human rights, both in the Church and in society. Emblematic of her theological/sociological approach was her 1977 book, *A Socio Theology of Letting Go*, where she applies the method of the liberation theologians within the first-world context of the United States. It is the responsibility of a first-world church, she said, faced with the needs of the third world, to relinquish its hold on power, prestige, and wealth.

Themes of Her Lifetime: Renewal in Religious Life

Sister Marie Augusta Neal both lived through and facilitated the dramatic changes that took place in religious life in the post–Vatican II years. She advocated a spirituality focused on alleviating this-worldly injustice rather than being exclusively focused on otherworldly salvation. She had an enormous personal impact not only on those she encountered in the classroom but also through her lectures and writings. Sister Helen Prejean, author of *Dead Man Walking*, credits a talk by

Sister Marie Augusta as a conversion experience that transformed her vision of religious life and set her on to the path of social activism. Kip Tiernan, founder of Rosie's Place, the first women's shelter in Boston, and a powerful advocate for the poor and marginalized, both inspired and was inspired by her friend, Sister Marie Augusta.

But through these changes Sister Marie Augusta didn't lose the core values of her early community experience. While on her trips to South Africa and Brazil, and on other travels, she wrote back frequently to her community to share her experiences. Sister Janet Eisner, president of Emmanuel, recalls being surprised, as a newly appointed and very young college president, when Sister Marie Augusta asked her permission to travel and provided her with a detailed itinerary of her trips. And Sister Marie Augusta's activism was always rooted in prayer, in scripture, and in the mission of the poor of the Sisters of Notre Dame. She frequently evoked the Leviticus theme of the Jubilee year, which she interpreted as calling "for a return to the people of what is rightfully theirs, what they need for human development." Sister Janet Eisner said at the launching of *Themes of a Lifetime*, a collection of Sister Marie Augusta's works, that "Sr. Marie Augusta's passion for justice and her conviction in the power of education reflects St. Julie's [the founder of the Sisters of Notre Dame] vision. Like Sr. Marie Augusta, St. Julie was moved by God to act to correct the wrongs done to the poor in her day."

Elegant, soft-spoken, and radical, as one of her former students described her, Sister Marie Augusta insisted that withdrawal from the world and its most critical issues was no longer an option for an authentic spirituality in today's Church and world. Women religious are called to be in the forefront of the struggle for justice and human rights that is the gospel mandate for the whole Church.

28

African American Catholics

Witnesses to Fidelity

CYPRIAN DAVIS, O.S.B.

I fell in love with the Catholic Church when I was fifteen years old. This was not just the pre–Vatican Church; it was the medieval Church, the Church of pageantry and monasticism. I was a history buff. It was my uncle who took me to Mass one Sunday morning. I was about twelve years old. I was enthralled. To the dismay of my mother, I soon began to attend Mass on my own. My grandfather had left the Catholic Church when she was a baby. She was reared as a Presbyterian. Only later did she discover the Catholic Church and then become a very devout Catholic.

A Different Church

The first Catholic church I came to know was St. Augustine's Church at 15th and M Street in downtown Washington. It was one of the oldest black Catholic parishes in the United States. The parishioners were freed blacks who before the Civil War had raised money to build a church where they could have Mass every Sunday, with their own pastor and choir. Abraham Lincoln permitted the parishioners to raise money by giving a party on the White House lawn on July 4, 1864. It seems that the president and Mrs. Lincoln were among the thousand or so visitors. Financially, it was a success.[1]

The nation's capital has always had and still has a sizable black population; the number of black Catholics has always been large and influential. Many black Catholics, like my grandfather, were descendants of slaves from the Jesuit-owned plantations in southern Maryland. Washington, in fact, was a southern city. It was segregated, but there were no "colored" or "white" signs. It was a benign segregation. Not all Catholic churches welcomed African Americans. In fact, in some places the pastor pointed out to African Americans that the Catholic church for blacks was down the street. In other places there was segregated seating; even worse, there were some pre–Vatican II churches in which blacks had to receive Communion after whites had received. On the other hand, many black Catholic churches like St. Augustine's were well known for their music, their vibrant liturgy, and their social justice leadership.

Segregation and Civil Rights

In the case of St. Augustine's, the parish church was known not only for its music but also for its active participation in the civil rights movement. Howard University, one of the historic black colleges established after the Civil War, was one among many educational institutions in the city. Thomas Wyatt Turner (1877–1978), a black Catholic lay leader, worked tirelessly for an end to racism within the American Catholic Church. He had been a student at the Catholic University of America at the beginning of the twentieth century. Lack of funds forced him to leave Catholic University. He would eventually obtain his doctorate from Cornell University and become a professor at Howard University and later at Hampton University. Always a fervent Catholic, he began his fight for racial justice within the Catholic Church during the first World War when he was a parishioner at St Augustine's Church. He challenged the racism found in the American Catholic Church and spoke of the "dessicating [sic] race prejudice at every stage of our religious observance."[2] He founded the "Federated Colored Catholics" as an activist organization working for a "greater participation of black Catholics in the cause of racial justice."

Just as Washington was a segregated city, so was the Catholic Church in Washington. Catholic University closed its doors to African Americans in the first decades of the twentieth century.[3] The admittance of African American students began again in the 1940s. Georgetown University was closed to blacks well into the 1960s. Ironically, one of the most eminent presidents of Georgetown University (the title at the time was "Rector") was a former slave who became president in 1874.[4] Because of his light complexion, few knew that Patrick Francis Healy was the brother of James Augustine Healy, the first black bishop in the United States. Patrick Francis resigned as president in 1882. He died in 1910. Most of the private Catholic schools in the United States—primary schools, high schools, academies, prep schools—were closed to African American students until the 1960s.

Black and Catholic

Xavier University in Louisiana was founded by Mother Katharine Drexel (who has since been canonized) in 1925. It was and still is the only black Catholic university in the United States. Katharine Drexel (1858–1955) began her congregation, known as the Sisters of the Blessed Sacrament for Indians and Colored People, in 1891. It was dedicated to the evangelization and education of Native Americans and African Americans. This modern American saint worked for social justice with prophetic zeal. She contributed to the NAACP; she supported anti-lynching legislation in the U.S. Congress. She urged her sisters to do the same.

In 1938, Mother Grace Damman, president of Manhattanville College in New York, announced the acceptance of a young African American woman as a student in the prestigious Catholic liberal arts college operated by the Religious of the Sacred Heart. Mother Grace Damman wrote that a young Catholic woman who met all the requirements had a right to admittance whether she was African American or white. It was time for a young Catholic woman to accept not only the teaching of Catholicism but also its practice.[5]

In the 1940s and 1950s, Catholic leaders like Mother Katharine Drexel; John LaFarge, S.J.; George K. Hunton; Dorothy Day; the Baroness Catherine de Hueck; and members of the hierarchy such as Cardinal Joseph Ritter; Cardinal Patrick O'Boyle; and Archbishop Joseph Francis Rummel worked for the black community and stood up for justice and Catholic teaching.

In May of 1953, Vincent Waters, bishop of Raleigh, North Carolina, traveled to the small town of Newton Grove, North Carolina. Waters, a southern bishop, had learned to overcome his own background and southern sentiment. He had grown to understand what it meant to be part of the Body of Christ. He had called for desegregation in the

Catholic churches in the diocese, and he wanted to be present when the two frame Catholic churches merged in Newton Grove. These two churches, St. Benedict's Church for blacks and Our Holy Redeemer Church for whites, were only two hundred yards from each other. In April Bishop Waters had written a pastoral letter to the people of North Carolina, saying, "There is no segregation of races to be tolerated in any Catholic Church in the Diocese of Raleigh . . . A Church not uniting all races and peoples in one body could not be Christ's Mystical Body."[6] The reaction of the white parishioners in Our Holy Redeemer Church was anger and bitterness. Standing outside, they shouted and jeered at those going into the church. There were three Masses at Our Holy Redeemer Church. As many as one hundred whites gathered outside while Bishop Waters preached at two of the Masses. Inside, there were only twenty-nine people, black and white, who sat in separated groups.[7] Convinced that segregation was immoral and contrary to the Church's teaching, Waters believed that obedience to the authority of the Church was sufficient to bring about change. He considered that racism was heresy, pointing out that the Second World War was fought against the notion of a "master race."

African American parishioners, on the other hand, were affected in a different way. In most instances, the black community was moved into the white parish. They were not welcomed but only tolerated. An African American priest, Monsignor Thomas Hadden, the first black priest in the diocese of Raleigh, noted that "African-American Catholics who found themselves in an integrated parish often did not participate fully in the life of the parish." He went on to say that often there was "little sensitivity to . . . Black Catholic culture and distinctiveness." It is worth noting that African American parishes after the second Vatican Council easily introduced black culture and music into the liturgy. [8]

African American Priests

The history of African American priests is a long and painful one. When I recognized my vocation to priesthood, I had to face the fact that it was not easy for young black men and women to realize their religious vocation. I was told that only certain dioceses and only certain monasteries accepted African Americans. In fact, when I first became interested in monasticism, I wrote to the abbot of a monastic community asking whether a black would be accepted into their community. I had been told to state clearly that I was a "Negro." The response was also clear. It would be better for me to enter the Josephites. Angry and disappointed at first, I would later have the joy of entering St. Meinrad Archabbey. It must be stated, moreover, that after graduating from high school I received a scholarship to the Catholic University of America.[9]

Black American Catholic men sought to enter the priesthood even before the Civil War. William Augustine Williams, who was from Virginia and converted to Catholicism, became a student for the priesthood at the Urban College in Rome in 1855, hoping to be adopted by an American bishop. Despite his efforts, Williams was rejected for priesthood on the grounds that American Catholics—that is white Catholics—would not accept a black priest.[10] The first black priests in our history were the three Healy brothers—the previously mentioned James Augustine Healy and Francis Patrick Healy as well as Sherwood Alexander Healy—all the slave offspring of a slave-holder in Georgia. Brilliant and ill-fated, they did not identify with fellow African Americans. On the other hand, Augustus Tolton, born a slave, eventually became a student at the Urban College in Rome and was made a pastor of a black parish in Chicago. A man of gentleness and generosity, he had a heart open to all African Americans. The number of African American priests grew slowly in the period before the Second Vatican Council and then began to increase in the 1960s.

Some would say that African American Catholics are merely the stepchildren of American Catholicism, usually forgotten and overlooked. Nevertheless, there is no question that their presence in the Church has been a witness to fidelity and to hope. African American Catholics like Mary Lou Williams, Llewellyn Scott, Lena Edwards, A. P. Tureaud, Claude McKay, Ralph Metcalfe, Earl Johnson, and so many others made significant contributions to American Catholicism in the Church before the Second Vatican Council.

"Chastised a little, they shall be greatly blessed because God tried them and found them worthy of himself" (Wisdom 3:5).

Notes

1. Morris J. MacGregor, *The Emergence of a Black Catholic Community: St. Augustine's in Washington* (Washington, DC: Catholic University of America Press, 1999), 36–39.

2. Cyprian Davis, O.S.B., *The History of Black Catholics in the United States* (New York: Crossroad, 1990), 220.

3. Roy J. Deferrari, *Memoirs of the Catholic University of America. 1918–1960* (Boston, MA: Daughters of St. Paul, 1962), 281–90. See also C. Joseph Nuesse, *The Catholic University of America. A Centennial History.* (Washington, DC: Catholic University of America Press, 1990), 190–91.

4. Albert Foley, S.J., *Dream of an Outcaste: Patrick F. Healy: The Story of the Slaveborn Georgian who Became the Second Founder of America's Great Catholic University, Georgetown.* (Tuscaloosa, AL: Portals Press, 1989).

5. Davis, *The History of Black Catholics*, 254.

6. Quotation from the pastoral letter as found on page 325 of Mark Newman's "Toward 'Blessings of Liberty and Justice': The Catholic Church in North Carolina and Desegregation, 1945–1974," *The North Carolina Historical Review* 85 (2008): 317–51.

7. Ibid.

8. Ibid., 348, n. 72. Thomas P. Hadden, "A 'catechism' on African-American Ministry and Evangelization," *North Carolina Catholic*, August 26, 2001 (Hadden interview).

9. Catholic Scholarships for Negroes, Inc., was established to provide financial aid for African American Catholics who had promise for advanced education. It was sponsored by Mrs. Roger Putnam and Richard Cardinal Cushing.

10. Stephen Ochs, *Desegregating the Altar: The Josephites and the Struggle for Black Priests, 1871–1960* (Baton Rouge, LA: Louisiana State University Press, 1990), 29–31. The work by Ochs is a detailed history of black Catholic priests in the United States.

29

Dorothy Day and Peter Maurin

Twentieth-century Prophets

ROBERT ELLSBERG

She was a thirty-five-year-old single mother, a journalist with a background in the labor movement and radical politics, and a recent convert to Catholicism. He was a Frenchman twenty years her senior, a self-described "peasant philosopher" with a thick accent, an overcoat stuffed with pamphlets, and a rumpled suit that looked as if he had slept in it (as he had). She had just returned from covering a Communist-organized "Hunger March of the Unemployed" in Washington, DC. He was waiting for her in her New York apartment, convinced, on the basis of a recommendation from the editor of *Commonweal,* that she was the one to set his ideas in motion. It is hard to imagine a more unlikely partnership. And yet that meeting between Dorothy Day and Peter Maurin in December 1932 must be counted as one of the most significant events in the history of American Catholicism.

Dorothy Day: Reconciling Faith with Commitment to the Poor

For Dorothy Day, the meeting with Peter Maurin seemed like an answer to prayer. Literally. While covering the march in Washington she had found herself wondering why Catholics were not leading the struggle for social justice. She had made her way to the Shrine of the Immaculate Conception (auspiciously it was December 8, the very feast day of that Marian dogma), and had prayed with tears in her eyes for some way to reconcile her Catholic faith with her commitment to the cause of the poor and oppressed.

She had come to that prayer by an improbable road. Born in 1897 to a respectable middle-class family, she had dropped out of college and gravitated to New York where she worked for a succession of radical journals and causes. She was arrested twice. She took part in marches and demonstrations. But there was always something that set her apart from her radical friends. As one of them observed, she was always "too religious" to make a good Communist.

Not that she had much use for any church. As a teenager she had renounced Christianity, on the grounds that Christians seemed to have little to say about the burning social issues of the day. She had admired the lives of the saints and the stories of their heroic charity. "But where were the saints to change the social order, not just to minister to the slaves, but to do away with slavery?"

The turning point in Day's life came with the birth of her daughter Tamar, in 1926. The child's father was an anarchist and atheist, whom she deeply loved, though he had no interest in marriage. The experience of pregnancy filled her heart with such a sense of gratitude that it awakened her instinct for reverence and prayer. She found herself wanting to have her daughter baptized a Catholic, a step she eventually took herself, even when it required the painful separation from her "common-law husband." That loss was compounded, in her mind, by a feeling that in joining the Church she was betraying the cause of the working class—crossing over to an ally of the rich and powerful. That is how her friends viewed it, and she saw their point. So with her conversion she entered a lonely period, searching in the wilderness for some sign of her true vocation. That search had led to her providential meeting with Peter Maurin.

Peter Maurin: Blowing the Lid Off the Dynamite in the Gospels

And what of him? Peter Maurin was born in 1877 to a peasant family in southern France. Educated by the Christian Brothers, he had made an unsuccessful stab at a vocation in that teaching order. He had participated in "Le Sillon" (the Furrow), a movement of lay Catholics in France who tried to reconcile their faith with their commitment to democracy and social reform (only to be condemned by the Vatican). In 1909 Maurin had immigrated to North America. He had spent many years tramping around the country, engaging in hard labor of various kinds while living in poverty. All the while he was reading and studying. Drawing on the best—mostly European—Catholic thinkers of the time, he was devising his own synthesis in the area of Catholic social theory.

By this time it was the heart of the Depression. Millions of people were unemployed. Maurin believed the source of these social problems came from the separation of sociology, economics, and politics from the gospel. In the process, society had lost any sense of the ultimate, transcendent purpose of human activity. Social life had come to be organized around the drive for production and the search for profits, rather than the full development of persons. The Church, he believed, had an answer to all this, but it had failed to act on it. There was "dynamite" in the gospels, but for the most part the clergy preferred to keep it under lock and key. What was necessary was to "blow the lid" off that dynamite.

This was the message he was eager to share with Dorothy Day. When she returned from her trip to Washington and found him waiting in her apartment (her brother having let him in), he began at once to speak with her about his vision, quoting from an assortment of thinkers such as Eric Gill, Vincent McNabb, and Jacques Maritain. Maurin had a whole program laid out, beginning with the need for a newspaper to promote the social vision of the Church, houses of hospitality to practice the works of mercy, farming communes where "workers could become scholars and scholars could become workers." He had even formulated his ideas in the form of sing-songy verses, ideal for street-corner declamation: "The world would become better off / if people tried to become better. / And people would become better/ if they stopped trying to become better off."

Maurin had been preaching this message for years before finding anyone who would take him seriously. In fact, it would be some time before Day herself fully appreciated his ambitious vision. (And, even then, she had to ask herself whether she really liked him.) But she was quickly won over by his notion of starting a newspaper that would offer solidarity with workers and a critique of the social system from the radical perspective of the gospel. Maurin, as she later put it, had given her "a program," a "Catholic view of history," broader than the "class struggle" framework in which she had been formed. Drawing on the lives of the saints he had shown her that it was not necessary to wait for official permission to live by the teachings of Christ. One could begin today, with the means at hand, "building the new world in the shell of the old." In effect, he gave her permission to invent her own vocation.

The Catholic Worker: Serving the Poor and Challenging Society

Five months later, on May 1, 1933, *The Catholic Worker* newspaper was launched at a Communist rally in Union Square. If Maurin had provided the "program," it was Day who set it in motion. The paper was the organ of a movement based in houses of hospitality— first in New York, and then in other parts of the country—where lay Catholics lived in community among the poor, feeding the hungry, offering shelter to the homeless. Through these works of mercy, Catholic Workers responded to the needs of their neighbors. As Dorothy wrote, "The mystery of the poor is this, that they are Christ, and what we do for them we do to Him." But through the paper and other forms of direct action Catholic Workers also challenged the values, the structures, and the institutions that gave rise to so much poverty and need.

In the early years of the movement the circulation of the paper quickly swelled, as many bishops and clergy embraced Day's model of social activism. But over time, as her pacifist position became more pronounced, especially during World War II, she was increasingly relegated to a marginal position in the Church. In the 1950s she was arrested numerous times for protests against nuclear weapons. During the years that followed she was outspoken in her opposition to the Vietnam War, her support for the civil rights movement, and her solidarity with the United Farmworkers Union. By that time opinion had begun to shift; if she was still regarded warily by many in the Church, she had been embraced as grandmother to a new generation of peacemakers and social activists.

Dorothy Day died in 1980 at the age of eighty-three. Peter Maurin had long since passed from the scene—having died in 1949 after several years of infirmity.

Commenting in *Commonweal,* David O'Brien called Day "the most significant, interesting, and influential person in the history of American Catholicism." It was an extraordinary statement on behalf of someone who had occupied no official position of authority, and whose views, after all, had met with widespread rejection throughout most of her career. In 2000 the Archdiocese of New York proposed

Dorothy Day for canonization—the recognition that there is a kind of authority in the Church that has nothing to do with office or contemporary popularity.

On an obvious level, Day and Maurin did more than almost anyone in America to promote awareness of the social dimension of the gospel. This went beyond propagating traditional "Catholic social teaching." In effect, they anticipated themes that would not form part of official teaching for decades to come: the principle of solidarity, the preferential option for the poor, concern for ecology, a "seamless garment" approach to the protection of life, an emphasis on gospel nonviolence. Building on the best Catholic thinking of the time, they also advanced themes that would not be widely embraced by the Church until Vatican II: the role of the laity, the priority of conscience, ecumenical dialogue, liturgical reform, the return to scripture.

In accepting Dorothy Day's cause for canonization, the Vatican has recognized her importance as a model of holiness for our time. In fact, one of her constant themes was that we are all, as Christians, called to be saints. But she preferred to deflect attention to her holy mentor, Peter Maurin—another "St. Francis" for our time. She called him "most truly the founder of the Catholic Worker movement . . . He opened our minds to great horizons, he gave us a vision." Whether he was truly the founder of the Catholic Worker, he will always be remembered as the true founder of Dorothy Day.

30

Mary Luke Tobin, S.L.

About Her Father's/Mother's Business

THERESA KANE, R.S.M.

Sister Mary Luke Tobin was a woman who lived her entire life in the twentieth century; Mary Luke was, however, a woman whose spirit, vision, energy, and enthusiasm for life and its future qualified her fully as a Twenty-First Century Woman!

Ruth Tobin was born May 16, 1908, in Denver, Colorado. She was educated in Denver public elementary and high schools. After two years at Loretto Heights College (Denver), Tobin entered the novitiate of the Sisters of Loretto in Nerinx, Kentucky. At her reception into the congregation, she received the name Mary Luke.

She served for some years as principal in several Loretto high schools when, in 1952, she was elected to the general council of the Sisters of Loretto. In 1958 she was elected superior general, in which position she served two six-year terms. From 1964 to 1967 Sister Mary Luke was president of the Conference of Major Superiors of Women (now the Leadership Conference of Women Religious, or LCWR). As leader of women religious in the United States at the time of Vatican II, Sister Mary Luke was invited to the last two sessions of the council. She was one of fifteen women auditors. Later, drawing upon her early friendship with Thomas Merton during her years at the motherhouse in Kentucky not far from Gethsemani, she directed the Thomas Merton Center in

Denver until 1995. Throughout her years she championed issues of peace and justice, including the dismantling of racism, women's rights, and abolition of the death penalty. She died on August 24, 2006.

Spokeswoman for Vatican II

I first met Mary Luke in the late 1960s and early 1970s when she and Ann Patrick Ware, also a Sister of Loretto, took up residence in New York City to engage in ecumenical work with Church Women United and the National Council of Churches. By the mid-to-late 1980s, a number of religious communities of women would broaden their ministries to include work with other Christians and interfaith groups and to establish a presence as a non-governmental organization at the United Nations. However, in the late 1960s, it was a creative and visionary step for the Sisters of Loretto and for Mary Luke to take almost immediately at the conclusion of the Vatican Council II. No doubt, such a step was related to the fact that she had been a most active and engaged observer at the council's second session.

Mary Luke was, without a doubt, a passionate and vibrant Vatican II spokeswoman at the council. Although the very few women who were present were prohibited from speaking publicly in the general assembly, they were allowed to participate in working committee sessions. Mary Luke never missed a session or an opportunity for dialogue at the gatherings on the concilar document, The Church in the Modern World.

Mary Luke was a short woman, yet she walked with great determination. In fact, my impression of Mary Luke in the 1970s and well even into the late 1980s is that she seemed to be always walking very fast; maybe even a run would better describe her movements! She was always about "her Father's/Mother's business." She had much to say, to do, and to accomplish, not for herself but for others—for our religious communities, for our church, for our society! I do not recall any agitation or impatience; however, I sensed she had little time or appreciation for slowness or indecisiveness. She was far ahead of many of us—thinking well into the future, not only thinking ahead but actually envisioning a future many of us were just beginning to imagine!

Woman of Fidelity

As a consequence of qualities so evident throughout her entire life, Mary Luke was a sterling example of fidelity. When she had an idea, she would share and discuss it with a few significant people—if nothing seemed to be an overwhelming obstacle, she would enable the idea to develop, to unwind; then, backed by her drive and determination, it would take on a life of its own.

In October 1979, as president of the Leadership Conference of Women Religious, I was invited to greet Pope John Paul II at the Shrine of the Immaculate Conception in Washington, D.C., on October 7, the last day of the pope's first visit to the United States. There I voiced the following words: "As women we have heard the powerful message of our church addressing the dignity and reverence of all persons. As women we have pondered these words. Our contemplation leads us to state that the church in its struggle to be faithful to its call for reverence and dignity for all persons must respond by providing the possibility of women as persons being included in all ministries of the church."

The LCWR National Board, the Executive Committee, and I met with our members throughout the fifteen regions in the following months to relate the events and to receive members' responses. We also met with every cardinal in the United States before they left for an upcoming meeting with the pope in November.

At our meetings in the fifteen regions, there seemed to be some questions and concerns. In August 1980 we held our annual assembly in Philadelphia. My papal greeting had been a source of much public discourse. At the conclusion of our assembly, most though not all of the LCWR members present were overwhelmingly positive and supportive of the greeting—its style, its content, and its timing.

Now Mary Luke Tobin enters into the experience! As I was completing my leadership of the LCWR, Mary Luke approached me and said she was initiating a conversation among the LCWR past presidents and executive directors at her home in Denver, Colorado. She was most eager for Vatican officials to realize that my greeting was representative of the organization and supported by it, especially by its presidents and directors. She thought such an action needed to be taken while I was still in a leadership position.

It was her vision that we gather in prayer and in friendship, that we share our vision of religious life and express our gratitude for our many blessings, and that all of us simply have the opportunity to experience a wonderful time together.

Mary Luke worked very hard to organize that gathering, bringing women from all across the United States. Most of the invitees were present; we had two or three glorious days and each one of us wrote reflections on the papal greeting. Mary Luke, with the Loretto Sisters, was totally responsible for this Denver gathering. She then asked one of the Loretto Sisters to write an article about the experience and request it be published in the *National Catholic Reporter.*

Mary Luke's Spirit Lives On

I share this story to give an example of the powerful presence Mary Luke was in my life and the lives of so many others. She had determination, she had grit, and she certainly had endurance; she was "a woman of substance," to quote the title of a popular book that was adapted for TV mini-series some years ago.

Mary Luke was vitally interested in politics and was acutely knowledgeable about the realities of the political world. In the fall of 2004, it was predicted Mary Luke would not live much longer; however, she followed the national elections avidly and lived to see the results—which were not to her liking! How thrilled she would have been to have supported and voted for Barack Obama as president in 2008! Such an election in the United States was, I am sure, not beyond her vision or dream but how delighted she would have been to experience such a historic American paradigm shift!

Mary Luke was an outstanding human being, an extraordinary woman, and a zealous, devout religious—a very proud Sister of Loretto. She was so proud of her religious order and equally proud of the other religious orders in the United States and throughout the world. She believed very strongly in this form of life and believed just as strongly that radical changes had to be made for renewal to become truly a reality—renewal at the very roots of our spirits. She was committed to creating an environment where women religious could be adult, responsible, conscientious agents and decision-makers regarding the events in their lives and no longer passive recipients of a "male-defined society and church"! Her spirit and that of many other great religious women before us should sustain us now in these times of Vatican review of our lives and ministries.

How alive Mary Luke still is in the hearts, minds, and lives of myriad women religious! Mary Luke, we applaud you and we thrill to think of our reunion with you once again some day!

31

Theodore M. Hesburgh, C.S.C.

Leadership Spanning Two Centuries

Richard P. McBrien

There is no question in my mind that the leading Catholic educator in the pre– and post–Vatican II years has been Theodore M. Hesburgh, a priest of the Congregation of Holy Cross and for thirty-five years president of the University of Notre Dame. More than that, he is the twentieth century's and the early twenty-first century's most significant U.S. Catholic leader, bar none, whether in religion, politics, business, or the professions.

Ordained on June 24, 1943, he has been a major presence in the U.S. Catholic Church and in the United States generally for much of the pre-conciliar period and for all of the post-conciliar period thus far.

Soon after ordination, with the Second World War still raging, the young Father Ted, as he has always preferred to be called, asked his superiors in the Congregation of Holy Cross if he might serve as a Navy chaplain. But those superiors had other plans for him, and he was sent instead to study for a doctorate in theology at the Catholic University of America.

He would excel in his studies there, as he would excel in everything else that he has done in life, but he had difficulty obtaining approval for his doctoral dissertation topic: the theology of the laity. Some of his professors at the Catholic University regarded the topic as not sufficiently academic.

A Man ahead of His Time

One needs to be reminded that in the early and mid-1940s the laity were still looked upon as second-class members of the Catholic Church. The "real" Church consisted of the hierarchy and other clergy. Lay people were simply the beneficiaries of their teachings and spiritual ministrations. As one cynical wag once famously put it, the laity existed to "pay, pray, and obey."

There was also a movement at the time known as Catholic Action. Its strength was that it found a place for the laity in the Church. Its weakness was that it regarded lay activity as completely dependent on the hierarchy.

In fact, Catholic Action was defined as "the participation of the laity in the work of the hierarchy." The "real" work of the Church was done by, or under the direct supervision of, the hierarchy. The laity were at best the helpers of the bishops.

Critics twisted the definition to fit their own idea of the actual situation in the Catholic Church of that period, namely, "the *interference* of the laity in the *lethargy* of the hierarchy." But the young Father Ted knew in the mid-1940s, long before it was theologically fashionable, that there was much more to the role of the laity in the Church than what even the Catholic Action movement allowed for, and certainly more than the ministerial opportunities that were open to the laity at the time afforded.

So, after something of a struggle with members of his dissertation committee, but with the support of his dissertation director, Paulist Father Eugene Burke, Father Hesburgh produced his theology of the laity. So popular was the finished product that the university bookstore could not keep printed copies in stock.

Father Hesburgh later received a request from the Vatican for a copy of the dissertation. The young priest dutifully sent it off to Rome but heard nothing more about it—until two decades later, when he read the Second Vatican Council's Decree on the Apostolate of the Laity and recognized his ideas incorporated therein, without a single footnote of attribution.

He had surely been ahead of his time, even ahead of the great Dominican theologian (later Cardinal) Yves Congar, whose book, *Lay People in the Church*, became the standard work on the theology of the laity upon its publication in 1953.

It was prescient of the young Father Hesburgh, who was destined for such greatness in the Catholic Church and in the world community (where he would befriend presidents, other heads of state, and popes and cardinals alike), to have recognized at the outset of his priestly life and ministry that priests exist for the sake of the laity, not vice versa. Indeed, we are all laity, or people (*laos* in Greek) of God. As much as Theodore Hesburgh cherished his priesthood, he realized that the fundamental sacrament is Baptism, not Holy Orders.

God, Country, and Notre Dame

Theodore Hesburgh rose quickly in Notre Dame's academic and institutional ranks, becoming chair of the Department of Theology, executive vice president, and then in 1952 president of the University of Notre Dame. He has always regarded his greatest achievements as Notre Dame's president to have been the transfer of control of the university from his own Congregation of Holy Cross to a lay board of trustees in 1967 and the admission of women to the university in 1972.

He also ensured the academic vitality of Catholic higher education, both before and after Vatican II, by bringing together other leading Catholic educators in 1967 to craft the celebrated Land O'Lakes statement that applied the principles of academic freedom and institutional autonomy to all Catholic universities and colleges. His academic outreach, however, went far beyond the shores of the United States, particularly in his seven-year role as chair of the International Federation of Catholic Universities.

After being compelled to retire from the Notre Dame presidency in 1987 because of age, he continued to lead an exceedingly active life in service to the academy, his country, and the Church. He was elected to the Board of Overseers at Harvard University—the first priest to be so honored—and in 1994, at age 77, he became chair of the board for two terms. He also received more than 150 honorary degrees from various colleges and universities in the United States and around the world.

His national stature, beyond education and the Church, is reflected in some sixteen U.S. presidential appointments to working groups in such areas as the peaceful use of atomic energy, Third World development, immigration, and civil rights. Indeed he was a charter member and then chair of the Civil Rights Commission.

In July of 2000 Father Hesburgh received the Congressional Gold Medal, the highest form of recognition that the U.S. Congress can bestow upon a civilian for distinguished achievements and contributions to the nation. George Washington was the first of some 250 recipients of the award in the nation's entire history.

At the Congressional Gold Medal award ceremony in the Capitol rotunda, President Bill Clinton captured the essence of Father Hesburgh when, after calling attention to his extraordinary contributions to his country and to world peace, he said: "The greatest honor you'll ever wear around your neck is the collar of a priest." Father Hesburgh readily agreed, noting that the most significant day of his life was the day of his ordination to the priesthood.

This natural leader, both inside and outside the Catholic Church, is a man not only of extraordinary vision and a remarkable capacity to inspire but also of confidence and hope, both of which are rooted in his deep Catholic faith.

His daily prayer is "Come, Holy Spirit." That prayer emanates from his long-held conviction that it is the Holy Spirit—not the clergy, not the bishops, not even the pope—who ultimately determines the Church's course in history and its final destiny.

Those who wish to preserve the best of the pre–Vatican II Church in order to apply its spiritual assets and its wisdom to the present and future Church need look no further than to Father Theodore M. Hesburgh, C.S.C., as both a model and a beacon for all of us to follow.

When the history of twentieth-century and early twenty-first-century Catholicism is written, his name will loom large upon its pages.

III

PRACTICES

32

Questions and Answers—Again— from the *Baltimore Catechism*

THOMAS H. GROOME

A Confident Faith

In Shakespeare's opinion, "To be or not to be; that is the question," while the philosophers ask it as "Why is there anything and not nothing?" The *Baltimore Catechism*, however, posed the ultimate question as, "Why did God make you?" And it offered an unsurpassable answer: "God made me to know, love, and serve Him in this world, and to be happy with Him forever in the next."

Many times when presenting on the holistic nature of Christian faith—to know, love, and serve God, engaging head, heart, and hands—I've posed this old catechism question to participants. The response grows fainter with the years but those of a vintage to have learned it "by heart" shout it out with confidence, to the envy of the youngsters who never did. Perhaps that's the best gift that the question-and-answer catechisms gave people, the security that they "knew their faith" and could recite its core dogmas and doctrines, sacraments and prayers, values and ethical teachings—on cue.

As children moved along in the *Baltimore Catechism*, they would memorize the attributes of God and of themselves, the paschal mystery of Jesus Christ, the gifts and fruits of the Holy Ghost, the "marks" of the Church, the sacraments and commandments, the corporal and spiritual works of mercy, the "last things," and more. And the intent was that they learn the answers not only by rote but truly "by heart"—thus shaping their identity as Catholic Christians.

Good Memories

Surprise, surprise: I won the prize in first grade for "best in catechism"—a portent, surely, of a lifetime in catechesis. My fondest memory, however, is of a particular evening when my mother inquired, as she typically did, "What questions do you have for tomorrow?" and I said something like "137 to 140." Whereupon she, without even opening the book, asked, "What is calumny?" I was flabbergasted. How could she know what No. 137 asked, and, when I stumbled through the answer, could prompt me along?

Years later, I figured it out; in my Irish village one went through the *Maynooth Catechism* at least five times over the years of grade school. I was the youngest of nine children, so this was about her forty-fifth time to tutor the *Catechism*, besides having learned it herself. Beyond her good memory, my story makes the point that the catechism gave parents the confidence to participate in the formal catechesis of their children; there was a consistent set of questions to be asked and there were clear answers to be memorized.

Brief Historical Note

Before the Protestant Reformation, most people were able to recite the Ten Commandments, the Lord's Prayer, and either the Apostles or Nicene Creed—the latter learned by recitation at Mass. With Reformation-era polemics, however, it became urgent for people to know more precisely the data of their faith; claiming two or seven sacraments could decide which side you fought on when the wars broke out. It was Luther who created the first easy-to-memorize, question-and-answer book and called it *The Short Catechism*. It had phenomenal success. Catholicism soon responded in kind; the two most notable early catechisms were penned by Peter Canisius (1559, popular in northern Europe) and by Robert Bellarmine (1598, favored in southern Europe). Many of the national catechisms that followed were indebted to either or both of these two.

At the First Vatican Council (1869–1871), some bishops proposed a universal question-and-answer catechism but the council failed to reach agreement on this. Instead, it encouraged each national episcopacy to write its own catechism. The outcome for the American church was *The Catechism of Christian Doctrine, Prepared and Enjoined by Order of the Third Plenary Council of Baltimore*—known simply as the *Baltimore Catechism*. It was first published in 1885. Cardinal McCloskey of New York gave the imprimatur, and Archbishop Gibbons of Baltimore, as apostolic delegate, gave approval (note, however, that although official approval by Rome was requested, it was never received). Of the *Baltimore Catechism*'s 421 questions and answers, only 10 percent were original, with the rest borrowed and primarily from *Butler's Irish Catechism*—also parent to the *Maynooth Catechism* that I learned as a child.

Limitations of the Baltimore Catechism

The U.S. Church is one of the most vibrant Catholic communities in the history of the world; it stands on the shoulders of "catechism Catholics." As noted earlier, the *Baltimore Catechism* gave people security in the knowledge of their faith and parents a user-friendly way to participate with confidence in the formal catechesis of their children.

However, from the time it was first published, the *Baltimore Catechism* has had its critics and rightly so; I suggest five limitations.

First, its 421 questions and answers were excessive, with many of very limited relevance. For example, it had a whole section on what happened to Jesus between Good Friday afternoon and Easter Sunday morning (where did he spend his time?) as if this were of major concern to people's life in faith.

Second, its selection and presentation of topics reflected no sense of a "hierarchy of truths" to Catholic faith, a core point of Vatican II and of the *Catechism of the Catholic Church* (1994). So, limbo and indulgences are presented as if they are equal in importance to the paschal mystery or the real presence of the Risen Christ in the Eucharist.

Third, and following on, what was emphasized and neglected could actually give a distorted understanding of the Catholic faith. For example, there are eleven questions and answers on purgatory and limbo and seven on indulgences, yet there is *no* direct question on the meaning of Easter.

Fourth, the *Baltimore Catechism* pays no attention to the life and teachings of the historical Jesus. It mentions his birth, of course, but then skips straight to his passion and death on the cross. While its focus on the Christ of faith is valid, its neglect of the Jesus of history leaves a lacuna around how to live as his disciples, the core mandate of Christian faith.

And fifth, one could know the *Baltimore Catechism* backwards and forwards and yet be biblically illiterate. It taught nothing of scripture, only occasionally citing a proof text to verify some Catholic doctrine (e.g., the words of consecration). This oversight was borne out in a religious survey conduced among Catholics in the 1960s; the vast majority could name neither who gave the Sermon on the Mount nor the first book of the Bible.

What to Bring with Us

The critiques notwithstanding, there is a wisdom that we American Catholics should bring with us from the *Baltimore Catechism* even as we leave its text behind. In short: Catholic Christians should know well and be able to recite the core formulas, symbols, and ethics of our faith, and likewise some key Bible verses. Ideally these summaries should be "learned by heart"—in ways that reach far beyond people's heads and memories to the very marrow bone of their lives. Before moving on to make some proposals, I offer two nuances lest we simply settle again for memorizing data.

First, Catholic identity and commitment are nurtured through the socialization of lived faith within family and community. The social sciences regarding identity formation assure us of this, though most of us know it well from our own experience. It was the shared faith that we encountered through parents, parish, and program/school that nurtured our own faith. The "catechism era" was itself the epitome of such socialization in faith. People who urge a return to the *Baltimore Catechism* as a panacea forget that it played only a minor role in nurturing people's faith. Returning to the intentional socialization of its era—practicing Total Community Catechesis—is much more imperative than memorization.

Second, cognitive psychologists and neuroscientists now make an empirical distinction between "explicit" and "implicit" knowledge. The former is what people can readily remember and recall linguistically; the latter has to do with procedures and principles that people internalize, though they might not be able to recite these on cue. I recently had a student I taught twenty-five years ago return to thank me for having changed his life. When I inquired, he could scarcely remember the name of the course, let alone my lecture on Aquinas's theology of nature and grace. And yet, he may have been telling the truth—that I had been an instrument of God's grace to enable him to internalize his faith. That's the "learning outcome" that matters most in catechesis.

A Religiously Literate Catholic

This being said, all Catholics should be "religiously literate" in the essentials of Catholicism and be able to recall their explicit knowledge as needed, whether in response to an invitation, a challenge, or an opportunity. So, what might be some "essentials" that Catholic Christians should be able to recite by heart? Here I make only a few suggestions.

As dogmas and doctrines, Catholics should know a formula that reflects the oneness and threeness of God—the Blessed Trinity; that the one person Jesus Christ was fully divine and fully human; that his death and resurrection were God's definitive catalyst of salvation history; that God's grace in Jesus continues to work through the Holy Spirit; that the Risen Christ is truly present in the Eucharist; that the Church is to be a sacrament of God's reign of holiness and justice in the world.

Regarding worship and prayer, Catholics should be able to name the seven sacraments and have a basic knowledge of the particular grace that each one confers; they should know the centrality of Sunday worship to living as a Catholic Christian; they should be able to recite both Creeds, the Lord's Prayer, the Hail Mary, an act of contrition, a grace before meals, and a morning and evening prayer.

For values and ethical teaching, Catholics should know by heart the Ten Commandments, the great commandment of love, the Beatitudes, the Golden Rule, the cardinal virtues, the Church's teaching on the sanctity of life, and the principles of the Church's social "doctrine."

As we renew the "linguistic literacy" of Catholics, we must honor the intent of Vatican II to re-center the Bible in our faith. Among the core gospel texts that we should know by heart, my list would include:

From Matthew: 7:12 (the golden rule); 22:36–40 (the greatest commandment); 25:40 ("what you did for the least"); 26:26–28 (institution of the Eucharist); 28:18–20 (the great commission)

From Mark: 1:13–15 (reign of God is at hand); 8: 34–35 (take up your cross to follow Jesus); 10:43 (the greatest serves the rest); 15:40–42 (the women at the foot of the cross)

From Luke: 1:30–35 (the Annunciation); 2:4–7 (the birth of Jesus); 4: 16–21 ("the Spirit of Lord is upon me"); 6:27–31 (love of enemies); 24:50–53 (the Ascension)

From John: 1:14 ("Word was made flesh"); 3:16 ("God so loved the world"); 10:10–11 (life abundant and the good shepherd); 11:27 (Martha's confession of faith); 14:6 ("I am the way"); 14:34–35 (new commandment); 20:18 (resurrection confession of Mary Magdalene)

To these we should add some memorable texts from the Hebrew Scriptures and from the rest of the New Testament. So may we bring with us from the catechism era its commitment to linguistic literacy regarding both scripture and tradition.

33

Catholic Schools

Daily Faith

Karen M. Ristau

In the period before Vatican II, especially the 1950s, Catholics in places like Boston, Chicago, New Orleans, Philadelphia, and large urban cities primarily in the East and Midwest lived in an almost totally Catholic world. They bought clothes from Catholic merchants, were treated by Catholic doctors, even went to grocery stores operated by Catholic people. The parish, usually populated exclusively by one particular nationality—Irish, Polish, German, or Italian—was the center of their lives and every parish had a school attended by all the Catholic children in the area. In a given location, the Catholic school might be much larger than any public school. (In 1958, there were nearly 300,000 students in Chicago's Catholic schools.) Catholics were reminded mid-summer by the pastor speaking from the pulpit that all children were to attend the parish school, which more often than not included a secondary school. To do otherwise was to put the child's immortal soul in danger. Parents for the most part accepted all this unquestioningly.

This was not exactly my experience. I grew up in a small town in the Midwest. Our town had a public school, a Lutheran school but not a Lutheran high school, and a Catholic school, elementary and secondary. I did not know if my doctor was a Catholic or where the shopkeepers worshiped unless I saw them by chance in my church.

Mine was not an exclusively Catholic world. But the pastor of our parish—which was comprised of Irish, Germans, Poles, and people from a smattering of other nationalities—always made the mid-summer admonishment to send all children to the parish school. And all the Catholic children I knew attended the parish school. Many of us who began together in first grade (Catholic kindergartens were quite rare—as kindergarten was still not legally required by most states) graduated together twelve years later.

Once I was inside the school-house doors, my experience was more like than unlike that of students in any Catholic school. Now I was in a Catholic world. All the teachers, with rare exceptions— mine being the football coach/homeroom teacher—were members of a congregation of religious women. The school's outward sign of identity was the habit of the sisters and our uniforms, navy plaid. My education provided me with a great deal of information about all things Dominican—the founder, the saints of the congregation, the meaning of the habit, and the way of life. The sisters were particularly important in our lives. We knew they were more than the regular teachers one might have in a public school. We knew they gave their lives to us to teach secular subjects that we would need to be considered educated and to teach us about God and the Church— absolutely essential knowledge for living in this world and in the next!

The normal school day included daily Mass attended by the entire student body and classroom prayers. Religion class was first memorizing and then reciting the questions and answers of the *Baltimore Catechism*—and doing everything possible to get Sister off the lesson by asking every preposterous question we could dream up: If your aunt who isn't Catholic serves hot dogs on Fridays, which is worse, to insult her and make her feel bad or knowingly eat the meat?

School life included preparation for the sacraments—Penance, First Communion, and Confirmation—the latter scheduled for whenever the bishop could get to our parish. Recess often included a visit to the Blessed Sacrament next door in our church. Monthly, class by class, we went to confession; the whole school attended Stations of the Cross during Fridays in Lent; and we crowned the Blessed Mother during May. We were prepared to defend our Catholic faith in any situation and avoided anything that might lead us astray—entering a Protestant church, for example, or seeing a movie condemned by the

Legion of Decency—but we were also busy saving others by collecting money to buy and name a "pagan baby in Africa."

Academic subjects were taken very seriously; effort, utmost effort was expected. Nothing less would be tolerated because we were doing everything—absolutely everything, including perfect Palmer penmanship—for the greater glory of God. The admonition "to whom much is given, much will be expected" was a frequent and believable mantra because each one of us knew we were being given the very best education one could have—a Catholic education that shaped how one would live one's life and arrive at eternal salvation.

Fostering Faith in a New Generation

In the setting of pre–Vatican II Catholic education, the question of Catholic identity was unknown. There was little concern about the non-Catholic in the Catholic school nor, to my knowledge, was there any worry over enrollment numbers. These are today's considerations. Catholic schools once staffed by members of religious communities are now directed and taught mostly by lay persons or religious in secular garb. After years of content-less experimentation in the 1970, the rote question-and-answer learning style of the *Baltimore Catechism* has been replaced by an age-appropriate curriculum that presents religious content, scripture study, and activities to help the student understand faith and apply it to daily life.

Today's schools are staffed primarily by lay people (95.9%).[1] They give witness to the importance of passing on the Catholic faith in a different way than did the members of religious congregations. While living lives much like everyday citizens, living lives similar to those of the students' parents, these teachers nonetheless demonstrate their commitment to students, to furthering both their academic and faith development. Catholic school students still do well academically—99.1 percent graduate from high school in four years, 97 percent go on to post-secondary education. This high number is a credit in no small part to the teachers—who still demand "the very best" from students.

The parish priest—and there were usually several priests in addition to the pastor—was a familiar person to both teachers and students in Catholic schools during the 1950s and 1960s. The pastor was often present in the religion class to hear the students' recitation of the catechism; priests were usually present at school activities—athletic events, plays, and concerts. In many places, the pastor visited each classroom to distribute report cards. Because of the present shortage of priests and the fact that today many priests serve more than one parish, the role of the priest in the school has of necessity changed.

Successful Catholic schools still enjoy the support of pastors who appreciate the value of Catholic education. Strong endorsement has been given by the United States Conference of Catholic Bishops for Catholic education:

> ... Catholic schools afford the fullest and best opportunity to realize the fourfold purpose of Christian education, namely to provide an atmosphere in which the Gospel message is proclaimed, community in Christ is experienced, service to our sisters and brothers is the norm, and thanksgiving and worship of our God [are] cultivated.[2]

Nonetheless, some priests are less than enthusiastic about the Catholic school, citing concerns about the cost of operations. While no one would expect the pastor to speak about mandatory attendance, especially since he also must support all programs of the parish, convincing support from the clergy is imperative and should be expected.

That the Catholic school system continues despite considerable odds gives remarkable testimony to the value and success of its mission. In spite of the severe reduction in the numbers of teaching religious and the decrease in parish financial support, Catholic schools still make up the nation's largest private educational system. Today the schools are less "parochial" and set apart. Serving the broader world provides an opportunity of evangelization and witness beyond ethnic enclaves. Learners spend their days immersed in a Catholic environment with a sense of sacramentality—knowing God in all things. Crucifixes and religious art adorn classrooms, regular celebration of liturgy and daily prayer are part of school life. While the reputation for excellence cannot be taken for granted, no one is providing more affective and intellectual development for the new immigrants—urban minorities—than are Catholic schools. The schools are a demonstration of the Church's commitment to the underserved. Despite challenges of leadership, finances, continued professional and faith development for teachers, and disagreements of some laity with the Church, Catholic schools provide an excellent holistic education for those who choose them and are today an exceptional source of vitality for the Church.

Notes

1. All statistics are from Dale McDonald, P.V.B.M. and Margaret M. Schultz, *United States Catholic Elementary and Secondary Schools, 2007–2008* (Washington, DC: National Catholic Educational Association).

2. United States Conference of Catholic Bishops, *Renewing Our Commitment to Catholic Elementary and Secondary Schools in the Third Millennium* (Washington, DC: USCCB, July 2005), 1.

34

Amica Fidelis, Ora pro Nobis
Devotion to Mary

ADA MARÍA ISASI-DÍAZ

The picture shows a chubby girl dressed in a long white gown with a shiny sash around her waist. She is wearing a veil that also reaches her waist. The girl looks to be about ten years old. She stands as if ready to jump into action, seriously looking beyond the photographer. I look at myself in this picture and remember not the physical details that the camera captured but rather the sentiments and emotions of the moment. It was May 31 and for the second time in my life I was a "Maid of Honor of the Virgin Mary." Every year for the twelve years I went to Catholic school, during the month of May, I was intent on proving to everyone how much I loved the Blessed Virgin Mary.

The Virgin Mary as Childhood Friend

The month of May provided me with the opportunity to show everyone I was a good friend of the Blessed Virgin Mary—a most faithful friend. The system set up by the nuns "to honor the Virgin" was simple but powerful. The idea was to make a "sacrifice for Mary," because, in the pre–Vatican II spirituality of those days, "sacrifice" was the way of showing love. The sacrifice that they asked us to make was one they could measure: we were to keep silence at all times except when participating in class with the teacher's permission. This meant no talking from 8:10 AM when the class bell rang until the end of the school day at 4:10 PM, except for the fifteen-minute mid-morning recess and the lunch break. Looking back on those days I can see that the sacrifice the nuns encouraged us to make in honor of the Virgin Mary was also an effective pedagogical tool. The goal of the nuns was to make us strong women, women of conviction who could make a difference in society. Having us perfectly abide by the school rule on silence was a way of teaching us self-control and self-discipline.

Many of the five hundred girls in the school set out every year on May 1st to show their devotion to the Virgin Mary by becoming one of her "Maids of Honor." Those who kept silence perfectly were rewarded throughout the month. Every day the whole student body would assemble facing the graceful statue of Mary in the middle of the school patio and we would sing and pray to Mary while a floral offering was made by the different classes in the school. On Fridays, the school principal would call out over the loudspeaker the names of the girls who had kept perfect silence. Each would receive a medal of Mary hanging from a tiny silky pale blue bow, which we wore proudly on the lapel of the school white blouse. Every week the medal would be a little bit bigger but—and here was the catch—you could get the second-week medal only if you had gotten the first-week medal and so forth.

However, if you had slipped and you did not get the medal, you still had a chance of being one of the two Maids of Honor selected from each class as the girls who had made the greatest sacrifice, not necessarily the ones who had kept perfect silence. I received many May medals during my twelve years in school and twice I was a Maid of Honor of the Virgin Mary. The nuns hardly ever gave me more than a B- in "deportment," and at least once I got a D (a terrible stain in my record since the passing grade in the school was C). But every year, during May, I had an opportunity to redeem myself. I could show them all that I was a good girl and that I loved the Virgin Mary so much that I could keep perfect silence, and that even if I failed, I would keep trying.

For the Love of Mary

The Virgin Mary was my friend and I proudly showed her my love by earning those May medals. I might not manage to be disciplined the rest of the year, but during May, for love of the Virgin Mary, I could keep quiet. I do not remember a single year when I considered giving up trying. On the contrary, year after year I would throw myself wholeheartedly into my May project. For me this had nothing to do with the nuns or school rules. May was about the Virgin Mary and me. She was a very personal friend and in times of trouble—when I had broken some school rule or was being punished by Mamá for fighting with my brothers and sisters or disobeying her—I always turned to the Virgin Mary. I was always making deals with her. I would ask her to do the impossible: "Please, could you make Mother Raphael forget she punished me for having the back of my blouse full of scribbles? Look, if you help me, I promise to say twenty Rosaries today before going to sleep."

Of course, by the time Mamá came for me and my sisters at the end of the school day, the principal had already called her, and on top of my having to go to school in a dress instead of the school uniform—which hurt me so very much besides shaming me—Mamá added her own punishment, and I had to put on my pajamas and go to bed as soon as I came home from school. Yet, for some reason I do not know even today, I never got upset or angry with the Virgin Mary. On the contrary, I was most generous in my relationship with her. For example, when I was in distress, it never occurred to me that to say the Rosary twenty times would take me five hours and there was no way I could do it before falling asleep. Having failed to keep such a promise, I would seriously ask her pardon and renegotiate my promise. "Look, Virgin Mary, I am sorry I fell asleep but you know that I am good for what I promise. Listen, let me make it up to you. I will add twenty more Rosaries to the eighteen I owe you from yesterday." I kept strict count and I remember accumulating in several years a debt of more than fifty Rosaries!

Though undoubtedly all of this was childish, the Virgin Mary became a friend forever. I trusted her unconditionally. I had no doubt that she was as faithful to me as I was to her. I never related to her as "mother." I suppose because I had a very good relationship with my mother, who loved me, valued me, and cared for me, I did not need another mother. The Virgin Mary was my friend. Beliefs about her being the Mother of God, her virginity, her being free from original sin, and her being assumed into heaven body and soul at the time of her death—all of it was irrelevant to me. None of this influenced me in picking her as a very special friend. Mary was my friend because she understood me, cared for me, thought I was worthwhile—she never would give me a D in deportment! She knew I was a good girl. My unruliness was just a matter of my enthusiastic way of being and had much to do with my always wanting to be involved, my being curious, and my having a good dose of not being challenged sufficiently. Yes! Perfect silence during May was a strong challenge and I rose up to that occasion year after year.

Mary: My Friend in the Struggle for Justice

Years later I entered the convent, for in the 1960s there was no other way for a Catholic girl to be involved in the ministry of the Catholic Church. From the beginning, I struggled to fit into the mold, to be a good nun according to the canons of that time. The fact is that I did not succeed. Very early on, one of the nuns in charge of formation chided me by throwing in my face my devotion to Mary. "You say you have so much devotion to the Blessed Mother, why are you not obedient like she was?" I was so pained by this comment. I was also furious, furious! Later that day I went for a walk down a long road lined with trees on both sides and surrounded by open fields beyond flimsy fences. I cried and cried. I do not remember praying, or even thinking. I never really articulated it clearly, even to myself, but from that day on I began to draw away from Mary. I felt I had to choose between being myself and trying to imitate Mary. I knew I had to be faithful to myself and I could not embrace the submissive Blessed Mother who was being proposed as a model. I did not consciously stop praying to Mary. As a matter of fact, I continued for many years to say the Rosary every day. But for the longest time I just did not confide in Mary, I did not talk to her, I did not strike any deals with her.

Years later I went to Peru as a missionary, became involved in the then incipient liberation movement, and confirmed what I had suspected all along: the message of the gospel is one of justice, not one of obedience and submission. I still remember clearly the first day I heard a hymn to Mary that used her words in the Magnificat. *"En mi Dios, mi Salvador, me salta el alma de gozo, pues el Santo y Poderoso, ha hecho en mí maravillas, por ser pequeña y sencilla."* ("In my God, my Savior, my soul leaps with joy for the Holy and Powerful One, has done marvels in me because I am small and simple"). Somehow the simple melody soothed the hurt I had been carrying for several years and I was able once again to begin claiming my friendship with Mary. To this very day I often sing the chorus of this song, reveling in Mary's unbelievably truthful simplicity and humility, in her never sacrificing her mind or her will. She was no malleable clay in God's hands but a clear-headed woman who asked questions, learned what she needed in order to make an informed decision, and then decided for herself. "The Holy and Powerful One has done marvels in me," are the words the gospel puts on her lips. She does not deny her greatness; she does not fall into any pious self-obliteration.

Mary continues to be the friend she always was. I greet her every morning under the invocation of Our Lady of Charity, patroness of my birth country, Cuba. She comforts me in my disappointments and losses. She challenges me, as only a friend can, to an ever stronger commitment to the kin-dom of God, to the *familia de Dios* whose first-born she birthed and whose disciples she has always encouraged. Mary, whose Maid of Honor I was in my growing up years, yes, she is my friend!

35

Contraception

Conflict and Estrangement in the Recent Catholic Past

Leslie Woodcock Tentler

The American Historical Background

Catholic teaching on contraception—that no means of fertility control is morally licit save for prolonged or periodic abstinence—is almost as old as the Church itself. But for long stretches of the Church's history, the teaching did not figure prominently in terms of pastoral practice. As late as 1910, the American laity heard few if any sermons in which birth control was addressed. (Mission sermons were sometimes, but only sometimes, an exception to the general rule.) Nor was the sin of contraception usually mentioned in the printed "examinations of conscience" available to those who were preparing to go to confession, or even discussed at length in handbooks for confessors. Contraception was simply not a topic of polite public discourse. And apparently many priests believed that some of their immigrant parishioners were ignorant of the various means of birth control. Talking about it might inadvertently lead them into temptation.[1]

Matters had changed dramatically by the early 1930s. The rise of a pro-contraception movement in the United States, something that dated from the time of the First World War, was seen by many church leaders as requiring a vigorous Catholic response. In the 1920s, mission preachers routinely inveighed against birth control in frank and

graphically condemnatory language. The Catholic press and a growing pamphlet literature denounced contraception too. Surviving evidence does suggest that confessors were still quite reticent, seldom in-
terrogating penitents with regard to this particular sin and even
responding in cursory fashion when the sin was actually confessed. But
evasive strategies like these were much less common after *Casti Connubii*, Pope Pius XI's encyclical on Christian marriage, published in
the last days of 1930. *Casti Connubii* affirmed, in clear and unmistak-
able terms, the Catholic prohibition on contraception. (Interestingly,
it was the first papal encyclical to do so.) It also summoned confessors
to do battle against what the Vatican apparently regarded as widespread ignorance of the teaching.

For roughly the next forty years, the teaching on contraception
stood at the heart of Catholic life and practice in the United States. This
does not mean that the teaching was universally observed. Catholic birth
rates and the testimony of confessors, not to mention common sense,
tell us that it was not. But especially in the late 1940s and the 1950s,
with a revivified economy and broad cultural support for large families,
a great many Catholics tried to live this demanding and increasingly distinctive aspect of their faith. (Most Protestant denominations made public peace with contraception over the course of the 1930s.) Only 30 percent of the married Catholics queried in a 1955 study acknowledged
ever having used a means of fertility control forbidden by their Church.
In that same year, college-educated Catholic women—particularly those
who were graduates of Catholic institutions—were among those who
had the nation's highest birth rates, even though college education for
women nearly always correlates with low fertility.

Catholic compliance with the teaching rested in part on fear—
specifically, the fear of hell. Contraception was always a mortal sin,
motives and circumstances notwithstanding. But fear was only part of
the story. In these same years, the teaching on contraception was increasingly presented to the laity in attractively personalist terms. Couples were less and less likely to hear that marital sex was potentially
dangerous, coarsening in its effects if the spouses indulged too
freely—an argument favored by clerical writers as late as the 1930s.
After 1945, and especially in the context of groups like Cana Conference and the Christian Family Movement, they learned instead that
martial sex was akin to prayer—a means of communion not just with
one's spouse but also with God. It was meant to be joyous, spontaneous, and—presumably, given the analogy—frequent.

The Crisis and Its Aftermath

Highly educated young Catholics were particularly grateful for this newly positive assessment of marital sex. But, as they sooner or later learned, the fertility of a healthy couple who, like most Americans in the 1950s, married young made frequent sex a risky business. One might turn after several children to the "rhythm method," a physiologically plausible version of which was first publicized in the 1930s. But rhythm nearly always required a lengthy period of abstinence every month. Sex on a rhythm schedule was less-than-frequent and inevitably less-than-spontaneous. It did not much resemble the vision implicit in the gospel according to Cana.

Other factors pressed on Catholic couples in the post-war period, too: the expectation—new to their generation—that all their children needed college; more exacting standards of child nurture; even worries—again, new to their generation—about global population growth. It was probably inevitable that the frustrations bred by this concatenation of circumstances would eventually go public. By 1964, Catholic periodicals and even the secular press were carrying what soon became a flood of lay criticism with regard to church teaching on contraception. The rhythm method, according to many, put intolerable strains on a marriage—not just physically but emotionally as well. And because it was widely regarded as an unreliable mode of family limitation, it was also said to endanger the well-being of children, who might as a result of too frequent births lack adequate nurture and education. Testimony of this sort, ubiquitous by 1966, was sufficiently frank and theologically literate that it altered the practice of countless confessors, not to mention the thinking of prominent moral theologians. By 1967, even quite moderate theologians were willing to call the teaching "doubtful." As for confessors, growing numbers either absolved without comment when a penitent confessed to birth control or—if their counsel was sought—advised the penitent to follow his or her conscience.

Pope Paul VI was certainly aware of this unprecedented tide of lay dissent. It had clearly shaped the thinking of the advisory commission on birth control he inherited from his predecessor—Pope John XXIII had established that commission in 1963, thereby removing the topic of birth control from the agenda of the Second Vatican Council—and which Paul VI had greatly enlarged. It is true that Pope Paul reaffirmed the traditional teaching in *Humanae Vitae*, issued in the summer of 1968. But that encyclical also acknowledged the new lay assertiveness in its positive language regarding marital sex and in its pastoral sympathy extended to couples in hard circumstances.

Still, many laity felt in the wake of the encyclical that the pope had not heard them. Lay dissent by the late 1960s had moved beyond complaints that the traditional teaching was inhumanly difficult to a moral indictment of the teaching, which more and more laity seemed to regard as pernicious in both its assumptions and effects. Marriage is fundamentally a sexual relationship, the lay dissenters said; sexual expression in marriage has its own integrity, to which procreation is essential but of which it is only a part. We need a theology of marriage that is grounded in our experience as Christian spouses and parents, one that speaks to the complex realities of our lives in the world. It must simultaneously address both respect for life and the embodied nature of human love.

For all its pastoral sensitivity, *Humanae Vitae* was not congruent with such a theology. As Garry Wills has aptly noted, it ultimately judges marriage by celibate standards.[2] The "unitive" aspect of the marital act can never stand alone, according to the encyclical; contraceptive sex, in part because of its presumed frequency, was described as undermining a husband's respect for his wife; periodic abstinence was said to have beneficial effects not just on a couple's relationship but also the emotional climate of the home. Such assertions were for a great many laity not only demonstrably false but morally mischievous. Even the pope's justifiable worries about the negative social effects of the contraceptive revolution—worries that nearly all Catholic parents shared—could not win assent for *Humanae Vitae* among most American laity, 54 percent of whom told Gallup's pollsters in August 1968 that they disagreed with the encyclical. Only 28 percent of those polled were willing to give it their assent.[3]

A good many priests disagreed with the encyclical, too—about half of them by 1970, according to Andrew Greeley.[4] And even those who supported the pope were often reluctant to enforce the teaching, either in the pulpit or in the confessional. Why risk further alienating an already prickly laity? It did not help that fewer and fewer penitents were frequenting confession, a trend that seems to have first been evident in 1966 but which accelerated sharply after *Humanae Vitae*. Nor were the laity generally disposed to consult the clergy about contraception in other settings. Having made up their minds on the matter, they now kept their own counsel. With an initial sense of relief, the clergy did too. Even liberal priests were not eager to be flagged as dissenters on an issue that had evident staying power in Rome.

Thus, shortly after *Humanae Vitae*, public silence descended on the subject of contraception. Moral theologians turned to what they frankly regarded as more interesting matters. Having issued a compromise statement in support of *Humanae Vitae*, the American hierarchy was largely silent too. The silence did buy breathing room—a space in which angry laity might make their personal peace with the Church. But at a very high cost. The enduring silence on *Humanae Vitae*—and that is what has prevailed, despite occasional iterations of its central prohibition—means that Catholics since the 1970s have formed their consciences on matters sexual without much input from their Church. How could it be otherwise, given that their clergy have been so effectively muzzled? If one can't speak honestly about contraception in terms that the laity regard as moral, one can't really talk about sex at all.

Wisdom from a Conflicted Past

What, if anything, can we retrieve from so widely discredited a teaching? (Adjusting for income and education, Catholic contraceptive use has long been indistinguishable from that of other Americans.) We obviously don't want to return to the rigid, act-centered moral theology in which the teaching was embedded. Motives and circumstances do matter. Nor do we want to infuse married life with the guilt and tension the teaching often gave rise to. But that teaching, whatever its inadequacies, did embody a high moral seriousness about sex. It made clear that sex is in fact a "life issue"—that whatever its role in enhancing a couple's relationship or indeed in making life pleasurable, sex is most fundamentally the means by which human life is transmitted. A truly Christian sexual ethic must take this reality into account.

Back in the mid-1960s, when the intra-Catholic debate over contraception was at its height, lay Catholics often spoke in terms of a renewed theology of marriage. Marriage is our principal route to sanctity, they argued. We have learned from our own experience and indeed from our Church that joyous sexual communion is essential to the growth of marital love and hence, quite literally, to our salvation. Perhaps this truth might best be expressed—and this was a widely popular formulation—by insisting that every marriage, rather than every sexual act, must be open to conception. Children are indeed gifts from God, to paraphrase the argument. But spouses are also gifts to each other.

The conversation just described did not address today's most contested questions. No one spoke about non-marital sex, much less homosexuality. Nonetheless, that conversation is a model for us in two important ways: first, because it *was* a conversation—made possible by the honesty of all parties to it and their willingness to listen and learn; and second, because all participants accepted as a fundamental premise that the Christian tradition possesses enduring wisdom with regard to sex. Can we revive such a conversation in our own time? That, it seems to me, is one of the most important questions facing today's Church.

Notes

1. Information in this and the following paragraphs comes from my *Catholics and Contraception: An American History* (Ithaca, NY: Cornell University Press, 2004).

2. Garry Wills, *Bare Ruined Choirs: Doubt, Prophecy, and Radical Religion* (Garden City, NY: Doubleday & Company, 1972), 186.

3. Figures quoted in Maurice J. Moore, "Death of a Dogma? The American Catholic Clergy's Views of Contraception" (PhD dissertation, Department of Sociology, University of Chicago, 1972), 19.

4. Andrew M. Greeley, *The Catholic Priest in the United States: Sociological Investigations* (Washington, DC: United States Catholic Conference, 1972), 106.

36

The Last Sacrament

From Extreme Unction to the Anointing of the Sick

WILLIAM MADGES

Extreme Unction was the name Catholics used prior to the Second Vatican Council to refer to what today is called the sacrament of the Anointing of the Sick. As the name "Extreme Unction" suggests, this sacrament involved a final anointing before death; for this reason, it was also called "last rites" or "the sacrament of the dying." My first experience with this pre–Vatican II ritual of the sacrament was also my most personal.

In the early morning hours of June 30, 1956, our house in Detroit was astir with anxious activity. A siren blared outside, signaling the arrival of the Fire Department's Rescue Squad. They had been called because my father had suddenly been stricken ill. At the time, we did not know what the problem was. My father Mike had awakened with a very stiff neck. In response to his complaint, my mother Mary went quickly to the medicine cabinet in the bathroom to retrieve a tube of Ben-Gay, thinking that his neck was stiff from the hot and physical work of loading and unloading the ovens at the Silvercup Baking Company. As my mother rubbed the ointment into his neck, he let out a groan and his head slumped back against the headboard of their bed. My mother quickly determined that he was unconscious.

At about the time the firefighters arrived, our parish priest, Father Szelc, rang the doorbell. We lived on the second floor of a two-family house, which we shared with my aunt and uncle. At the time, I was three-and-a-half years old. I don't recall who greeted Father Szelc at the door, but I do remember how he was welcomed. Either my mother or my aunt met our parish priest at the door with a lit candle. The "sick kit," consisting of two candles and a crucifix, had already been set up in the bedroom within sight of my parents' bed. This was standard procedure when someone was taken gravely ill at home and a priest had been summoned to administer Extreme Unction. After a few quick words spoken in an attempt to reassure my mother, Father Szelc came upstairs, entered the bedroom, approached my father's prone form, and began the rite of Extreme Unction.

Because of my age, I did not understand what was taking place. I did not know what was wrong with my father and why he would not wake up, despite the commotion in the room. All I knew was that something serious had happened and Mom was very upset. A couple of firefighters were in the bedroom as well. My memories of the performance of the rite are quite fuzzy, but some of the graphic images that stayed with me include the priest saying some words (I later learned that they were prayers), sprinkling with holy water, and anointing. When Father Szelc was finished, the firefighters quickly loaded my father's body onto a stretcher, carried him down the steps, out of the house, and into the waiting red truck, whose siren started up again as it raced away from our house.

My mother returned home in the evening, bringing with her the very sad news that my father had died. Dead at the age of 39, killed by a cerebral hemorrhage. Up to that point, I knew nothing of death and I certainly had no idea what the words "cerebral hemorrhage" meant. All I knew was that my mother had come home alone. She constantly dabbed her eyes, as she alternated between uncontrollable sobbing and some level of composure. I thought that Dad was sick, but that, when he got better, he would come home.

A Suitable *or a* Necessary *Sacrament?*

As I think back to that day many decades later, I am somewhat surprised by what I do remember. The images of our parish priest, the lit candles, the somber procession of the priest into my parents' bedroom, and the "strange" ritual of sprinkling and rubbing oil on my father are all extant in my memory.

Because Dad was already unconscious, Father Szelc did not hear his confession nor did he give him "Viaticum," that is, Holy Communion, which, as the Latin word suggests, was intended to be "food for the journey" from this life to the next.

What was done sacramentally with my father and why was it done? How did these actions fit into the belief system and religious practice of Catholics before the reforms of the Second Vatican Council?

Three characteristics define the belief system that undergirds the pre–Vatican II practice of the sacrament. First, it was the sacrament that was administered to those who had reached the end of their life, those who were on the very threshold of death. Second, the sacrament was desired, both by the person dying and by his or her family, because it was intended to free the dying person of the last remnants of sin, thus preparing him or her for entrance into the glory of heaven. In the pre–Vatican II Church, great emphasis was placed on the need to perform good works to attain an increase in grace and to overcome sin. To be in full communion with the God who is sinless, one needed to be purged of sin. Reception of the sacraments helped one to achieve this end. Third, the rite of Extreme Unction occurred usually in the company of one's immediate family or closest relatives. As a person departed from this life, he or she naturally wanted to be encircled by the love of family.

With the changes effected by the Second Vatican Council, those three characteristics were modified. First, the sacrament is no longer regarded as appropriate only for those who are at the point of death. According to the new rite, the sacrament should be administered to anyone who is seriously ill. This shift is reflected in the change of the sacrament's name from Extreme Unction or the sacrament of the dying to the sacrament of the Anointing of the Sick. This sacrament can be administered to those who are about to undergo surgery and it can be received more than once during the same illness. Second, the new rite exhibits a more holistic understanding of the person who receives it and, concomitantly, a more holistic understanding of the sacrament itself. The prayer for blessing the oil in the new rite (no. 75) prays that the person receiving it may "be freed from pain, illness, and disease and made well again in body, mind, and soul."[1] By contrast, in the pre–Vatican II era it was the penitential-spiritual aspect of the sacrament that was almost exclusively emphasized. Third, the context in which the sacrament is administered today has expanded from a tightly familial to a more broadly communal context. As Vatican II's Constitution on the Sacred Liturgy (*Sacrosanctum Concilium*) states, liturgical services are not private functions, but are "celebrations of the Church." Consequently, whenever rites make provision for communal celebration involving the active participation of the faithful, this way of celebrating is to be preferred to a celebration that is individual and quasi-private.[2]

Retrieval or Rejection?

Is there anything in the pre–Vatican II experience of the sacrament that ought to be retained? Or should much or all of that previous rite be rejected? A salutary development that occurred with the Second Vatican Council was the attempt to regain balance in understanding the purposes of this sacrament. Although the penitential aspect of the sacrament should be retained today, the earlier rite's overemphasis upon the gravity of sin needs to be rejected. The consciousness of sin and of the need for forgiveness needs to be balanced with an affirmation of faith in God's mercy. Moreover, the prayer for the remission of sin needs to be augmented with a prayer for strength and healing, in body as well as in soul. The Second Vatican Council sought to restore a balance between the spiritual and the physical, the heavenly and the earthly. Consequently, the current rite is more holistic and therefore more appropriate, not only to our context today, but also to the early history of the Church when the anointing was administered to the sick, not simply the dying, and when there was prayer for healing in body as well as soul.[3]

Another aspect of the pre–Vatican II rite that can be retained is an appreciation of the power of the sacrament in bringing solace and comfort not only to those who receive it but also to their families and loved ones. In the twentieth century prior to the Second Vatican Council, Catholics often carried cards in their wallets or wore medals around their necks that stated "I am a Catholic. In the event of an emergency, call a priest." These cards were meant to help ensure that emergency personnel or police officers would call a priest to administer Extreme Unction to the Catholic in need. Few Catholics today carry such a card or wear such a medal. I think that this is an indication that, in the pre–Vatican II Church, there was a much stronger sense of the "necessity" of the sacrament in bringing appropriate closure to this life. This sense of the sacrament's importance, an appreciation of the psychological as well as the religious benefits of the sacrament in preparing the recipient to face serious illness or death with strength and hope, are features of the pre–Vatican II rite that can be meaningfully retrieved. If that appreciation is joined to Vatican II's understanding of the grace conferred in sacraments, not as a thing but as a gracious encounter with the divine Spirit through Christ, then this sacrament of the sick can become a powerful and effective symbol of God's love. "Christ" means "the Anointed One." For the person of faith, then, receiving the anointing with oil can be a powerful experience of feeling the healing touch and loving embrace of Christ and the Christian community.[4] In times of serious illness, such a feeling is most welcome.

Notes

1. *Anointing and Pastoral Care of the Sick: Commentary on the Rite for the Anointing and Pastoral Care of the Sick* (Washington, DC: U.S. Catholic Conference, 1973), 22.

2. Second Vatican Council, Constitution on the Sacred Liturgy, nos. 26 and 27, in *Decrees of the Ecumenical Councils,* 2 vols., ed. Norman P. Tanner (Washington, DC: Georgetown University Press, 1990), 2:826.

3. James L. Empereur, *Prophetic Anointing: God's Call to the Sick, the Elderly, and the Dying* (Wilmington, DE: Michael Glazier, Inc., 1982), 25–64. *Anointing and Pastoral Care of the Sick,* 18–21.

4. Peter E. Fink, "Anointing of the Sick and the Forgiveness of Sins," in *Recovering the Riches of Anointing: A Study of the Sacrament of the Sick* (Collegeville, MN: Liturgical Press, 2002), 27–33.

37

All the Angels and Saints

What Happened to Them?

DOLORES R. LECKEY

During the years of my growing up Catholic in the pre–Vatican II period, the first part of the Mass almost always included a short, but to my mind, powerful prayer: the Confiteor. It was prayed in Latin but my missal had a translation. A more recent post–Vatican II translation (1973, ICEL) is as follows:

> I confess to almighty God,
> and to you, my brothers and sisters,
> that I have sinned through my own fault,
> in my thoughts and in my words,
> in what I have done and in what I have failed to do;
> and I ask blessed Mary, ever virgin,
> *all the angels and saints,*
> and you, my brothers and sisters,
> to pray for me to the Lord our God.

As a child I focused on the unseen but very real presence of angels and saints. It was important to me, especially since I lived in an urban setting with parents who were older (and so in my mind, closer to death) and with brothers who were serving in World War II. In the midst of all this uncertainty I could reach out to the spirit-world for help, guidance, solace.

Angels

Like most Catholic children, I learned at an early age the prayer to my guardian angel.

Angel of God, my guardian dear,
to whom God's love commits me here,
ever this day be at my side,
to light and guard, to rule and guide. Amen

We were taught that we each had our own angel who was very close at hand.

At some point I reasoned that if I could ask *my* angel for help of all kinds I could also pray to my endangered brothers' angels who were with them in the war zones. The invisible angelic guardians were a source of comfort during the years of my childhood.

As I moved into adulthood, and with a certain amount of exposure to theology, the angelic world grew more remote to me. My experience is to a certain extent reflected in the four paintings of the American artist Thomas Cole called "Stages of a Man's Life." The paintings are in a permanent exhibit at The National Gallery of Art in Washington D.C.

In the first painting a young boy is in a boat, setting out from shore, and close by an angel keeps watch. This is the "childhood" painting. The second painting is "adolescence," with the angel more distant from the young man. In the third stage, "adulthood," the angel is barely visible, far from the boat, on the margins of the man's life. Finally in the fourth painting, "old age," the angel is once again a close companion.

Guardian angels returned to prominence in my own life when I had children. During one of the sessions of the Second Vatican Council, word came to Washington from Rome that the words of absolution in the sacrament of Penance—traditionally in Latin—could now be said in the vernacular, in this case, English. However, when I arrived at the confessional I learned that the priest was a visiting German Franciscan, and while the absolution was in his language (German), his exhortation to me was in strained and hesitant English. Still, I understood the meaning. He told me to develop a devotion to my children's guardian angels, casting that in terms of the greatest gift I could give them. I received those German-English words with seriousness and gratitude. Guardian angels were back in my life—at least for my kids.

With the Second Vatican Council urging Catholics to read and reflect on the Bible, a more scriptural presentation of the celestial world was available. We encountered the archangels, messengers from God who often appeared in human guise urging biblical characters, and by extension us, not to be afraid. The message, in its essence, was (and is) to trust God and to trust the inner word that reverberates in all of us. We are told to extend hospitality to strangers because many have entertained angels in such gracious outreaches.

Over the years I have come to appreciate the archangels Gabriel and Raphael in their difficult assignments. The repercussions of Gabriel's encounter with Mary of Nazareth continue to this day. Everything that we as Catholic Christians believe is linked to that moment when Gabriel announced God's plan for Mary, and for the world.

And Raphael's task, that of accompanying Tobias on a perilous journey and facilitating his eventual marriage to Sarah (a love story full of suspense and mystery), is deserving of admiration. Surely the value of perseverance in matters of love is demonstrated in this story.

I have sometimes wondered if all our prayers to Michael the archangel, prayers that in pre–Vatican II years we said at the end of every Mass did, indeed, move Communist Russia to a form of conversion. Might the archangels be called upon today to help our broken world heal and achieve some modicum of peace?

As great emissaries of God, could Raphael walk through Gaza? Gabriel linger awhile in Jerusalem? Michael hold back forces bent on war? Why not?

Saints

Saints shared my childhood world as well. My first experience of answered prayer occurred when I was eleven years old. I had been introduced to Mary's title Our Lady of Good Counsel in religion class where it had been explained that Mary can guide us to solve problems that are upsetting. I had a problem and was very upset. The problem was jealousy. I was jealous of the attention that a favorite nun was showing to another student. I reacted by withdrawing from all contact with the nun and the student (thus engaging in what I can recognize now as passive/aggressive behavior), and as a result I was disconsolate and inwardly agitated. One evening, in desperation, I fell to my knees and asked Our Lady of Good Counsel what I should do. Before long I stopped crying because I had a clear idea of what was needed. An apology. I would apologize to Sister. The decision to do so brought peace and the act itself deepened the peace. Mary, first among the saints, led me to needed action. And today, Mary is my doorway to the communion of saints.

My childhood bedroom housed a collection of plaster statues of saints who stood watch on my dresser, knowing and wise. I was happy to have St. Anthony there, because he could help me find lost things, and Joseph, whom I knew to be the patron of a happy death (but I didn't want to think about that too much). One of my favorites was Thérèse of Lisieux who taught how little acts of care and responsibility (for example, picking up after oneself) could lead to sainthood. St. Thérèse's doctrine of "the little way" was a relief to me because as I grew older I knew that I did not want to emulate the idiosyncratic behaviors of many saints (such as St. Francis of Assisi's taking off all his clothes in the public square to make a point with his father). My non-Catholic friends were enchanted to learn that we Catholics have a patron saint for every need: St. Genesius for stage jitters and other theater-related problems; St. Appolonius for courage when facing the dentist; St. Dorothy for eye problems; St. Brendan for the protection of sailors—and on and on, into eternity.

Communion of Saints

In recent years there has been expanded theological reflection on the Christian doctrine of the communion of saints. Dr. Elizabeth Johnson, C.S.J., is in the forefront of this particular area of study.[1]

I have recently written about my own personal experience of the communion of saints in the context of Vespers (the evening prayer of the Church), which I prayed regularly following the death of my husband. My major discovery was that I was not alone. I wrote:

> In these times of prayer, the communion of saints, a cornerstone of Catholic belief, enshrined in Christian creeds, became palpable. Traditionally the communion of saints referred to the dead only. The communion I experienced included not only my husband, but friends, public figures, culture in its many forms, and the social contexts in which we all live. The difference between loneliness and aloneness took on a new clarity as

my life experience expanded into communion. I began to probe the meaning of resurrection, our resurrection . . .

and

Whom do we count in the communion of saints? Surely the canonical saints, and surely our own beloved dead, all of them silently moving in and out of our daily lives. But there are the living, too. Known and unknown to us personally are those whose simple, ordinary lives give glory to God.[2]

The Catholic symbol of the communion of saints reflects the conviction that the bond of Baptism is never broken, not even by death. So, those now in the eternal presence of God can continue to intercede for us.

Angels and Saints Today

What, then, has happened to all the angels and saints? They are where they have always been, in the horizon of our personal and public worlds, an ever-expanding cloud of witnesses. These friends of God exercise a watchful love and, representing God's effective love for us in the everyday, encourage us to trust in God. They inspire us to purposeful lives, not in the context of first century Palestine or Asia Minor, but in this time and in many diverse places and cultures. Their presence is a blessing. *Deo gratias.*

Notes

1. Elizabeth Johnson, C.S.J., *Truly Our Sister: A Theology of Mary in the Communion of Saints* (New York: Continuum, 2003)

2. Dolores R. Leckey, *Grieving with Grace* (Cincinnati, Ohio: St. Anthony Messenger Press, 2008).

38

Catholic Eucharist, before and after Vatican II

RICHARD ROHR, O.F.M.

"Lord, I Am Not Worthy to Receive You"

When I was growing up in the 1940s and 1950s in Kansas, I think you could say that "going to Mass" and being a Roman Catholic were pretty much the same thing. Everything seemed to circle around when, where, how much, if, and how worthily you "attended Mass." You could perhaps call it religion as "attendance" and preparation for attendance. The Eucharist gave us our corporate, spiritual, and social identity, and did it quite well on many levels. It rightly said that true religion was about "going to Communion."

Lines formed outside confessionals on Saturday afternoons and even before weekday Masses to prepare us to "receive in the state of grace." Fasting was strictly observed from midnight, so Masses were usually early in the morning for those who wished to communicate. I remember when the Monsignor yelled at me for drinking from the school water fountain, and said "I better not see you in the communion line!" I was rightly shamed. There was no wine for anyone but the priest in those days. All was done in silence except for the reverent murmuring of the priest and the organ songs that we listened to in the background. It was actually quite contemplative or at least pleasing to introverts.

Coming in and going out anonymously and quietly was almost considered part of the reverence. You came for God and not for community. Most of the Eucharist's transformative work seems to have been at the subliminal level; the medium was the message, with no great emphasis on sermon or lectionary, adult education, or personal involvement with the parish beyond offering the Sunday "envelope." The priests were the ministers, nobody else. It was definitely the "mystical" Body of Christ. But believe it or not, it kept the edges of Catholic identity "hot," clear, and even vibrant for many. The power of agreed-upon and shared ritual is far more powerful than most people realize.

Many—if not most—moral obligations and spiritual teaching were largely tied up with worthiness to receive Communion or not, and attendance at Sunday Mass was one of the six "commandments of the Church." So well taught was this commandment that most confessors to this day would find "missing Mass on Sunday or a holy day" the number-one sin confessed. We were required to actually go to Communion only once a year, however, and that during the Easter Time. No one told us that there were at least fifteen other "rites" of the Mass, fully honored by Rome. It was a bit of chosen ignorance and arrogance on the part of the Latin Rite, and still a source of insult to many groups from Maronite to Malabar Catholic traditions.

Transcendent Catholicism

The repetitious and routine words of the Mass (only one Eucharistic Prayer was known) in a foreign "sacred" language lent it a profound sense of an otherworldly mystery that we were privileged to observe, "understand," and enjoy. While it kept us grounded, it also allowed us to remain largely "unconscious" as to any specific mission or message beyond "keep coming back." Only the feasts and seasons changed—but not the substance or the words of the Mass. The colors of the vestments, the readings from a single cycle, the number of candles, the feast day variations were all anticipated by the fervent, often by nine days of preparation, called novenas; major feasts were anticipated by vigils or vespers. This gave many of us a sense of the eternal, the cyclical, and the calming that comes from order and definition. The priest and his role in the transubstantiation of the bread and the wine into the Body and Blood of Jesus Christ created a personal and corporate *axis mundi*, an objective center for everything Catholic. Our hierarchical figures held us together as one. The priest dressed differently and didn't marry; lots of us fully believed that he was almost metaphysically different.

"This is the day we bless the throats, this is the day of the May Crowning, this is the parish feast day, these are the 'Rogation Days,' this is when we process through the streets displaying the Blessed Eucharist." We knew these days and traditions by heart, and we looked forward to them, almost as if they defined the very nature of the cosmos. On this day or that, special graces were granted as on no other day, because of this patron, this promise, this indulgence, this shrine. It all created immense and immediate expectation—now, here, today—*this* is the day of salvation (an expectation we seem to have lost). Rituals, repetition, and remembrances such as these work at profound levels in human consciousness.

The Mass held us together inside of a "numinous" world and also somehow inside of ourselves. It gave a sacred meaning to most human suffering. It created a Catholic people that transcended nationality and race and century. Transcendence was made available in a way that no one doubted. The vertical line of salvation was very clear; not so much, however, the horizontal. Ironically we did not talk about Jesus that much, or even his practical teaching. The common phrases were "Our Blessed Lord," "The Lord," "Christ," or "Our Lord and Savior." It was a pretty formal and awesome relationship we had, nothing too personal or active, except for some pious types.

In most places religion appeared to be more a civil matter than an encounter with the living Jesus. Jesus' concerns for peacemaking, humility, a simple life style, and present-day healing were not high on our list (in terms of healing, "Extreme Unction" was enough). Jesus was surely more in the Eucharist than in us. The Eucharist was the "true body," *corpus verum*; people were merely the *corpus mysticum*. This was a strange transposition if you believe that the Eucharist is to feed the people and not the other way around.

I was a fervent altar boy in 1950s Topeka and rose early to ride my bike to the church that faced the Kansas capitol building. Like all altar boys of that time, I knew my role, gestures, and prayers perfectly, and would not have thought of being late or bothering Father or talking loudly in the sacristy. As soon as we rang the sanctuary bell, the well-trained organist began the same "Introit" to the same Mass formula (on almost all days except first class feasts), the Requiem Mass. We ordinarily set out the black vestments for Father, because much of our concern was rescuing the poor souls from purgatory. Without exaggeration, the typical parish had become a funeral society showing more daily concern for praying for the dead than healing the living.

Some parts of the country actually had separate Eucharists and churches for the different ethnic groups, especially blacks and Mexicans. I recently heard of one church in Colorado where the Anglos sat in the center pews and the Mexicans on the sides as late as the 1960s. It makes one wonder how effective the Eucharist was in changing society beyond its message of personal salvation.

Mystification or Mystery?

So what was lost and what was gained by the liturgical reforms of the Vatican II? I think we lost community as a free and solid given. Today we "create" community by choice, study, action, or conversation, and not totally by the rituals. We also lost any strong sense of group identity, which was very effectively maintained by uniform practices and agreements. Now Catholic community and identity are much more fluid, fragile, and voluntary.

The most common phrase among critics is that as a result of the liturgical reforms of Vatican II we lost a sense of "mystery." I both agree and disagree with that observation. I do think we lost a sense of worshipful and pregnant silence. We also share in America's general disrespect for most authority and for tradition. This is a major regression, it seems to me.

Mostly, however, we let go of a sense of mystification, but not necessarily real religious Mystery. *Mystification is actually a non-experience of Great Mystery and the disillusionment that follows from this non-experience.* Holy Mystery elicits a strong sense of inner clarity, direction, enlightenment, and invitation to it. It calls forth intellectual curiosity and spiritual searching and study, not glib or smug certitudes. Engaging with True Mystery is not a matter of loving amorphous belief systems or obscure traditions onto which we can project anything we want. Rather, Holy Mystery calls forth inner accountability and responsibility for what we have actually experienced. For example, it is inconceivable that Eucharist truthfully experienced would allow one to be a racist. Yet rampant racism remained quite common among communicants in most Catholic countries I have visited. Mystification has to do with pseudo mystery and may be even the opposite of encounter with True Mystery. I think we have more Mystery now, and much less mystification.

The idealized silence, the non-dialogue, the obscure symbols (disconnected to any narrative), the anonymous saints' lives (nothing beyond a name and a legend), the prohibition of questioning authority—all sent everything underground. It allowed most peoples' unconscious and personal ego or cultural assumptions to set the actual direction and avoid any clear or shareable meaning at all (note that to this day Catholics are generally reticent to talk about their inner life or their relationship with God). The de facto value systems of most Catholics have been indistinguishable from those of most other Americans, except on a couple of hot button issues, usually having to do with sexuality or Mass attendance itself.

We became good at denial and repression of *what we really believed, really felt, and really experienced.* There was a giant cover available for not being in touch with our inner life and our actual belief systems. It seems *there is a silence that is deeper consciousness and there is a silence that is merely unconsciousness.* It probably was true religious Mystery for people with sincere prayer and inner lives, but for many of us it was mystification. I admit that even mystification held us fast inside of a certain salutary container. We could probably use that holding tank now, as we have become cynical and skeptical about any meaning at all. I can even see why some want to go back to the "good old days."

Today's Eucharist—yes, overly chatty sometimes and even trivial—still hopefully includes a preached Gospel on a triple-cycle lectionary in understandable language, and is based much more in actual community relationships. No more "God without God's world," no more vertical priestcraft without a horizontal Body of Christ, no more mystification substituting for mystical union with God and all that God loves. A Eucharist that is both "vertical and horizontal" tells us that the Christian religion has an actual and accountable message for our lives and for society. It is now much more a transformational system than merely a belonging system or an external belief system.

Encounter with Holy Mystery always makes one humble and keeps one seeking and searching for the *Ever More* of that enticing Mystery. Authentic Eucharist allows every age to hold, learn from, and suffer the same contradictions that Jesus held and suffered in his life and on the cross. Such a Eucharist is both a banquet for the universe and an exercise in sacrificial letting go in any age or time or culture. It cannot be anything less, if it is to be true. The Eucharist is always Jesus' and our "one and eternal sacrifice," and any age dare not make it into anything either more convenient or less comforting.

39

First Confession

"Bless Me Father, for I Have Sinned"

KATE DOOLEY, O.P.

Ready to Go

In the decades before Vatican II, preparation for children's first confession placed great emphasis on "how to go to confession." Children practiced with "made up" sins, which unfortunately were often repeated as the actual confession. Another part of the preparation included taking the children to the church in order to become familiar with the space, the sliding panel, and the darkness of the confessional. Children were usually given a very detailed set of instructions to memorize, instructions that took absolutely nothing for granted. The handout began with: "I go into the confessional and kneel down. When the priest opens the slide, I make the sign of the cross and I say, 'Bless me Father, for I have sinned. This is my first confession. My sins are . . .'"

The story is told of one teacher, kneeling near the confessional, hearing a child repeat the wording of the handout as far as "When the priest opens the slide . . ." Then the child, in her anxiety not remembering what came next, began repeating "When the priest opens the slide" louder and louder. The confessor gently said, "Yes, go on," and finally in a firm voice said, "The slide IS open!" The child, who by this time was quite agitated, replied in a loud voice: "Well close it, so I can start over!"

Primary teachers of the pre–Vatican II era had an abundance of amusing stories about first confession. For children, the experience of first confession was one that more often than not generated fear and anxiety.

The *Baltimore Catechism* or material based on it was the primary source of preparation for the sacrament. Simple line drawings augmented the printed text. The illustration of a hand was a means of remembering the five things necessary for a good confession: to examine one's conscience (thumb); to be sorry for one's sins (index finger); to resolve not to sin again (middle finger); to tell one's sin to the priest (fourth finger); and to remember to do the penance given by the priest (little finger). The degrees of sinfulness were displayed by three milk bottles: one bottle with some small black specks (venial sin); another with many large black specks (mortal sin), and finally a bottle that was pure white (soul in grace). A common image used to present the sacrament to children was a court trial. The confessional is the judgment seat; the confessor is the judge; the penitent is the accused; confession of precise individual acts is the accusation; the exhortation of the priest to the penitent is similar to the judge's admonition; absolution is the verdict; and penance is reparation.[1] This analogy corresponded to the understanding of sin as a violation of rules and regulations. In this analogy, however, the image of the merciful loving God of the scriptures was sometimes replaced in the child's mind by the image of a God seeking retribution and recompense.

Moreover, the catechism vocabulary of venial sins, mortal sins, actual sins, "falling into sin," was more than a little confusing to young children. Children could sometimes be heard asking each other: "How many 'mortals' did you do?" One child was greatly relieved after having been assured by his mother that the meaning of the word "original" was something that was new or something that had not been done before. Reciting a litany of the transgressions of his classmates, he knew his actions were certainly not original sins! Moreover, since the focus was on externals, children often were confused and assumed that actions that annoyed adults were sins.

The religion texts offered a guide for the examination of conscience with simple questions that reflected the Ten Commandments: "Did I say my prayers every day? Did I take God's holy name in vain? Did I miss Mass on Sunday or on a holy day? Did I misbehave in church? Was I obedient? Did I get angry? Was I pure in touch and thought? Did I steal anything? Did I tell lies? Did I say mean things? Did I eat meat on

Friday?" The teacher explained the meaning of each of the commandments from a doctrinal perspective and then summarized by using examples from the scriptures, from the lives of the saints, or most often
from vignettes created by the teacher, stories that reflected the children's
experience. The purpose of the sacramental preparation was not just to
prepare for first confession but to establish a lifelong practice of exam-
ining one's conscience in order to participate with the family in the
weekly or monthly reception of the sacrament of Penance.

From Confession to Reconciliation

The Second Vatican Council (1962–1965) revised all of the sacramental rituals, including the sacrament of Penance in 1973. Pope John
Paul II in his 1984 exhortation on Reconciliation and Penance in the
Mission of the Church described the sacrament in this way: "It is in
the light of God's mercy and love that we examine our actions, both
the good and the bad, take responsibility for them, are sincerely sorry
and amend our life. The sign of absolution, a visible sign of God's
faithfulness and forgiveness, completes the sacrament."[2]

The revised Rite of Penance (RP) presents the sacrament as liturgical prayer, as an act of worship and an expression of the faith of the
Church (RP, 4). The dominant theme in the Rite of Reconciliation is
that God is the God of mercy and love. The ritual provides three forms
for the celebration of the sacrament: individual confession, communal
celebration with individual confession, and (to be used in special circumstances) a communal celebration with general absolution. The
second form of communal prayer is generally used for the children's
first confession. The scriptures are proclaimed to affirm that it is God's
initiative that calls us to conversion and to trust in God's mercy and
love. To celebrate the sacrament is to obtain pardon through God's
mercy for offenses committed but also to be "reconciled with the
church which they have wounded by their sins and which by charity,
by example and by prayer labors for their conversion" (RP, 4). The
communal form is a reminder that the sinfulness of one harms others
just as good actions benefit others. The sacrament is not just about the
individual; it is about the person through Baptism as a member of the
Christian community. To truly achieve its purpose, this sacrament of
healing must take root in the life of the individual so that by God's
grace that person "may work with all people of good will for justice
and peace in the world" (RP, 10).

From Reconciliation to Renewal

Teachers today prepare children to receive the sacrament through instruction and through prayer services such as those found in Appendix Two of the Rite of Penance. These examples, directed to different age levels, serve as preparation for the celebration of the sacrament. The prayer service assists children in the formation of conscience through reflection on scripture in terms of their relationships with God and with others. Reconciliation underlines God's initiative as found in the beautiful parables of the forgiving Father or of the Shepherd who looks for the lost sheep as well as in stories such as the call of Zacchaeus. The focus on reconciliation does not replace the aspects of penance or confession but indicates that they are part of a process that culminates in our reconciliation with God and with one another. The sacrament is not simply a matter of admitting one's sins; it includes a regret that leads to a change in attitude and behavior. It means taking on the likeness of Christ. Through these prayer services, children acquire a sense of belonging to the community and an awareness that their choices affect others.

The penitential celebrations build up a vocabulary of both sign and word that enable the child to enter more fully into the Church's rite of sacramental forgiveness. In the sample celebrations given in the Rite, it is recommended that a specific action of service—visiting the sick, caring in some way for the poor—be suggested as a tangible sign of conversion and love. A concrete work of charity helps children to understand that forgiveness and reconciliation "must take root in their whole life and move them to more fervent service of God and neighbor" (RP, 7b). The reconciled are to become reconcilers. In a world so in need of forgiveness and reconciliation, perhaps it will be children who will lead the adult faith community to a renewed appreciation of the sacrament of healing.

Notes

1. Josef Goldbrunner, *Teaching the Sacraments* (New York: Herder and Herder, 1961).

2. John Paul II, *Penance and Reconciliation in the Mission of the Church* (Washington, DC: United States Catholic Conference, 1984).

40

Asceticism

Then and Now

WILKIE AU

Every year when Lent rolls around, Catholics (especially those of us who grew up in the pre–Vatican II Church) almost instinctively ask themselves: "What am I going to give up?" This question reflects the Lenten emphasis of earlier times, when Lent was seen as a time of abnegation, renunciation, penance, and acts of mortification. As Catholics, we were urged to intensify our spiritual efforts during Lent and to focus with gratitude on the passion and death of Jesus who died for our sins. Lenten practices were meant to teach us how to follow the example of Jesus, who endured suffering and pain out of his love for God and his commitment to lay down his life for us, his friends. In imitation of Jesus, we were exhorted to show our love for God by making some kind of personal sacrifice, like fasting, abstaining from meat, giving up candy, not going to movies, or saying more prayers and attending daily Mass. These ascetical practices, like acts of penance, would help us make reparation for our sins, deepen our life of faith and virtue, strengthen us against temptation, and unite us in solidarity with the poor souls in purgatory, whose painful time of purification could be shortened by our meritorious deeds on their behalf.

These pre–Vatican II Lenten practices present a snapshot of the ascetical approach to spirituality that dominated the times. This essay will discuss the nature of Christian asceticism as a means of spiritual growth and suggest how some of its past shortcomings can be avoided in an attempt to reclaim what is of perennial value in our ascetical tradition.

A Renewed Asceticism for Today

Christian asceticism embodies the guidelines and practices of Christians throughout the centuries who have attempted to conform their lives to the teachings of Jesus. Positively, ascetical teaching and practices support us in our vulnerability and weakened condition due to "original sin," and reinforce the values of self-knowledge, discipline, restraint, vigilance, and persistent effort. Today a renewed asceticism as a response of love flows from a commitment to grow in human authenticity and to build community through the promotion of justice and peace. Asceticism can be an important means of liberating us from inordinate attachments and debilitating addictions that hinder growth. It can provide invaluable guidance for us in our efforts to live as followers of Christ in a consumerist and materialistic society. It cautions us to guard against a self-centeredness that focuses on individual pleasure at the cost of caring for our neighbor. It alerts us to our tendency to place our trust in the false gods of material possessions and power, instead of trusting in the living God. In our post 9/11 world, fractured by divisive forces and threatened by an ecological crisis of global proportions, Christian asceticism encourages us to love God and neighbor by moderating our desires and preventing greed from damaging others and harming the earth.

Asceticism in the past, negatively influenced by the stoicism of Greek philosophy, has at times been tainted by a "no pain, no gain" mentality that exalts suffering as the path to holiness. At its worst, the ascetical tradition placed an unhealthy emphasis on self-mastery and self-control, based on a Platonic devaluation of earthly values and pleasures, a suspicion of human feelings, and a denigration of the body and sexuality. Monastic practices of traditional asceticism, once a useful means of purifying the self from egocentric obstacles to loving like Christ, have at times been so distorted that degrading humiliation masqueraded as humility, natural and life-enhancing impulses were rejected as sinful desire, and submissive acceptance of abuse or deadening self-sacrifice were confused with Christian love. Fortunately, with the enlightenment brought about by Vatican II reforms and modern psychological as well as theological insights, such distorted ascetical views have largely been demystified and exposed as dangers to healthy Christian and human growth.

Asceticism: A Focus on Vigilance and Fidelity

The word "asceticism" comes from the Greek root *askesis*, the training that athletes go through to prepare for competition. It is applied by Paul to the Christian life, viewed as a race for an imperishable reward (1 Cor 9:24-27). Reflecting this Pauline metaphor for the Christian life, the ascetical way emphasizes self-control, discipline, assertion, and renunciation focused on achieving the goal. Another metaphor that grounds an ascetical approach to the Christian life is that of a lifelong spiritual battle in which we struggle between forces of good and evil, light and darkness, grace and sin.

Paul graphically describes the nature of this spiritual struggle in his letter to the Romans in words that have an enduring ring because they resonate deeply with the personal experience of people throughout the ages. Like Paul, we too live with a divided self. We encounter warring forces within ourselves so strong and autonomous that we often feel helpless and weak. Like Paul, we are perplexed by the mystery of our interior fragmentation. When the apostle declares, "I cannot understand my own behavior," we know what he means. "I fail to carry out the things I want to do, and I find myself doing the very things I hate . . . for though the will to do what is good is in me, the performance is not, with the result that instead of doing the good things I want to do, I carry out the sinful things I do not want . . . What a wretch I am!" (Rom 7:14–15, 18). The self-sabotaging self wages war within every man and woman. Christian asceticism is meant to support our attempts to fulfill the commandment of love in the midst of weakness and struggles.

Perhaps the most concise gospel illustration of ascetical practice is found in the "way section" of the Gospel of Mark (8:22–10:52). In this part of his gospel, Mark uses the words "*ho hodos*" (meaning "the way") a total of seven times as he illustrates what is entailed in following Jesus. To be a disciple of Jesus requires that we "take up our cross daily" in imitation of Jesus whose love was sacrificial because he remained faithful to proclaiming the good news of God's unconditional and merciful love, even at the cost of personal suffering and death. By his example of unswerving fidelity to God's will, Jesus showed how we are called to surrender our lives over to God, trusting in the divine promise to always bring new life from death. Jesus had to repeat his instructions three times, because his disciples were slow to understand and resisted such a radical trust in God.

Christian spirituality acknowledges that our struggles today are identical to those of Jesus' disciples. The process of loving according to the way of Jesus involves a slow and lifelong process of recognizing that our tendency towards selfishness, control, ambition, competition, and our desire to be the first and the greatest can stand in the way of loving like Jesus. Thus, there is a need for ongoing fidelity and vigilance in order to stay as faithful disciples to the message of Jesus and to avoid the temptations of "the world, the flesh, and the devil."

Spiritual Disciplines: A New Name for Traditional Practices

In contemporary Christian spirituality, traditional ascetical practices—such as various forms of meditation and contemplation, spiritual reading, individual and group retreats, and so on—have been retrieved and renamed "spiritual disciplines." These ancient spiritual practices have regained their valuable place in Christian life today because of a renewed understanding of them as positive means for fostering spiritual growth.

When ascetical practices were followed as a matter of routine, like Lenten practices unthinkingly carried over from childhood, they lost much of their relevance and usefulness in the eyes of many Christians. Greater appreciation for the contribution such practices make to Christian growth comes from keeping in mind the following principles:

- *Ascetical practices or spiritual disciplines should always be linked to heartfelt spiritual desires. They are means to an end, not ends in themselves.* We should always first ask what we want to achieve in our spiritual growth, and only then discern what practice would be the best means of achieving it. Ascetical practices risk becoming meaningless and inane when they are disconnected from the desired goal they were intended to serve. If, for example, we want to heighten our sensitivity to the presence of God in daily life, we need to decide upon what would best help us do this. Would prayerfully reviewing the day for fifteen minutes every evening before going to sleep in order to monitor how God was present throughout the day be the best way

for us to do this? Or would briefly abstaining from some activity—like listening to our iPod, checking our e-mail, or
watching television—for the sake of some silent reflection
in the midst of a busy day work better? Or would doing a
bit of spiritual reading every day best serve our purpose? Or
would skipping lunch occasionally best help us stay in touch
with our hunger for God and alert us to how God actually
meets and nourishes us through ordinary encounters?

- *Spiritual disciplines need to be freely chosen, not done out of
  obligation; they should feel liberating, not burdensome.*

- *Spiritual disciplines need to fit our unique personality and religious sensibility as well as the concrete circumstances of our
  personal and work life.* Because "one size does not fit all,"
  we need to experiment with various spiritual disciplines and
  adopt only those that we discover to be fruitful and lifegiv-
  ing in light of ongoing personal experience.

Ascetical practices or spiritual disciplines are meant to serve us as
the sycamore branch served Zacchaeus, the tax-collector who was too
short to see Jesus above the crowd and needed help to get a glimpse
of Jesus passing by (Lk 19:1–10). They are meant to be means that
help us recognize and respond to God in the parade of events that
make up our daily lives. If these methods take on exaggerated importance, they can turn out to be hindrances rather than helps. Ascetical
means can help dispose us to receive God's self-disclosure and love;
they can be a means of opening ourselves to God's grace in our lives.
But they can never replace grace, which alone can bring about spiritual transformation.

An ancient Chinese proverb is very instructive here: "Only the
fool stares at his finger when it is pointing to the moon." Ascetical
practices are like fingers pointing to God. To become preoccupied
with them is to be foolishly distracted from our heart's true desire.

41

The Rosary

"A Treasure to Be Recovered"

Thomas H. Groome

Childhood Memories

Like many Catholics of my vintage, I grew up in a family that recited the nightly Rosary. And we knew why we did: as Mom would
often assure us, the most effective person to bring our prayers to Jesus
was his own mother. As a good son, how could he refuse her? (And
we got the double message.)

As children, we often came to it in protest—"In a minute, Ma"—
but once we had settled on our knees, I remember it as a lovely quieting time, one that bonded our large family (nine kids) at the end of a
day that had generally been filled with the usual sibling squabbles.
Years later, when we gathered—from the four winds—for my parents'
wakes, and then for those of siblings, it bonded us again. The Rosary
crusader Father Paddy Peyton was right: "The family that prays together, stays together"—in spirit if not location.

In my native Irish home, the leaping flames of the turf fire combined with the gentle drone of the Hail Marys to introduce me to
what I later knew as meditation, even contemplation. My mother
would often encourage us to "just think about the mysteries." And
how wise she was. In his apostolic letter, *Rosarium Virginis Mariae*

(hereafter *RVM*) of Oct 16, 2002, Pope John Paul II proclaims the Rosary as a "treasure to be rediscovered" and particularly as a "path of contemplation."

If one of us missed the family recitation, our mother's goodnight was always accompanied by "be sure to say your Rosary." We knew that she kept her own beads under her pillow, at hand for waking moments. And my grandmother loved to assure us that "if you start the Rosary and then fall asleep, the angels will finish it for you."

From my childhood, then, I experienced the gift of the Rosary as both communal and personal prayer, as a quieting mantra-like mode of recitation and contemplation. The Rosary also taught me the responsibility of being a person of prayer myself and that I can pray just about anytime and anywhere. Even then I knew that I wasn't literally praying to Mary, since only God can answer prayer. But I was confident that Mary was praying with me to Jesus, and was surely effective in this role. I really did think of her as a "second mother" and the Rosary as the mode of our conversation.

History and Legacy

The word "Rosary" comes from the Latin *rosarium* meaning "rose garden." We cannot pinpoint how or when the Rosary began as a popular Catholic devotion. The old tradition that it was personally delivered to St. Dominic by the Blessed Mother is now seriously questioned. On the other hand, the Dominicans certainly helped to standardize and popularize it during the sixteenth century. Pope Pius V—a Dominican—instituted the feast of Our Lady of the Rosary (now celebrated October 7); he credited the defeat of the Turks at the battle of Lepanto in 1571 to the efficacy of the Rosary.

Around the year 1000, ordinary people began to recite 150 Our Fathers, divided into three sets of fifty and counted on strings of beads called "paternosters." This became known as "the poor persons' Psalter" because they were copying the monks and nuns who recited the 150 psalms each day in their monasteries. As Marian devotion increased in the twelfth century, the Carthusians and Cistercians helped develop and popularize a Rosary of Hail Marys, keeping an Our Father at the beginning of each decade.

The Hail Mary came together from the angel's salutation to Mary at the Annunciation (Lk 1:28), and Elizabeth's greeting to

Mary at the Visitation (Lk 1:42). Though this first half of the Hail Mary had been a popular prayer in the West since the eleventh century—and as early as the sixth century in the East—the second half was not added until the sixteenth century. At about that time the Dominicans organized Rosary confraternities, encouraging people to commit to praying it daily.

Though exactly how the Rosary emerged remains unclear, to remember why it emerged can help us recognize its spiritual legacy for today. It arose from the instinct of ordinary Christians that they, too, were called to lives of prayer and to sanctify their time throughout the day. They knew the monks and nuns were doing so with their recitation of the 150 psalms as the Divine Office of the Church. But the peasant people didn't have time to pause for choral reading, and if they had, they didn't have books and most couldn't ready anyway. Yet, their good instinct was that Baptism calls all Christians to holiness of life, demanding the regular practice of prayer. And what a gift it was to have a mantra-like meditative prayer that they could recite alone or together, at work or at rest, anywhere and any time, confident that Mary, the "holy mother of God" and theirs, was praying with them.

We can still be inspired by their wise instincts, for the regular practice of prayer will always be essential to sustain the Christian life. We need to be conscious of God's presence in the ordinary time and activities of our lives—not just in church. We Christians cannot delegate others—like monks and nuns in monasteries—to pray instead of us; we need to pray ourselves, both "with" and "as" Church.

Even if the Rosary is not a person's regular prayer of choice, one would do well to find another way to fulfill those good baptismal instincts of our fore-parents in faith. But I'd propose that the hassle of daily life can still be calmed by a gentle and meditative prayer as "user friendly" as the Rosary. And, as my mother counseled, to have Mary pray with you to Jesus her son must surely be effective.

Mysteries Old and New

The Rosary's widespread popularity fell off after Vatican II—an unintended outcome of the council's good efforts to refocus Catholics on Jesus, on sacred scripture, and on the liturgy. But as John Paul II noted in *RVM*, the Rosary "though clearly Marian in character, at heart is a Christocentric prayer" and "has all the depth of the Gospel message in its entirety" (#1). Likewise, "it serves as an excellent introduction and a faithful echo of the Liturgy" (#4).

While heralding the Rosary' spiritual legacy, Pope John Paul II also recognized a deficiency in its listing of "mysteries." For some five hundred years, the full Rosary consisted of fifteen decades of one Our Father and ten Hail Marys, each decade focused on some event from the life of Jesus or Mary. The fifteen decades were grouped into three sets of five called "chaplets" (crowns), named as the Joyful, Sorrowful, and Glorious mysteries; these focus on the incarnation, passion, and glorification of Jesus respectively.

Traditionally, the fifth Joyful mystery concludes with "Finding Jesus in the Temple" at age twelve, and the follow-on Sorrowful mysteries begin with "The Agony of Jesus in the Garden." In other words, there was no mystery among the fifteen that contemplated the public life and ministry of Jesus. Considering that many ordinary Catholics encounter their "working" Christology through reciting the Rosary, to skip over the public life of Jesus leaves a huge lacuna. Recognizing this deficiency, Pope John Paul II introduced five new "Mysteries of Light" that focus on five great events in the public life of Jesus. Catholic consciousness may now more adequately reflect the Jesus of history as well as the Christ of faith.

Praying the Rosary Today

Thus, the Rosary now consists of four chaplets of five decades each, focusing on the Joyful, Luminous, Sorrowful, and Glorious mysteries. The decade of the Rosary devoted to each specific mystery begins with an opening Our Father, is followed by ten Hail Marys, and ends with the doxology or "Glory be . . ." Though all twenty mysteries can be prayed at one time and in sequence, the usual format is some opening prayers, then five particular decades, and some brief closing prayers.

It is customary, too, to assign each chaplet to a particular day of the week. When he added the Luminous mysteries, Pope John Paul II suggested that the Joyful mysteries be prayed on Monday and Saturday, the Luminous mysteries on Thursday, the Sorrowful mysteries on Tuesday and Friday, and the Glorious mysteries on Wednesday and Sunday.

The Mysteries as Suggested in *Rosarium Virginis Mariae*

THE JOYFUL MYSTERIES

1. The Annunciation by Gabriel to the Virgin Mary
2. The Visitation of Mary to Elizabeth
3. The Birth of the Savior of the World
4. The Presentation of Jesus in the Temple
5. The Finding of Twelve-year-old Jesus in the Temple

THE LUMINOUS MYSTERIES

1. The Baptism of Jesus
2. Jesus at the Wedding in Cana
3. Jesus Proclaims the Kingdom of God
4. Jesus' Transfiguration
5. Jesus Institutes the Eucharist

THE SORROWFUL MYSTERIES

1. The Anguish of Jesus in Gethsemane
2. Jesus is Scourged
3. Jesus is Crowned with Thorns
4. Jesus Carries his Cross
5. Jesus Dies on the Cross

THE GLORIOUS MYSTERIES

1. The Resurrection of Jesus from the Dead
2. Jesus Ascends into Glory
3. The Spirit Outpours upon Mary and the Disciples at Pentecost
4. Mary is Assumed into Heaven
5. Mary Shines forth as Queen of the Angels and Saints

There are varied customs with regard to the opening and closing prayers. One popular version is to begin with the first verse of Psalm 70, "O God, come to my assistance, O Lord make haste to help me," followed by an Our Father, three Hail Marys, and a "Glory be..." Then take note of the chaplet for meditation and the first mystery, for example, "The five Joyful mysteries, the first mystery, the Annunciation."

And there are a variety of ways to conclude. Indeed, in my family the "trimmings to the Rosary" could take almost as long again, depending on my Mom's "intentions." Typical, however, is to end with the Hail Holy Queen or *Memorare*, followed by a closing prayer.

And one's prayer mode throughout the recitation of the Rosary? The tradition is to meditate or contemplate on the mystery of each decade—rather than focusing on the words of the prayers. So, with the first Joyful mystery, "The Annunciation," one can think about God's extraordinary initiative toward humankind, about Mary's openness to doing God's will, her role in the work of our salvation, and so on. Or, more contemplatively, one can imagine and enter into the setting as the angel Gabriel appears to Mary and listen to the exchange between them, with a sense of presence to the scene. The purpose of all such meditation or contemplation is to encourage discipleship to Jesus in daily life. Indeed, in the Rosary we have "a treasure to be rediscovered."

42

Catholics Growing Up

The Legion of Decency

RICHARD A. BLAKE, S.J.

When he was defending *The Last Temptation of Christ* against its critics, Martin Scorsese maintained: "My whole life has been movies and religion. That's it. Nothing else." The former aspiring Catholic seminarian was indulging in a bit of exaggeration, no doubt. He did, however, point out the powerful influence of those twin institutions in the life of young American Catholics growing up in the Church of the 1950s. Odd as it may seem, religion and the movies have enjoyed a mutually constructive relationship, or so it seems as I look back.

Within a twenty minute walk from my home in Brooklyn, I could go to the movies at the Alpine, the Bay Ridge, the Electra, the Stanley, the Dyker, the Shore Road, or the Harbor. Since tickets were fifty cents or less for children, the usual Saturday "kiddie" shows—two ancient Westerns or horror films, a serial, newsreel, coming attractions, and ten cartoons—were all part of the cinematic diet. The movies were the normal way to pass a rainy Saturday or Sunday afternoon or a school holiday during the winter or to enjoy an air-conditioned respite from the oppressive heat in summer. And for teenagers, especially after television took over the family living room, the movies provided the usual, cost-efficient first steps away from parents and into the dating game.

On the way to the theater of choice, I might have passed by St. Ephrem's, Our Lady of Angels, St. Anselm's, or St. Patrick's, each with a huge parochial school perched next to the church. The parish complex, with Mass on Sunday, confession and the posting of the Mass servers' schedule on Saturday, and in my pre-teen years school on weekdays, was in every sense the daily hub of my social universe. It sponsored the scout troops and the CYO teams, produced annual talent shows around St. Patrick's Day and dances for teenagers, young adults, and married couples.

A Moral Code for the Movies

For Catholics of that period, religion and the movies converged most obviously through the Legion of Decency. In this universe, few saw the Legion as oppressive or as restrictive of artistic freedom as the Legion is commonly viewed today. Catholics in my neighborhood never expressed doubt about taking the annual oath during Sunday Mass: "I wish to join the Legion of Decency, which condemns vile and unwholesome moving pictures. I unite with all who protest against them as a grave menace to youth, to home life, to country and to religion." Who could argue with that? It was an age of muscular, confrontational Catholicism, and everyone had a duty to join the campaign against "godless atheism," as the then current pleonasm had it. Every Saturday *The Brooklyn Tablet* was delivered to the door, and since I wasn't much interested in seeing what pastors were being transferred, I went directly to the youth pages to see if any movies had been condemned that week. I was generally disappointed. For all its reputation today, it's really amazing to see how few movies actually received the "C" rating.

As much as any other institution in the American Catholic Church, the Legion provides an indicator of change not only in the Church's relationship with the secular world but in its own internal self-awareness. In 1934, only a few years after the movies learned to talk, it became quite clear that the industry had absolutely no inclination to observe the Production Code formulated in 1929 with the help of Father Daniel Lord, S.J., and Martin Quigley, the outspoken Catholic editor of the *Motion Picture Herald*. Then, as always, sex and violence sold tickets. Understandably feeling betrayed by Hollywood's ignoring its own Code, Lord and Quigley retaliated. With the support of the American hierarchy they formed their own organization to rate movies on the basis of moral content. They christened the organization with the suitably military title, the Legion of Decency. Since Catholics in the large East Coast and Midwestern cities formed a significant percentage of its potential audience, Hollywood took notice. With its quasi-official standing within the Church, in the mind of many the Legion could in effect forbid Catholics from going to the movies.

Sensing the proverbial wolf at the box-office door, Hollywood responded by establishing the Production Code Administration (PCA), led by Joseph Ignatius Breen, an energetic Catholic layman with an identifiably Irish Catholic name. The Legion and the PCA operated on parallel tracks. The Legion offered objections and suggestions as an interested outside party, but the PCA with its own staff of reviewers working within the industry insisted on changes in scripts or cuts in films that were ready for release. If a studio refused to comply with PCA demands, the film did not receive a seal of approval, and the studios were fined if they chose to release the film without it. Rarely did anyone defy the PCA.

This was a remarkable development, but not for the reasons usually cited. The Catholic Church had a long history of banning books and scrutinizing those accused of heterodoxy. Nothing new on that score. With the Legion, however, the Church engaged a new popular art form that reached beyond the realms of academic discourse and touched the lives of ordinary Catholics. In an astonishingly short time it recognized the pervasive presence of this new medium, especially among young people. What's more, it understood the corporate nature of the industry and used its influence to threaten the profitability of objectionable films.

A Positive Legacy

Most film historians refer to the Legion as a "pressure group." It was that, of course. But it was much more. It enabled the Church to enter into a dialogue with a major cultural institution. It was one of the factors, and I would argue an important one, that helped American Catholics break out of their immigrant heritage of insularity. Through the Legion, Catholics did not withdraw from mainstream American culture, but addressed it by identifying and effectively expressing their areas of conflict with secular values in very concrete and specific terms. Yes, some of the objections were silly then and appear doubly silly now, but when one thinks of all the wonderful American films produced during the glory days of the Legion, it's hard to maintain that the Legion and the PCA conspired to stifle artistic expression to the extent some have claimed. Perhaps they even helped the movies step beyond their peepshow background and develop a capability for subtlety.

The conversation was not always adversarial. In the early 1950s my father and I attended the annual communion breakfast of the New York Motion Picture Holy Name Society. After Mass at St. Patrick's Cathedral, the group would fill the grand ballroom of the Waldorf-Astoria, where the dais would contain a mixture of clerics, including officers of the Legion, industry notables, and an occasional movie star. Many in attendance were not Catholic, but they came to listen to what Catholics had to say. And it was clear from the very fact that they were there that Catholics felt that the movies were important to them as church members.

The American Catholic Church matured through the experience. The Legion developed an extensive list of reviewers, which included lay people and clerics alike, many of whom were educators. After a private screening, each viewer wrote out reasons to explain the recommended rating. Without recognizing the fact at the time, the Legion was creating a cadre of quite sophisticated Catholic film viewers. From this grew the cinéclubs and discussion groups that sprang up in colleges, which in turn led to formal academic programs in film studies. If the Catholic universities did not assume a leading role in grappling with the communications revolution, at least it is clear that they were not left behind.

Some years later, when both American society and the film industry were going through the convulsions of the 1960s, the legacy of the Legion of Decency paid off. As social norms changed, the dialogue continued. The PCA lost its clout, and the Legion morphed into the National Catholic Office of Motion Pictures, whose oath, if administered at all, took a more positive tone: "I promise to promote by word and deed what is morally and artistically good in motion picture entertainment." Catholic audiences had become quite discriminating viewers, and reviewers like Moira Walsh at *America* or Philip Hartung at *Commonweal* persuaded their readers that films with adult themes made for mature audiences were not necessarily immoral. Many of their reviews seem quite progressive, even by today's standards. Both Catholic and industry rating systems became advisory. Today few Catholics speak of condemning movies.

For the most part, after a long and at times acrimonious dialogue, Catholics have built a comfortable relationship with the movie industry. But the more important result is internal. Through the experience of the Legion of Decency, American Catholics have engaged the popular culture on its own terms. In the process they have grown in their own self-understanding as both American and Catholic.

43

The Angelus

Praying throughout the Day

BISHOP ROBERT F. MORNEAU

Sanctifying Life

Our parish church and school stood on a small hill in the village of Bear Creek, Wisconsin. It was during the pre–Vatican II days of the 1940s and 1950s that my five siblings and I attended our Catholic grade school and the weekend liturgies at St. Mary's Parish. Mass was in Latin; our teachers, all women religious, wore habits; the priest and his housekeeper governed the parish. It was the days of no parish council, no lay lectors or Communion distributors, no finance council. It was a time of deep devotion (family Rosary every night) and strict observance of the Church's rules (attending Mass every Sunday and holy day and no meat on Fridays).

I remember those days with gratitude while appreciating that our participation in the life of faith was quite limited, given that the liturgy was in Latin and the participation of the laity in the life of the Church was minimal. Yet people prayed, reached out to the poor, were generous with their time and talent and treasure, feared the Lord, and honored their faith as being extremely important, if not the most important aspect of their lives. The pluralism and relativism of our current times had not eroded belief in God nor made irrelevant one's practice of the Catholic faith. It was a good time; it was a time of grace.

One pre–Vatican II devotion that was passed on to me was "The Angelus." This prayer was based on the annunciation story (Lk 1:26–38). The angel Gabriel appeared to the virgin Mary with the request that she become the mother of Jesus. Though fearful and not knowing how this could happen, Mary gave her consent. The mystery of the incarnation was honored and recalled by a triple repetition of the "Hail Mary," preceded by an introductory verse and followed by a concluding prayer. This devotion was repeated three times a day as the church bells rang, in early morning, at noon, and in the evening. It helped ordinary people sanctify their everyday lives with regular pauses for prayer. Here is that devotion:

Verse: The Angel of the Lord declared unto Mary,
Response: and she conceived of the Holy Spirit.

All: Hail Mary, full of grace, the Lord is with thee. Blessed art thou among women and blessed is the fruit of thy womb, Jesus. Holy Mary, mother of God, pray for us sinners now and at the hour of our death. Amen.

Verse: Behold the handmaid of the Lord,
Response: be it done unto me according to thy word.

All: Hail Mary, . . .

Verse: And the Word was made Flesh,
Response: and dwelt among us.

All: Hail Mary, . . .

Verse: Pray for us, O Holy Mother of God,
Response: that we may be made worthy of the promises of Christ.

All: Let us pray. Pour forth, we beseech Thee, O Lord, Thy grace into our hearts; that we, to whom the incarnation of Christ, Thy Son, was made known by the message of an Angel, may by His passion and cross, be brought to the glory of His resurrection. We ask this through the same Christ our Lord. Amen.

The origin of this devotion is obscure, but it probably arose out of the monastic tradition. Whatever its origin, for more than five centuries this prayer nourished the faith life of Christians as they paused to honor the mystery of the incarnation three times a day (for some, just once a day). In Vatican City, the Angelus bells still chime three times daily as they do in some parishes throughout the world.

An Evangelizing Prayer

In 1975, Pope Paul VI wrote an apostolic exhortation *Evangelii Nuntiandi* (Evangelization in the Modern World). It is one of the Church's most accessible and theologically rich documents. In that post-synodal exhortation, the pope stated that one of the eight methods of doing evangelization is popular piety. At the Second Vatican Council tremendous emphasis was put on the sacraments and scripture, and rightly so. For many years, devotions such as the Rosary, the Stations of the Cross, novenas, and the Angelus had been the main means for many Catholics to stay "connected" to God. Since the pre–Vatican II celebration of the Mass was in Latin, as was the celebration of the other sacraments, and since the scriptures also were proclaimed in Latin and there was little if any encouragement to do Bible study, popular devotions filled the vacuum.

With the implementation of the sixteen Vatican II documents, there has been a major focus on God's word and on full, conscious, active participation in the sacramental life. While this is well intentioned and correct, there is a problem. How can people stay "connected" to God and their faith life on a daily basis in-between the celebrations of the sacraments? There is room—indeed, need—for devotions and practices lest we forget the presence of the Lord in our daily life; lest we fail to nurture a strong personal relationship with God that is expressed in action. So, we may well ask the question: Does the devotion of the Angelus merit a retrieval?

For centuries the Angelus served us well. It contains the whole dynamic of the spiritual life. The opening verse and response are all about God's initiative; God sent the angel Gabriel to Mary. In the spiritual life, God always takes the initiative and we are, at best, responders. The Angelus reflects the central chapter in salvation history and pondering it three times a day enriched our faith journey.

In the second verse and response we witness Mary's obedience of faith. Mary's response to the angel and Mary's statement at Cana

("Do whatever he tells you" Jn 2:5b) provide a model for all Christians. Here we have a positive response to the divine invitation. God's will is paramount, and Mary embraces it with her whole being. We have here an attitude of faith that can transform our lives and the world.

The third part of the Angelus plunges us into the mystery of the incarnation. All history changed when God became incarnate in the person of Jesus. The Word became flesh and took on our human nature, even unto death. We must not hurry over this profound mystery. There is a "scandal of particularity" here: that God would come at this time, to this people, in this land, in this manner boggles the imagination and challenges our faith. Our finite intelligence and our limited love stumble before the extravagant love of God.

The devotion ends with a prayer that reminds us of the paschal mystery. We ask God for the grace to participate in the life, death, and resurrection of Christ. Only in this way can we come to God's glory and find peace. Though we are graced persons, we are aware of our sinfulness and know we are not worthy, but with God's mercy we can be reconciled to God and know the gift of eternal life.

Interspersed with the devotion is the "Hail Mary." In this brief prayer we acknowledge a number of things: that Mary is filled with God's love (grace); that she is the most blessed of all women; that she is the mother of God; that we are sinners ever in need of her prayers. It is Mary's intercessory prayer that helps us to do what she did: hear and live God's word. The Angelus is truly a treasure that deserves our attention and our practice.

A Healthy Devotional Catholicism

We must be clear that the sacraments and scripture are foundational to the spiritual life (as are asceticism and service). Devotions, though helpful and nurturing, do not have the centrality of God's word and sacramental life. Yet, when devotions are grounded in scripture and when devotions dispose us to celebrate the sacraments more fully, they should be given due consideration. I maintain that the retrieval of the Angelus has the power to transform our individual lives, our communities, and our world. The Angelus makes us recognize that God is always active and inviting us into the life of grace; the Angelus calls us to a life of obedience to God's will; the Angelus has us re-experience the central mystery of the incarnation; the Angelus invites us into the paschal mystery and divine glory; the Angelus reminds us to raise our minds and hearts to God throughout the day. All this in three minutes, several times a day.

The story is told that Edgar Allan Poe (1809–1849) heard the chimes of Fordham University ringing out three times a day. Not knowing why the bells were rung, he inquired and was informed that these bells were inviting people to stop and pray the Angelus. Impressed with this practice, Poe wrote the following poem—indeed, the following prayer:

Hymn

At morn—at noon—at twilight dim—
Maria! thou hast heard my hymn!
In joy and woe—in good and ill—
Mother of God, be with me still!
When the Hours flew brightly by,
And not a cloud obscured the sky,
My soul, lest it should truant be,
Thy grace did guide to thine and thee;
Now, when storms of Fate o'ercast
Darkly my Present and my Past,
Let my Future radiant shine
With sweet hopes of thee and thine!
   (1835)

It is good to give the poets the last word. No more need be said.

44

The Eucharistic Fast

A Long Past into the Present

Berard L. Marthaler, O.F.M. Conv.

It is now seventy-five years since, in the language of the time, I "made my First Communion." My memory of the event, except for two things, is lost in the mist of time. One is the frequent reference to Napoleon Bonaparte who was reputed to have said that the day of his First Communion was the "happiest day of his life." The other was the preoccupation with the eucharistic fast lest swallowing a few drops of water or taking a piece of candy after midnight would disqualify me from participating in the solemnity with the rest of my first-grade classmates.

It was not only first-communicants, however, who were preoccupied with the eucharistic fast. Until Pope Pius XII in effect abrogated it in the 1950s, ramifications of the eucharistic fast generated endless casuistry and fostered scrupulosity among clergy and laity alike. It admitted of no exceptions and made no allowance for *parvitas materiae*—a few drops of water broke the fast as effectively as a whole glass! It shaped Mass schedules, the pastoral care of the sick, and the health and disposition of priests. A bride and groom who opted to solemnize their wedding and receive Holy Communion at a nuptial Mass could not drink or eat until after the ceremony.

A Long and Strict History

The custom of fasting from food and drink before receiving the Eucharist had a long history. It was so common by the end of the fourth century that St. Augustine suggested that it must have originated as a result of divine inspiration. The 1917 Code of Canon Law formalized the regulations of local councils in stating that anyone who does not fast from midnight is not to receive the Eucharist except when in danger of death or the need to prevent irreverence toward the sacrament requires it (c. 858).

In practice this meant that priests who celebrated Sunday Mass often did not eat for sixteen to twenty hours after the meal on Saturday evening. (I remember a housekeeper/cook in one parish who, despite my protests, served the same menu, a *breakfast* of eggs and bacon, toast and coffee, whether I celebrated the early Mass or was eating for the first time in mid-afternoon after the late Mass and baptisms.) Priests only a few years older than I told of celebrating an early Mass in one place and then traveling to a mission church—sometimes two—to celebrate another Mass many hours later. Not having imbibed or ingested anything since the previous evening, their stomachs growled, their heads ached, and sunny dispositions suffered.

Pastoral manuals interpreted the law for every imaginable circumstance and went into minute detail as how to calculate midnight. (Does the first or last striking of the clock at twelve signal midnight?) Most manuals agreed that the law applied only to digestible matter, so that putting toothpicks, buttons, coins and similar objects in the mouth (and biting ones' fingernails!) did not break the fast. Smoking did not break the fast; neither did snuff (in the nose) nor chewing tobacco. On the other hand, chewing before Communion appeared unseemly (*"indecens"*), and one who indulged in it was probably guilty of venial sin. Soups, juices, coffee, tea and all liquids, whether nourishing or not, were also prohibited.

The Catechism of the Council of Trent instructed the faithful that abstaining from food and drink from the preceding midnight is a way of preparing the body for Holy Communion. It adds, "The dignity of the sacrament also requires a certain abstinence on the part of married persons: they should abstain from marital relations for some days previous to their receiving Communion." Pope Pius X made no mention of such a restriction in describing the dispositions for frequent and daily reception of the Eucharist in the decree *Sacra Tridentina Synodus* (1905). In fact, the decree denounces the kind of rigorism that excluded whole classes of persons as, for example, "merchants or those who are married." Nonetheless, when I joined the faculty at the Catholic University of American in 1963 there was a professor (not in Religious Studies!) who taught students to keep the tradition of the Tridentine catechism alive—for both kinds of fast. And I have reason to believe there were others in classrooms and pulpits elsewhere of a similar bent.

Changes Emerge Slowly

Pius X also relaxed the eucharistic fast for the sick. The concession was later incorporated into the 1917 Code of Canon Law: "The sick who have been confined to bed for a month without certain hope of a speedy recovery may, with the prudent advice of their confessor, receive Holy Communion once or twice a week though they have taken medicine, or some liquid food beforehand" (c. 858, #2). The wording in the code raised a new series of questions: Did the concession apply only to those suffering from a serious illness? Under what circumstances could it apply to pregnancy? Did the reference to the "bed-ridden" (*infirmi qui discumbunt*) include persons who are ailing but who are confined to bed only a few hours each day? When in individual cases there was doubt, the sick person was instructed to ask for a dispensation from the fast.

More and more after the time of Pius X and the promulgation of the 1917 Code, dispensations from the eucharistic fast became common and were granted for reasons other than sickness. Priests, for example, who because of particular circumstances had to binate (celebrate Mass twice in one day), petitioned for a dispensation and generally received it. During the Second World War the law was relaxed for entire classes of people: notably, chaplains, those serving in the armed forces. and defense workers under certain circumstances.

After World War II Pope Pius XII recognized that "the peculiar conditions of the times in which we live have introduced many changes into the usages of society" that made it difficult for people to partake in the divine mysteries. He published two documents, the apostolic constitution *Christus Dominus* (1953) and a motu proprio, *Sacram Communionem* (1957), that mitigated the eucharistic fast in such a way that the faithful were able to observe it more readily. While reaffirming "the law of the eucharistic fast," *Christus Dominus*—in a radical reversal of past practice—lays down the general principle that "natural water does not break the eucharistic fast," and lists many examples of "special circumstances" in which the law does not apply. The constitution together with the motu proprio that followed a few years later in effect abrogated all previous concessions, faculties, and dispensations and rewrote the law governing the eucharistic fast.

The new law described in *Sacram Communionem* took effect in March 1957. Again citing "the notable changes which have occurred in private and public working conditions as well as in all branches of social life," it allows the celebration of Mass every day after midday "whenever the spiritual good of a considerable number of faithful demands it." No mention is made of midnight. The eucharistic fast both for priests who wish to celebrate Mass and the faithful who wish to receive Holy Communion, "is limited to three hours for solid food and alcoholic beverages, and to one hour for non alcoholic beverages." At the close of the third session of Vatican II, Pope Paul VI reduced the abstinence from food and drink to one hour, the norm that was later incorporated into the 1983 Code of Canon Law (c. 91).

The eucharistic fast, intended as a way of honoring and showing reverence to the sacrament, in the course of time had, in the words of Pope Pius XII, made it difficult for people to partake in the divine mysteries. His reform and the further refinement of Pope Paul VI helped make Pius X's ideal of frequent Communion a reality. Pius X had quoted the Council of Trent: "The Holy Council wishes indeed that at each Mass the faithful who are present should communicate, not only in spiritual desire, but sacramentally, by the actual reception of the Eucharist." Furthermore, the action of Pius XII and Paul VI undercut some of the worst examples of casuistry and helped individuals preparing for their first reception of the sacrament to focus on the Eucharist and not on whether they swallowed water while brushing their teeth.

The value of this old tradition of fasting before receiving is that it serves as a reminder of the reverence that Christians should have for the Eucharist.

45

Lent

No Feasting without Fasting

RONALD ROLHEISER, O.M.I.

What has Lent meant to me?

I had the kind of religious upbringing that you might order from the catalogue, if you were looking for a classical Roman Catholic background. I grew up in an immigrant Catholic family, inside a strongly ethnic, mainly Catholic, rural community. The parish was the center of everything. Everyone went to church and the Church's seasons, particularly Lent, were felt inside of daily life. There were no weddings or dances during Lent and the old rules of fasting and abstinence were pretty rigorously followed. I liked the season even as I disliked it.

On the one hand, Lent made me feel good, giving me a sense of discipline and sacrifice, like military boot-camp. On the other hand, I counted the days until it was over, preferring feasting to fasting. But, like all Roman Catholics of my generation, I never questioned its wisdom: *There can be no feasting unless there first is fasting.* My parents imprinted that into my very genes.

Deeper Appreciation of Meaning

Unlike a lot of my peers, I never went through any adolescent rebellion where, for a time, I felt that the demands of Lent were silly and that a more mature attitude would be one of defiance. Rather, I went straight from my childhood faith to the seminary and everything my family had instilled in me was reinforced by what I learned and lived in the years leading up to my ordination to the priesthood.

Partly this was good, though it had an underside: I was never particularly reflective about Lent during all these years. It was simply a given, like a northern winter whose cold needs to be endured until spring comes and whose barrenness makes summer seem all the sweeter. I gave little thought to either its deeper theology or its deeper spirituality.

Vatican II came along just as I entered the seminary and, within five years, the council's effects were very much felt in how we lived out Lent, even if I still wasn't particularly reflective in terms of its theology and spirituality. It wasn't my thinking that changed, it was my actions. The old rules regarding fasting and abstinence, except for Ash Wednesday and Good Friday, were lifted in Canada (where I lived), though Roman Catholics were still encouraged to fast and abstain as before, but it was no longer a requirement. This had a double effect on me:

Negatively, not having to fast every day lessened the hold that Lent had on my everyday consciousness and, except for the fact that Lent was emphasized in the liturgy, it became easy to simply forget that we were in a season of penance. Most days, life went on exactly as in ordinary time. Also, the culture was growing more secular and attuning itself to a calendar quite different from the Church's liturgical calendar. There were now weddings and dances and high banquets during Lent and, for me, as for many others, Lent effectively shrank from forty days to seven. I still bore down on Ash Wednesday and during Holy Week.

More positively, though, the lack of external laws regarding physical asceticism, eventually led me to do more inner work in terms of what Lent meant to me. Each year now, I find the season more meaningful. What does Lent mean to me? Two things: *Ashes* and *Desert*.

A Cinderella Story

We all know the story of Cinderella, this centuries-old wisdom-tale that speaks about the value of ashes. The name, Cinderella, itself already says most of it. Literally it means: *the young girl who sits in the cinders.* As the tale makes plain, before the glass slipper is placed on her foot, before the beautiful gown, ball, dance, and marriage, there must first be a period of being humbled. Cinderella's story is a story of Lent.

Lent, for me, is a season to, metaphorically, sit in the ashes, to spend time, like Cinderella, working and sitting among the cinders of the fire—grieving over what I've done wrong, renouncing the dance, refraining from the banquet, refusing to do business as usual, waiting while some silent growth takes place within me, and simply being still so that the ashes can do their work in me.

And the place to sit in the ashes is the desert. Just as my parents believed that nobody could truly feast unless he or she first fasted, I believe that nobody can enter the Promised Land without first spending time in the desert.

The desert, biblically and mystically, is not so much a geographical location as a place in the heart, a place where we go to face our demons, feel our smallness, and be in a special intimacy with God. I believe that, before you are ready to fully and gratefully receive life, you have to first be readied by facing your own demons and this means going "into the desert," namely, facing that place where you are most frightened and lonely.

And this is not a place within which I can decide how I want to grow and change, but a place that I undergo, expose myself to, and have the courage to face. The idea is not so much that I do things there, but that things happen to me while I am there—silent, unseen, transforming things. The desert purifies me, almost against my will, through God's efforts. My job is only to have the courage to be there.

The desert makes me feel small and empty. This is an important spiritual place. Christina Crawford once said: "Lost is a place too!" That's wise. Emptiness can be a womb. Barrenness can be fertile. Desert flowers are often the most beautiful of all.

Medicine for the Soul

The experience of emptiness and barrenness is often best for the soul. Why? Because when we are surrounded by emptiness—when, as Shelley said, "the lone and barren sands stretch far away"—the soul is by necessity re-gestated. The experience of emptiness writes into our spiritual DNA what was once imprinted into our chromosomes, namely, that we are small, alone, fragile, and in need of a great providence and a great love.

For this reason, among others, the idea of the desert has played a prominent part in the spirituality of all religions. Great religious persons, Jesus among them, have always sought out the desert. The idea is to go into a barren landscape, hole up in some cave or crag, and simply sit there—alone, without protection or sustenance, with only sand around you, scorched by day, freezing at night, soaking in the barrenness, waiting for something deep to shift inside of your soul. The hope is that by immersing oneself in such emptiness one's soul will empty itself of all that is false and prideful.

The desert is that place in the soul where I feel most alone, insubstantial, and frightened. What happens to me there? What do I experience in the emptiness of the desert?

Emptiness

I feel the depth of our own loneliness. In the desert, in the womb of emptiness, voices within me remind me of a painful fact: "I am not sufficient unto myself; I cannot keep myself alive. I cannot provide sustenance for myself. I depend on many things and many people—for life, support, love, friendship, meaning. Everything I rely on can easily disappear. It's fragile. I'm fragile. I could disappear."

These feelings of fragility help break down my carefully nurtured sense of my own specialness. In the desert a brutal truth hits me: "I do not stand out. Nothing I can do will ultimately make me special, beyond anyone else. I am only a tiny piece of a great fabric within which I can only take my place. I am one of billions, one among many, no more important than anyone else."

Finally, too, when I am surrounded by emptiness, my mortality seeps through, raw and painful. A voice long kept at bay begins to say: "I too am going to die. Almost nothing sits between me and death. I stand on the brink of nothingness." The desert is full of painful voices. They tell me of my smallness.

We have no real maturity until our souls are shaped by that realization. The desert, letting emptiness work in us, is what re-gestates the soul. Emptiness is a womb. It re-molds the soul and lets us be born again, adults still, but now aware, as we once were as small children, that there can be no life and meaning outside of acknowledging our littleness and reaching out, as do infants, to a great providence and a great love outside of us.

"Lost is a place too" . . . and Lent is about going there. It is still not my favorite season. Feasting is still what we are born to do, but, I know now, just more deeply than I did as child, that there can be no real feasting until there has first been some fasting. The sublime is contingent upon sublimation. That's the lesson of Lent.

Contributors

Mary Christine Athans, B.V.M., is Professor Emerita at the Saint Paul Seminary School of Divinity of the University of St. Thomas (Minnesota) and an adjunct faculty member at the Catholic Theological Union and Loyola University Chicago. Among her books and articles on Jewish-Christian relations, American Catholicism, and American Catholic spirituality are *The Coughlin-Fahey Connection: Father Charles E. Coughlin, Father Denis Fahey, C.S.Sp., and Religious Anti-Semitism in the United States 1938–1954* (New York: Peter Lang, 1991), and *A Holy Lineage: The Jewish Roots of Christian Spirituality*, forthcoming from Stimulus Books of Paulist Press.

Wilkie Au is professor of theological studies at Loyola Marymount University, where he teaches in the area of spirituality and coordinates the graduate concentration in spiritual direction. Author of four books on Christian spirituality, his *By Way of the Heart: Toward a Holistic Christian Spirituality* won the 1990 Book Award of the College Theology Society. His latest work (with co-author Jungian analyst Noreen Cannon Au), *The Discerning Heart: Exploring the Christian Path*, was awarded first place by the Catholic Press Association of the U.S. and Canada in the category of pastoral ministry in May 2007.

James J. Bacik, a priest of the Diocese of Toledo, serves as campus minister and adjunct professor of humanities at the University of Toledo. His books include *Apologetics and the Eclipse of Mystery*, *Contemporary Theologians*, and, most recently, *A Light Unto My Path: Crafting Effective Homilies*. He was the writer for the editorial committee that produced the American bishops' pastoral letter on campus ministry "Empowered by the Spirit."

John F. Baldovin, S.J., is Professor of Historical and Liturgical Theology at Boston College School of Theology and Ministry. He is also president of the international Jungmann Society for Jesuits and Liturgy and past president of the international ecumenical Societas Liturgica and the North American Academy of Liturgy (from which he received the Berakah Award in 2007). His most recent book is *Reforming the Liturgy: A Response to the Critics* (2008).

Dianne Bergant, C.S.A., is Professor of Biblical Studies at Catholic Theological Union in Chicago. She was president of the Catholic Biblical Association of America (2000–2001). She is now on the editorial boards of *Biblical Theology Bulletin* and *Chicago Studies*. She wrote the weekly column, "The Word," for *America* magazine (2002–2005). She currently works in the areas of biblical interpretation and biblical theology, particularly on issues of peace, ecology, and feminism. Her most recent publications include *Scripture* (Collegeville, MN: Liturgical Press, 2008) and *A Word for Every Season* (New York/Mahwah, NJ: Paulist Press, 2008).

Richard A. Blake, S.J., is currently co-director of the film studies program at Boston College. He previously taught at Georgetown University and LeMoyne College. After receiving a doctorate in film from Northwestern University, he joined the editorial staff of *America* and eventually became the magazine's executive editor. He now serves as editor of *Studies in the Spirituality of Jesuits* and continues to review films for *America*. His most recent books are *Afterimage: The Indelible Catholic Imagination* and *Street Smart: The New York of Lumet, Allen, Scorsese and Lee*.

Mary C. Boys, S.N.J.M., is Skinner and McAlpin Professor of Practical Theology at Union Theological Seminary in New York City. Among books she has authored or edited are four on Christian-Jewish relations. She is currently working on a Jewish-Christian-Muslim commentary on the Passover Haggadah as well as on a book on the death of Jesus.

Francine Cardman is Associate Professor of Historical Theology and Church History at the Boston College School of Theology and Ministry. Her recent publications include "Sisters of Thecla: Knowledge, Power, and Change in the Church," in *Prophetic Witness: Catholic Women's Strategies for the Church*, ed. Colleen Griffiths (Crossroad, 2009) and "Poverty and Wealth as Theater: John Chrysostom's Homilies on Lazarus and the Rich Man," in *Wealth and Poverty in Early Church and Society*, ed. Susan R. Holman (Baker Academic, 2008).

Mary Collins, O.S.B., a Benedictine Sister of Atchison, Kansas, is Professor Emerita of The School of Theology and Religious Studies at The Catholic University of America in Washington, D.C. Her decision to concentrate in sacramental and liturgical theology when she began her doctoral studies in 1963 was guided by her novitiate reading of the bound volumes of *Orate Frates/Worship* from 1926 forward, the period when the journal was being edited by Michel and Diekmann. She has edited and written for liturgical and theological journals and encyclopedias, authored several books, and lectured widely.

Donald Cozzens, a priest of the diocese of Cleveland, teaches in the religious studies department of John Carroll University. His books include *The Changing Face of the Priesthood* and *Freeing Celibacy*, both published by Liturgical Press, Collegeville, Minnesota.

Charles E. Curran is the Elizabeth Scurlock University Professor of Human Values at Southern Methodist University and a priest of the Diocese of Rochester, New York. He has served as president of three national professional societies—the American Theological Society, the Catholic Theological Society of America, and the Society of Christian Ethics. His latest books are *Catholic Moral Theology in the United States: A History* (2008) and *Loyal Dissent: Memoir of a Catholic Theologian* (2006), both published by Georgetown University.

Michael J. Daley is a theology teacher at St. Xavier High School in Cincinnati, Ohio. He is a widely published writer whose articles have appeared in *U.S. Catholic, St. Anthony Messenger, Religion Teacher's Journal,* and *National Catholic Reporter*, among other publications. His latest book is *Our Catholic Symbols: A Rich Spiritual Heritage* (Twenty-Third, 2009).

James D. Davidson taught sociology at Purdue University from 1968 until he retired in 2009. He specialized in the sociology of religion, with particular emphasis on studies of American Catholicism. He is author, or co-author, of nine books, including *American Catholics Today* (2007) and *Catholicism in Motion* (2005). He has been president of the Association for the Sociology of Religion, the Religious Research Association, and the North Central Sociological Association. In 2007, he received the Rev. Louis Luzbatek Award for Exemplary Research in the Church from the Center for Applied Research on the Apostolate.

Cyprian Davis, O.S.B., a monk of St. Meinrad Archabbey (Indiana), is Professor of Church History at St. Meinrad School of Theology. He also serves as Professor of Black Catholic History in the Summer Institute at Xavier University of Louisiana in New Orleans. His publications include *History of Black Catholics in the United States* (New York: Crossroad, 1990) and *Henriette Delille: Servant of Slaves, Witness to the Poor* (New Orleans: Archdiocese of New Orleans and Sisters of the Holy Family, 2004). He also edited a work with Jamie Phelps, O.P., entitled *Stamped with the Image of God: African Americans as God's Image in Black* (Maryknoll, NY: Orbis Books, 2003). In 2002, the Catholic University of America awarded him the Johannes Quasten Medal for Excellence in Scholarship and Leadership in Religious Studies.

Kate Dooley, O.P., is a Sinsinawa (Wisconsin) Dominican Sister who teaches in the Department of Theology at Dominican University, River Forest, Illinois. She has published widely in catechetical and liturgical journals and written a number of catechetical texts and resource materials. She is the author of *To Listen and Tell: Commentary on the Introduction to the Lectionary for Masses with Children* and is currently working on *Be What You Celebrate* on liturgical catechesis. In 2005 she received the Emmaus Award for Excellence in Catechesis from the National Catholic Education Association of Parish Catechetical Leaders and the Georgetown Center for Liturgy National Award for Outstanding Contribution to the Liturgical Life of the Church.

Cardinal Avery Dulles, S.J., (d. December 12, 2008) was the Laurence J. McGinley Professor of Religion and Society at Fordham University, Bronx, New York (1988–2008). Prior to that, he taught at Woodstock College and The Catholic University of America. He was the author of numerous books and hundreds of articles, perhaps the most noted and memorable one being *Models of Church* (1974). In 2001 Dulles was the first United States–born theologian who was not a bishop to be named to the College of Cardinals.

Robert Ellsberg is the publisher of Orbis Books. From 1975 to 1980 he worked with Dorothy Day as part of the Catholic Worker community in New York where he served for two years as managing editor of *The Catholic Worker*. He has edited *Dorothy Day: Selected Writings* and *The Duty of Delight: The Diaries of Dorothy Day*. His own books include *All Saints: Daily Reflections on Saints, Prophets, and Witnesses for Our Time*.

Thomas H. Groome is Professor of Theology and Religious Education at Boston College and chair of the Institute of Religious Education and Pastoral Ministry within Boston College's School of Theology and Ministry. His most recent book is *What Makes Us Catholic* (HarperSanFrancisco, 2002).

Jeffrey Gros, F.S.C., is currently Distinguished Professor of Ecumenism and Historical Theology at Memphis Theological Seminary and academic dean of the Institute for Catholic Ecumenical Leadership. Prior to that, he served ten years as director of Faith and Order for the National Council of Churches, and then fourteen years as associate director of the Secretariat for Ecumenical and Interreligious Affairs at the United States Conference of Catholic Bishops. Most recently, he co-edited with Stephen B. Bevans *Evangelization and Religious Freedom* (Paulist Press, 2009). A member (and former board member) of the Catholic Theological Society of America, National Association of Diocesan Ecumenical Officers (associate), and former board member of the North American Academy of Ecumenists, he has spoken to a wide range of religious groups, including the American Academy of Religion, the College

Theology Society, the Faith and Order Commission USA, and Councils of Churches in various states and many varied religious and educational groups throughout the world.

Christine E. Gudorf is a professor in and chair of the Religious Studies Department at Florida International University in Miami. Her latest book, *Boundaries: A Casebook in Environmental Ethics*, co-authored with James Huchingson, was published in Japanese in 2008 and will have a second English edition in 2009. She was president of the Society of Christian Ethics in 2007–2008 and writes on many different areas of ethics. Lately she has been teaching and lecturing in Indonesia and arranging graduate-student exchanges with India, Indonesia, Ghana, and Colombia. She has been married forty years, raised three sons, and has two grandchildren.

John F. Haught is Senior Fellow, Science and Religion, at Woodstock Theological Center, Georgetown University. His area of specialization is systematic theology, with a particular interest in issues pertaining to science, cosmology, evolution, and ecology. He is the author of numerous books, including *God and the New Atheism: A Critical Response to Dawkins, Harris, and Hitchens* (2007); *Christianity and Science* (2007); *God After Darwin* (2nd edition, 2007), and *Responses to 101 Questions on God and Evolution* (2001). He lectures internationally on issues relating to science and religion.

Zachary Hayes, O.F.M., is Emeritus Professor of Systematic Theology at Catholic Theological Union, Chicago. Over the years he has also taught at the Franciscan School of Theology (Berkeley, California); at the Franciscan Institute at St. Bonaventure University (Allegheny, New York); and at the University of Notre Dame. During his years in Chicago, he collaborated with the Chicago Center for Religion and Science where he treated aspects of the Franciscan intellectual tradition related to the scientific issues being discussed at the Center. At present he is working on translations of the writings of the great medieval theologian, St. Bonaventure. Among his publications are many articles, reviews, and sixteen books, including *A Window to the Divine, The Gift of Being,* and *What Are They Saying about the End of the World?*

Kenneth R. Himes, O.F.M., is a Franciscan friar and priest teaching at Boston College, where he is presently chair of the Theology Department. A friend of the late George Higgins, he has written extensively in the fields of Catholic social teaching and social ethics. Among his publications are *Modern Catholic Social Teaching: Commentaries and Interpretations* (Georgetown University Press, 2005) and *Responses to 101 Questions on Catholic Social Teaching* (Paulist Press, 2001). He is a past president of the Catholic Theological Society of America.

Mary E. Hines obtained her PhD at the University of St. Michael's College, Toronto. She is Professor of Theology at Emmanuel College in Boston. She is the author of *Whatever Happened to Mary?, TheTransformation of Dogma: An Introduction to Karl Rahner on Doctrine* and co-editor of *The Cambridge Companion to Karl Rahner.* She has written numerous articles on ecclesiology, feminist theology, and the theology of Mary. She has served on the board of directors of the Catholic Theological Society of America and on the Anglican-Roman Consultation in the United States (ARCUSA).

David Hollenbach, S.J., is director of the Center for Human Rights and International Justice and holds the Human Rights and International Justice University Chair at Boston College, where he teaches theological ethics and Christian social ethics. He recently published *Refugee Rights* and *The Global Face of Public Faith.* He has regularly been visiting professor at Hekima College in Nairobi, Kenya. He assisted the National Conference of Catholic Bishops in drafting their 1986 pastoral letter "Economic Justice for All: Catholic Social Teaching and the U.S. Economy." He received the John Courtney Murray Award for distinguished achievement in theology from the Catholic Theological Society of America and the Marianist Award from the University of Dayton for Catholic contributions to intellectual life.

Ada María Isasi-Díaz, who was born in La Habana, Cuba, has been Professor of Christian Ethics and Theology since 1991 at the Theological School, Drew University, New Jersey. After being a missionary in Peru from 1975 to 1983 she worked as parish minister in Rochester, New York, and on the staff of the Women's Ordination Conference. Since the 1980s she has worked in elaborating *mujerista* theology based on the religious understandings and practices of Latinas in the United States. She co-authored, with Yolanda Tarango, *Hispanic Women: Prophetic Voice in the Church* (1988), the first Latina theology book published in this country. Her latest book is *La Lucha Continues—Mujerista Theology* (Orbis, 2004). At present she is working on a book to be published in 2011 by Fortress Press, *Justicia: A Reconciliatory Practice of Care and Tenderness.*

Luke Timothy Johnson is the Robert W. Woodruff Distinguished Professor of New Testament and Christian Origins in the Candler School of Theology at Emory University. In addition to his many works devoted to the New Testament, he has addressed topics of contemporary theological and moral concern in books such as *The Creed: What Christians Believe and Why it Matters,* and *Scripture and Discernment: Decision-Making in the Church.*

Theresa Kane, R.S.M., is a Sister of Mercy and associate professor at Mercy College in Dobbs Ferry, New York, teaching in the areas of world religions, women's studies, and religion and psychology. In 2005 she received the Outstanding Teacher Award from the faculty there. Prior to that, in 1980, she was given the U.S. Catholic Award for Furthering the Cause of Women in the Church. Within her religious community she has served in a number of leadership roles over the years. Nationally, from 1979 to 1980, she served as president of the Leadership Conference of Women Religious. She continues to speak at conferences and workshops, and she direct retreats.

Dolores R. Leckey has been a senior research fellow at the Woodstock Theological Center since 1998 where she is currently working on a composite biography about the late theologian Monika Hellwig. Prior to that she served for twenty years as executive director of the Secretariat for Family, Laity, Women and Youth of the United States Conference of Catholic Bishops. She is the author of eleven books, the most recent entitled *Grieving with Grace* (St. Anthony Messenger Press, 2008). The recipient of twelve honorary degrees and numerous awards, she is the mother of four and the grandmother of seven. She is a long-time resident of Arlington, Virginia, and now, having recently remarried, also lives (part time) in the Hudson River Valley.

William Madges holds an MA (Div.) and a PhD degree in Christian theology from the University of Chicago. From 1983 to 2006 he taught theology at Xavier University (Cincinnati) and in 1999 he was a Senior Fulbright Scholar at the University of Tübingen in Germany. He is currently dean of the College of Arts and Sciences at Saint Joseph's University in Philadelphia. His recent publications include *Vatican II Forty Years Later* (Orbis Books, 2006) and *The Many Marks of the Church* (Bayard/Twenty-Third Publications, 2006), which was edited with Michael J. Daley.

Gail Porter Mandell is Professor of Humanistic Studies at Saint Mary's College, Notre Dame, Indiana, where she holds the Schlesinger Endowed Chair in the Humanities. She has published two books on Sister Madeleva, a lecture delivered on the tenth anniversary of the Madeleva Lecture Series on Spirituality, sponsored by the Center for Spirituality at Saint Mary's College (*Madeleva: One Woman's Life* [New York: Paulist Press, 1994]), and *Madeleva*, a full-length, illustrated biography of Sister Madeleva (Albany: State University of New York, 1997).

Berard L. Marthaler, O.F.M. Conv., is Emeritus Professor of Religion and Religious Education at the Catholic University of America. He has earned doctorates in theology and history and is well regarded as a historian for his work in catechetics and for his leadership in developing catechetical directories and commentaries for the Roman Catholic Church. He was the long-time editor of the national catechetical journal, *The Living Light*. One of his most popular publications is *The Creed*.

Mark Massa, S.J., is the Karl Rahner Professor of Theology and co-director of the Curran Center for American Catholic Studies at Fordham University. His two most recent monographs were *Catholics and American Culture: Fulton Sheen, Dorothy Day, and the Notre Dame Football Team*, and *Anti-Catholicism in America: The Last Acceptable Prejudice?* He is currently working on a monograph entitled *The Catholic Sixties: The Pill, the Guitar Mass, and the Battle for the American Church*.

Richard P. McBrien is the Crowley-O'Brien Professor of Theology at the University of Notre Dame and author of *Catholicism* (1980; rev. ed., 1994) and *The Church: The Evolution of Catholicism* (2008). He is the former chair of Notre Dame's Department of Theology, former Professor of Theology at Boston College and director of its Institute of Religious Education and Pastoral Ministry, former president of the Catholic Theological Society of America, and winner of its John Courtney Murray Award for distinguished contributions to Catholic theology. He is a priest of the Archdiocese of Hartford, Connecticut.

Bishop Robert F. Morneau is currently pastor of Resurrection Parish in Green Bay, Wisconsin. Since 1979, he has been the auxiliary bishop of the Diocese of Green Bay and has also served as vicar general. Over the years Bishop Morneau has directed retreats, participated in various committees for the United States Conference of Catholic Bishops, and written books on prayer and spirituality. His most recent work is *The Color of Gratitude* (Orbis Books, 2009).

Padraic O'Hare is Professor of Religious and Theological Studies and director of the Center for the Study of Jewish-Christian-Muslim Relations at Merrimack College. He has served as academic dean of Anna Maria College in Massachusetts and for ten years as academic administrator of Boston College's Institute of Religious Education and Pastoral Ministry. He received the Dr. Maury Tye Award for Promoting Human Rights in 1999 and the Leonard P. Zakim Humanitarian Award of the Anti-Defamation League of the North Shore (Massachusetts) Jewish Community Center in 2002. He is the author or editor of eight books in religious education, justice and peace, contemplation practice and compassion, and comparative theology and interfaith relations. His most recent book is *Spiritual Companions: Jews, Christians and Interreligious Relations* (2006).

Thomas P. Rausch, S.J., is the T. Marie Chilton Professor of Catholic Theology at Loyola Marymount University in Los Angeles. Long active in ecumenical work, he served on the Catholic/Southern Baptist Conversation (1994–2001), the Catholic/World Evangelical Alliance Consultation (2001–), and presently serves on the Anglican-Catholic Dialogue in the

United States. His books include *Catholicism at the Dawn of the Third Millennium* (1996), *Who Is Jesus? An Introduction to Christology* (2003), and *Towards a Truly Catholic Church* (2005).

Karen M. Ristau is currently the ninth president of the National Catholic Educational Association, Washington, D.C. During her years of service to Catholic education, she has served as both teacher and administrator in Catholic elementary and secondary schools; as a professor at the University of St. Thomas in St. Paul, Minnesota; and as vice president and dean of faculty at Saint Mary's College, Indiana. She is the author of books and articles on Catholic school history and leadership issues and has received numerous awards for service to Catholic education.

Richard Rohr, O.F.M., is a Franciscan of the New Mexico Province. He was the founder of the New Jerusalem Community in Cincinnati, Ohio, in 1971, and the Center for Action and Contemplation (CAC) in Albuquerque, New Mexico, in 1986, where he currently serves as founding director. He founded the Center to serve as a "school for prophetic thinking," to encourage lay leadership and what he calls "a new reformation from within." He is probably best known for his writings and numerous audio and video recordings, which are distributed by St. Anthony Messenger Press, Crossroad Publishers, and Orbis Books as well as through The Mustard Seed, the CAC's resource center. He divides his time between working at the CAC and preaching and teaching on all continents. His latest book is *Things Hidden: Scripture as Spirituality* (St. Anthony Messenger Press, 2007).

Ronald Rolheiser, O.M.I., a priest and member of the Missionary Oblates of Mary Immaculate, is president of the Oblate School of Theology in San Antonio, Texas. He is a community-builder, lecturer, and writer. His books are popular throughout the English-speaking world and his weekly column is carried by more than sixty newspapers worldwide. For most of the thirty-five years of his priesthood he taught theology and philosophy at Newman Theological College in Edmonton, Alberta.

Susan A. Ross is Professor of Theology and a Faculty Scholar at Loyola University Chicago. She is the author of *For the Beauty of the Earth: Women, Sacramentality and Justice* (Paulist, 2006) and *Extravagant Affections: A Feminist Sacramental Theology* (Continuum, 1998), numerous journal articles and book chapters, and is the co-editor of five books and journal issues. She is the recipient of a Louisville Institute Sabbatical Grant, the Book of the Year Award from the College Theology Society in 1999, and the Ann O'Hara Graff Award of the Women's Seminar of the Catholic Theological Society of America. She currently serves as chairperson of her Department of Theology.

Thomas J. Shelley, a priest of the archdiocese of New York, is Professor of Church History at Fordham University. He has a doctorate in church history from the Catholic University of America where his mentor was John Tracy Ellis. His most recent book is *The Bicentennial History of the Archdiocese of New York, 1808–2008* (Strasbourg, 2007).

Leslie Woodcock Tentler is Professor of History at the Catholic University of America. She is author of *Catholics and Contraception: An American History* (Cornell University Press, 2004) and editor of *The Church Confronts Modernity: Catholicism Since 1950 in the United States, Ireland, and Quebec* (Catholic University of America Press, 2007).

Christine Vladimiroff, O.S.B., is a Benedictine Sister of Erie, Pennsylvania. She joined the community in 1957 and, over the years, has fulfilled a variety of roles within the community. In 1998 she was elected to serve as prioress of her Benedictine monastic community, a position in which she continues in today; her third term will end July, 2010. In 2002, she was awarded the U.S. Catholic Award for Furthering the Cause of Women in the Church. In August 2003 she was elected vice-president of the Leadership Conference of Women Religious (LCWR), an organization of the congregational leadership that represents more than 76,000 women religious in the United States. In August 2004 she became the president of the LCWR. She was elected president of the Conference of Benedictine Prioresses in February, 2009 and will serve in that position until 2013.

Index